The Worlds o

Duke Monographs in Medieval
and Renaissance Studies 14

Editorial Committee
Caroline Bruzelius, Arthur B. Ferguson,
Joan M. Ferrante, Edward P. Mahoney, Chairman,
Lee W. Patterson, David C. Steinmetz,
Bruce W. Wardropper, Ronald G. Witt

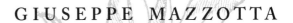

GIUSEPPE MAZZOTTA

The Worlds of
Petrarch

Duke University Press   Durham and London

1993

Second printing, 1999

© 1993 Duke University Press

All rights reserved

Printed in the United States of America on

acid-free paper ∞

Designed by Cherie Holma Westmoreland

Typeset in Caslon by Keystone Typesetting, Inc.

Library of Congress Cataloging-in-Publication Data

Mazzotta, Giuseppe, 1942–

The worlds of Petrarch / Giuseppe Mazzotta.

p.   cm. — (Duke monographs in medieval and

Renaissance studies ; 14)

Includes bibliographical references and index.

ISBN 0-8223-1363-4 — ISBN 0-8223-1396-0 (pbk.)

1. Petrarca, Francesco, 1304–1374—Criticism and

interpretation.   I. Title.   II. Series:

Duke monographs in medieval

and Renaissance studies ; no. 14.

PQ4540.M37   1993

851′.—dc20   —dc20

[851′.1]   93-19793 CIP

For my brother Lorenzo—
He knows
the heart of love.

Contents

Acknowledgments

In the astonishing passage of a letter (*Fam.* XV, 3) Petrarch imagines gathering the memories of the great cities of the past, his interlocutors from all places and from all ages, and all the friends he has or he has had, whose achievements, style, and wit he greatly admires. The pleasure he derives from conversing with them, he will say elsewhere, reaches to the marrow of his bones.

There have been many times since 1973, the year I began writing on Petrarch in Toronto, when I felt I understood exactly this passion of his mind, the joys and regrets induced by memories and anticipations of encounters and conversations with one's own friends. The work of Petrarch, which always evokes the links between friendship and conversation, memory and language, love and apprenticeship, has happily given me the occasion to engage in steady interactions with several friends, whom I remember one by one and from whom I have always learned without, probably, their even knowing it. Some of these "Petrarchan" friends are Guido and Olga Pugliese, the memory of whom brings me back to the time spent in Toronto. Other friends evoke the time spent at Cornell: John Freccero, whose seminars he gave on Petrarch while I was writing my dissertation on Dante I occasionally attended; Robert Durling, Piero Pucci, the late Eugenio Donato, Phil Lewis, who read and commented on my first papers, Richard Klein, the late Ted Morris who really loved Petrarch's poetry, Tim Bahti, Enrico Santi, Mary Ann Caws, the Aretine Donatella Stocchi-Perucchio, Robert Harrison, and Lynn Enterline. Still others, such as the late Bart Giamatti, who quickly understood my project, Vasily Rudich, Lowry Nelson, Nancy Vickers, and Virginia Jewiss belong to my Yale tenure. My dear friend Roberto González, who is now my colleague at Yale, was in my department also at Cornell and listened from the start to my early musings.

In the summer of 1989 I had the privilege to direct an NEH Yale Petrarch Institute. The excitement of that experience was heightened by the visitors to the Institute: Thomas Greene, John Freccero, María

Rosa Menocal, who spurred me to complete the book, Ronald Witt, who held a vibrant seminar on the historiography of the Humanists, Marcel Tetel, Aldo Scaglione, Dino Geneakopulos, Ned Duval, and Tim Hampton. Deanna Shemek, who was then a Yale colleague of mine, unofficially but with great intellectual enthusiasm attended the Institute and generously even proofread a chapter of this book. They all contributed to my understanding of Petrarch just as did the participant-colleagues such as Thomas Harrison, Brenda Schildgen, Diane Marks, Tony Roda, Ray Prier, David Baum, Dennis Looney, and, above all, my dear friend and long-standing intellectual interlocutor, Mihai Spariosu. Dina Consolini's commitment was remarkable.

It is a special pleasure to thank a distinguished Yale colleague and friend, Thomas Greene, who also lectured at the Petrarch Institute and who, years later, took time from his many obligations and gave me extremely helpful criticisms on the whole manuscript. Because his own work on Petrarch has set inimitable standards on most of us, I greatly appreciate his generous suggestions. William Kennedy of Cornell University and Rebecca West of the University of Chicago were marvelous readers for the press and I gladly acknowledge their acute comments. There is yet another reader that deserves to be singled out: Giovanni Sinicropi. In a spirit of fraternal friendship he pored over the manuscript with extraordinary diligence and made valuable suggestions.

The list would not be complete if I did not record two different encounters I had in Italy over the last few years. One took place in Padua in May 1987, when I listened with the care one reserves to what really matters to what I took to be a radical, Petrarchan reading of Leopardi by my friend Mario Andrea Rigoni. The other occurred one late summer evening of 1988 in Ravenna with a distinguished Petrarch scholar, Ugo Dotti, when we talked at length, and memorably, about Petrarch's politics. Over the last five years the inspiring friendship of a great Celtics fan, Doug Smith, made, unaccountably, the writing of this book easier.

Finally, it is my duty, and of course not just a duty, to acknowledge the endurance displayed by my wife, Carol, during the sabbatical year, 1992, that I passed writing this book. As always, she bears out for me the truth of 1 Cor.13. Last but certainly not least, Luisa Dato typed the manuscript, but she, who is a truly Petrarchan spirit, commented on and edited it. I am grateful to her more than I could ever say.

Some of these chapters were published in professional journals and critical anthologies. I republish them with only slight variations and gratefully acknowledge permission to reprint. Chapter 1 appeared as "Antiquity and the New Arts in Petrarch," reprinted in *The New Medievalism,* ed. Marina S. Brownlee, Kevin Brownlee, and Stephen G. Nichols (Baltimore, Md.: Johns Hopkins University Press, 1991), pp. 46–69. Chapter 2, in a much abbreviated shape, was published as "Petrarch's Thought," in *Mimesis in Contemporary Theory and Interdisciplinary Approach,* vol. 2: *Mimesis, Semiosis and Power,* ed. Ronald Bogue (Philadelphia: John Benjamins, 1991), pp. 27–43. Chapter 3, which is the first piece I wrote on Petrarch, appeared as "The Canzoniere and the Language of the Self," *Studies in Philology* 75 (1978), pp. 271–96. Chapter 6 appeared in a somewhat abbreviated form as "Orpheus: Rhetoric and Music in Petrarch," published in *Forma e parola Studi in memoria di Fredi Chiappelli,* ed. D. J. Dutschke, P. M. Forni, F. Grazzini, B. R. Lawton, and L. S. White (Roma: Bulzoni Editore, 1992), pp. 137–54. Chapter 7 appeared as "Humanism and Monastic Spirituality in Petrarch," *Stanford Literature Review,* vol. 5, nos. 1–2 (Saratoga, Calif.: ANMA Libri, 1988), pp. 57–74. Appendix 1 appeared in *Textual Analysis: Some Readers Reading,* ed. M. A. Caws (New York: Modern Language Association of America, 1986), pp. 121–31, with the title "Petrarch's Song 126." The translations from the *Canzoniere* are taken from Robert Durling's excellent *Petrarch's Lyric Poems* (Cambridge, Mass.: Harvard University Press, 1976). Permission to use the above material is gratefully acknowledged.

Note on Petrarch's Texts

Unless otherwise stated, all citations from Petrarch's works are taken from the following editions and translations.

Petrarch's Works

Bucolicum carmen e i suoi commenti inediti. Edited by A. Avena. Padua: Società cooperativa tipografica, 1906.

Canzoniere. Edited by Gianfranco Contini; annotated by Daniele Ponchiroli. Turin: Einaudi, 1964.

Collatio laureationis. In *Opere latine di Francesco Petrarca,* edited by Antonietta Bufano. 2 vols. Turin: Unione Tipografico-Editrice Torinese, 1975. 2:1255–83.

Contra eum qui maledixit Italie. In *Opere latine di Francesco Petrarca,* edited by Antonietta Bufano. 2:1153–1253.

De otio religioso. In *Opere latine di Francesco Petrarca,* edited by Antonietta Bufano. 1:567–809.

De sui ipsius et multorum ignorantia. In *Opere latine di Francesco Petrarca,* edited by Antonietta Bufano. 2:1025–1151.

De viris illustribus. Edited by G. Martellotti. Edizione nazionale delle opere di Francesco Petrarca, vol. 2. Florence: Sansoni, 1964.

De vita solitaria. In *Opere latine di Francesco Petrarca,* edited by Antonietta Bufano. 1:261–565.

Le familiari di Francesco Petrarca. Edited by Vittorio Rossi and Umberto Bosco. Edizione nazionale delle opere di Francesco Petrarca, vols. 10–13. Florence: Sansoni, 1933–42.

Invective contra medicum. In *Opere latine di Francesco Petrarca,* edited by Antonietta Bufano. 2:817–941.

Posteritati. In *Prose,* edited by G. Martellotti et al. La letteratura italiana. Storia e Testi. Milan-Naples: Ricciardi, 1955. 2–18.

Rerum memorandarum libri. Edited by Giuseppe Billanovich. Edizione nazionale delle opere di Francesco Petrarca, vol. 5. Florence: Sansoni, 1943.

Rerum senilium liber XIV. Ad magnificum Franciscum de Carraria Padue dominum. Epistola I. Qualis esse debeat qui rem publicam regit. Edited by V. Ussani. Padua, 1922.

Secretum. In *Prose,* edited by G. Martellotti et al. 7:22–214.

Sine nomine: Lettere polemiche e politiche. Edited by Ugo Dotti. Bari: Laterza, 1974.

Trionfi. In *Rime, trionfi e poesie latine,* edited by Ferdinando Neri et al. Milan-Naples: Ricciardi, 1951. 481–578.

Translations

Bergin, Thomas G., trans. *Petrarch's Bucolicum Carmen.* New Haven: Yale University Press, 1974.

Bernardo, Aldo, trans. *Rerum Familiarum Libri I–VIII.* Albany: State University of New York, 1975.

———. *Letters on Familiar Matters: Books IX–XXIV.* 2 vols. Baltimore: Johns Hopkins University Press, 1982.

Bishop, Morris, trans. *Epistle to Posterity.* In *Letters from Petrarch.* Bloomington: Indiana University Press, 1966. 5–12.

Carozza, Davy A., and H. James Shey. *Petrarch's "Secretum," with Introduction, Notes, and Critical Anthology.* Series 17. Classical Languages and Literature, vol. 7. New York: Peter Lang, 1989.

Durling, Robert M., ed. and trans. *Petrarch's Lyric Poems: The "Rime sparse" and Other Lyrics.* Cambridge: Harvard University Press, 1976.

Kohl, Benjamin G. *How a Ruler Ought to Govern His State.* In *The Earthly Republic: Italian Humanists on Government and Society,* edited and translated by Benjamin G. Kohl and Ronald G. Witt, with Elizabeth B. Welles. Philadelphia: University of Pennsylvania Press, 1978. 35–78.

———. "Petrarch's Prefaces to *De viris illustribus.*" *History and Theory* 13 (1974): 132–44.

Nachod, Hans, trans. *On His Own Ignorance and That of Many Others.* In *The Renaissance Philosophy of Man,* edited by Ernst Cassirer, P. O. Kristeller, and J. H. Randall, Jr. Chicago: University of Chicago Press, 1948. 49–133.

———. "A Self-Portrait." In *The Renaissance Philosophy of Man,* edited by Ernst Cassirer, P. O. Kristeller, and J. H. Randall, Jr. 34–35.

Rawski, Conrad H., trans. *Four Dialogues for Scholars: The Remedies.* Cleveland: Press of Western Reserve University, 1967.

Wilkins, Ernest Hatch, trans. *Triumphs.* Chicago: University of Chicago Press, 1962.

Zacour, Norman P. *Petrarch's Book without a Name: A Translation of the "Liber sine nomine."* Toronto: Pontifical Institute of Mediaeval Studies, 1973.

Zeitlin, Jacob. *The Life of Solitude by Francis Petrarch.* Urbana: University of Illinois Press, 1924.

Introduction

history + death

Most of the chapters in this volume were written over a long period of time. But although, at least at the start, they were conceived discontinuously as autonomous, isolated pieces, I have not substantially revised their original form. Nonetheless, in spite of the time gaps in my writing them, I believe that there is an underlying thread of themes and concerns that weave the chapters together in a network and give them the semblance of a unified work.

The thread that binds this book together can be called Petrarch's simultaneous thought of history and death. On the face of it, these two terms describe primarily the sharp opposition between, on the one hand, Petrarch's lifelong intellectual-political project to redefine the culture and language of his times and, on the other hand, his ironic, negative consciousness of the finiteness of existence, his deepest realization that he lived within the horizon of time's inexorable devastations. But history and death, which in their rich variations map the full trajectory of Petrarch's work, are not to be found at opposite ends of his thinking as merely two antithetical categories. Rather, they appear as two interlocked questions that infinitely repeat each other, as the double focus of an imaginary ellipsis around which the boundaries of Petrarch's poetry and thought are inexhaustibly drawn.

The metaphoric cluster of history and death, which this book explores by focusing largely on Petrarch's representation of self, casts its ambivalent light on every aspect of Petrarch's style of thought and reveals its essential unity. To be sure, unity is a concept Petrarch's diverse writings strongly resist. The very least that can be said of him, as a matter of fact, is that he recognized from the very beginning the crisis enveloping the concept of unity that historically can be said to belong to the "Dark Ages," to a time when an individual existence had an objective, firm, and congruent basis in a vision of a preordained wholeness. Petrarch perceives that the path to wholeness (and holiness) marked out by, say, Dante had already been traversed by Dante. What is left for him is to undertake, and he indeed undertakes, to

Christianity

open up a new, personal path. Like Dante, he has a definite Christian assumption about the transcendent meaning and destination of existence, but he maps the route of an existence caught up in the tortuous wanderings of history as a great venture unfolding over the seemingly random twists and turns of his wayward imagination.

Petrarch's awareness of the problematical nature and crisis of the principle of unity is apparent both through the material evidence of the structure of his texts and through the conceptual and metaphorical articulations of his vision. So many of his works—from the serial repetition of poems in the *Canzoniere* (interchangeably known as *Rerum vulgarium fragmenta* or *Rime sparse*) to the collections of disparate letters in the two volumes of *Familiares* and *Seniles,* from the epic fragment, *Africa,* to the unfinished *Trionfi,* which overtly attempts to recapitulate and unify the sundry themes of his works into a visionary whole, to the *Variae*—constantly dramatize how individual parts can be unified into a totality and end up showing how the unity of the work is made of fragments.

What I call the material or technical evidence of the fragmentary bent of Petrarch's imagination can, no doubt, be explained as a sign of the craftsman's tentativeness in composition, of the mind's steady pursuit of the pure and yet elusive formal perfection of design. This is certainly one reason that accounts for Petrarch's entanglements in countless minute revisions of style that heighten the impression that his writing is an ongoing process of purification of language wherein nothing or very little is left to the play of chance. The conceptual features of his poetry, however, suggest another probable cause for the meticulous care with which he tirelessly reelaborates his texts.

The radical, abiding novelty of Petrarch's intellectual vision is at one, as scholars have long acknowledged, with his discovery of the centrality of the individual. The breakdown of traditional structures of authority, his youth spent in a cosmopolitan city such as Avignon where he literally had to prove his mettle, the bewildering challenges and changes brought about by outside intellectual forces (which Eugenio Garin, reviving the old phraseology, refers to as the "barbarians" from the North) are some of the elements that trigger Petrarch's conviction that all events, beliefs, and values have to be refracted through the prism of one's own subjectivity. Accordingly, with his insistence on subjective individualism and his steady concentration on the innermost landscape of the mind, Petrarch is said to generate an

subjective individualism

epoch-making transition to modernity. The mark of the modernity he inaugurates lies in the transformed understanding of the self, in his self-projection, especially in his lyrical poems, as an autonomous, isolated subject who reflects on his memories, impulses, and desires and finds in the consciousness of his individuality, severed from all external ties, accidental preoccupations and concerns, his pure self.

This idea of the absolute self Petrarch supposedly forges has turned into the ultimate ground in which the principle of unity is rooted. We are all familiar with Gianfranco Contini's formulation of two distinct and antithetical categories—plurilinguism and monolinguism—as the two lines of force traversing the history of Italian literature. Plurilinguism, Contini says, is Dante's attribute and captures the multiple registers of his representation of reality, while monolinguism is the central trait of Petrarch's style. To be sure, Petrarch wrote, as Dante and Boccaccio did, in both Italian and Latin. But this bilingualism does not refute the fundamental monolinguism, which figures in the writing of the private, personal love poems of the *Canzoniere* and which denotes Petrarch's practice of methodical exclusion of heterogeneous realities from the realm of representation. "Monolinguism," more precisely, designates Petrarch's linguistic selectiveness, the homogeneity of a purified style that reduces diverse experiences to a uniform vision.

Contini's phenomenological description of the unified language of the *Canzoniere,* which is doubtless accurate, has been retrieved and extended by some readers of the *Canzoniere* (prominently among them and with considerable differences between each other, Robert Durling and John Freccero) to signal Petrarch's pursuit of an immobile esthetic form, his attempt to create a self-enclosed fictional universe that rejects time and history and makes the self the idolatrous counterpart of God. It is easy to see, beneath this moral definition of Petrarch's poetic project and style, a claim of unity and substantiality of self: in the sinful act of constructing a fantastical creation, the poet's self is invested with the authority and identity that are God's prerogative. This seductive theory notwithstanding, Petrarch also knows that this claim of unity is partial. The metaphoric patterns traversing Petrarch's poetry, in fact, radically challenge the possibility of idolatry, which is to be understood as the desire to give poetic fixity and substantiality to the multiple figments of his mind.

To say it in the textual terms of Petrarch's own poetry, the mobile

3

and delusory action of the imagination, the unavoidable intrusion of time as memory, the ceaseless dialectical movement of desire, and the shiftiness of poetic language counter Petrarch's willful plan to create a self-monument, and, in the process, they trace his sense of the impossibility to give a stable figuration of the self. Any idea of the self, as Petrarch lucidly intuits, can only be partial. Further, a number of poetic motifs such as the flight of time, mythic metamorphoses, the dislocations of desire, the absence of the beloved, the palimpsests of memory, and the posthumousness of self, to mention some that repeatedly circulate through his poems, reveal Petrarch's consciousness of what in its essence is the absolute limit of death on the tenuousness of life. The fragments of time and the divisions within experience, one may add, do not describe merely the phenomena in the outside world of nature and history. In Petrarch's poetry, time's ruptured dimensions (past, fleeting present, and expectation of the future) are internalized within the self, and they are even identified as the constitutive, broken pieces of oneself.

This perception of fragmentation, on which much of the present book focuses (ruins, antiquities, memories, time, desire, language, and sound, are some of the emblems of Petrarch's representation that the various chapters discuss), forces on us a redefinition of the essential unity of Petrarch's concerns. It is here, in his novel articulation of what constitutes "unity," that Petrarch's thought displays a high degree of complexity. Traditionally we tend to think of fragments as relics or vestiges of a lost whole (say, a monument), and they help us divine, by synecdoche as it were, the original artifice of which they were part. In a Platonic frame of reference, on the other hand, the part reflects the whole, just as the microcosm reflects, by analogy, the macrocosm. Petrarch, however, envisions a new possible way of articulating the relationship between fragments and unity. In fact, Petrarch allows us to speak of unity as a unity of fragments, as a unity of adjacent parts. What are these fragments or parts? I call them "worlds," and to clarify somewhat what is meant by this word, I must here explain the title of this book, *The Worlds of Petrarch,* which in itself is (to make use of one of Petrarch's own stylistic devices) something of an oxymoron.

The Worlds of Petrarch is an oxymoron in that it evokes, first, the plural "worlds" within the singularity of the epochal name, Petrarch, and seeks to define this singularity as the point of intersection of a cluster of particular, contradictory pulls and aspirations. Second, as a

Petrarch's worlds represent the various parts of society or his life that make up him

spatial metaphor, "worlds" also seeks to shift the center of gravity of the critical debates on Petrarch and on modernity away from the univocal, introspective subjectivism he forged for posterity to the external domains of history, such as the myth of Rome and the politics of culture. Finally, "worlds" suggests and brings to light the existence of disparate, fragmentary regions of experience within one's mind. These worlds or fragments are nothing less than the topics or parts scattered in the vast latitude of Petrarch's production.

Some of them are metaphorical worlds. There is a world of philosophy and there is a world of faith, and the two exist separate from and contrary to each other, though faith can encompass philosophy; there is a world of love, which, as we have seen, is a select, exclusive, and radically self-enclosed universe, and a world of books of classical scholarship; a world of delusory political engagements and a world of religious contemplation which the self longs for and from which the self is also excluded; a world of mechanical arts (medicine, law) and a world of liberal arts (grammar, rhetoric). Other worlds are literal, and yet they stand as emblems of a spiritual geography: there are the separate and competing worlds of Italy and of France; there is Greece and there is Rome; the nationalistic world defined and sheltered by the Alps and the world beyond the Alps; in classical times there were Rome and Carthage (or Babylon and Jerusalem) as two modalities of cultural values, and their list could continue. There is, to be sure, the nostalgia for the overarching spiritual unity of Rome which gives Petrarch the impulse to envision and establish his ideals of culture. Yet his myth of *cultura* is not at all the experience or outcome of a unified consensus; rather, it turns out to be a power play which perpetuates oppositions and divisions within competing paradigms of discourse.

Petrarchan scholarship at its best has been all too aware of the distinct and yet adjacent compartments that make up Petrarch's oeuvre. In the wake of Francesco Fiorentino's nineteenth-century study of the philosophy of Petrarch, Charles Trinkaus, for instance, has recently delineated the shape of the poet's philosophical thought. Hans Baron, Francisco Rico, and Bortolo Martinelli have explored the confessional experience of the *Secretum*. On the other hand, Ugo Dotti has intelligently investigated Petrarch's public role, his engagement as a fourteenth-century intellectual in the concrete, political context of the Avignonese papacy. Thomas Greene, in some seminal and exemplary

others who studied + wrote about Petrarch

What the book aims to do

studies on Petrarch's poetics of self-introspection, has brought to the surface what he calls the "lateral dispersion" and "flexibility" of Petrarch's figuration of self in its array of irreconcilable roles and interests. Giuseppe Billanovich has diligently studied Petrarch's philology and has reconstructed his library.

But there are fundamental questions that remain to be asked and that *The Worlds of Petrarch* directly confronts: How do Petrarch's fragmentary experiences relate to one another? How do these separate worlds communicate, if they do, with one another? Is there a conversation, to use a term Petrarch bequeathed to the Renaissance dream of possible conversations among different human beings and among the sundry disciplines of knowledge, possible between the various fragments of experience or, since the self is made of many parts, between self and self, and self and others? What exactly does the discourse of history or the assertion of culture have to do with Petrarch's discourse of death? These questions, and not just the perception of division and self-division, which really are the given of his mind, stand at the center of Petrarch's vision and determine the shape of his quest.

There has been a tendency among scholars to circumvent these questions. Traditionally, they have approached Petrarch's works through accounts of his biography and pretended that the dissymmetries and vagaries of his consciousness mechanically reflect and correspond to contingent vicissitudes of his restless life. Because Petrarch generally tells us about actual experiences from which his texts stem and fastidiously records the circumstances of their composition, he himself encourages the biographical fallacy, the notion that life and works constitute an inseparable, overlapping unity. Several scholars in our times (for example, Ernest H. Wilkins) have followed the poet's lead and have used his texts as literal evidence for the reconstruction of his life. An exception to this trend was Umberto Bosco, who, aware of the permanent impasse of Petrarch's will, of the lack of linear development in his ideas, and of the steady revisions to which he subjected his writings, denied even the possibility of writing a biography of the poet. I would add that it is certainly true, as this book argues, that for Petrarch no facile separation is possible between the world one carries inside oneself and the outside world. But this formulation has to be taken to mean, first, that one's own inner phantasms are just as real as the objective world and, second, that the objective world can be as ghostly as the figments of one's imagination.

[handwritten: What the book is about]

If the various separate realms of Petrarch's work are not arranged continuously within a transcendent whole, nor are they intelligible as if they were parts of an organic totality, and if they can be explained much less by the questionable assumption that art reflects the artist's life, how can they be related to each other? How can the distances between experiences remote from one another be covered? Each chapter of this book probes a different aspect of these multiple worlds Petrarch inhabits and seeks to answer the above questions. Some chapters, especially chapters 1, 4, 5, and 7, discuss the aesthetic implications of rhetorical forms such as, respectively, conversations, letter writing, polemics, the dialogue, prayer, and generally the style Petrarch deploys to communicate across vast stretches of time and space, with imaginary or real interlocutors.

He self-consciously refers to and defines his style as "vario stile" (varied style), as he announces on line 5 of the opening sonnet of his *Canzoniere*, and the qualifier gains in strength by its pointed contrast to Dante's "dolce stile"—the sweet style of the love book of his youth. Style for Petrarch, more precisely, is the transversal view that cuts across and unifies varied fields of experience. Most of the chapters in this book deliberately cut through different genres (tracts, poems, letters) or languages (Italian and Latin) in order to question the general assumption that these sundry texts exist, like hermetically sealed vessels, statically separated from one another. But the critical reflection on the possible relations among mutually foreign realms of experience, which are both within and outside the self, thoroughly structures the unfolding of *The Worlds of Petrarch*.

[handwritten left margin: these works are all related]

[handwritten: ✱]

The first chapter, which serves as an adumbration of the book's entire argument, begins by confronting the thorny question of historical periodization, of the disjunction between the "Middle Ages" and the "Renaissance," and it proceeds to show how the perception of ruins is the foundation of Petrarch's project of cultural renewal. Because he knew himself well (his life was the steady focus of his own thoughts), Petrarch sees his own world—the world of fourteenth-century Latinity that found in Rome its hallowed core—faced with the urgent task of revising its own conception of itself, and he sees himself faced with the obligation to carry out, almost single-handedly, the process of that revision. His project is not, however, one of encyclopedic, total inclusiveness of heterogeneous disciplines as Dante's is. Rather, it dictates exclusions of, say, medicine from the dignity of

[handwritten right margin: Ch. 1]

[handwritten bottom right: P's mission]

the arts of the soul; it seeks to retrieve the past as past, remote from the present, and to graft onto it the "new" arts, such as painting or music (as chapter 6 shows). Chapter 2 examines Petrarch's redefinition of philosophy and its relation to faith and rhetoric. By breaking up "philosophy" into its constitutive etymological components (love and knowledge), the chapter argues that Petrarch's poetry of love and thought recasts philosophy's quandary and aims. There is a passion for thinking, as Petrarch knows, and by this it is to be understood, against Guido Cavalcanti, whom Petrarch generally follows, to mean that one thinks when the mind is mobilized by love. Chapters 3 and 4 deal, from different perspectives, with Petrarch's idea of poetic self and ethical self, and together they show Petrarch's purpose to represent the self as the locus of inner tensions and relations, which are also projected onto the outside world. Chapter 5 recapitulates the political myths and themes raised in the previous four chapters and shows how Petrarch, who seeks to impose his style on his times, intuits in his historiographical texts the unavoidable links between biography, history, and finitude. Chapter 6 analyzes Petrarch's insight into the links between rhetoric and music. Chapter 7 studies the relationship between poetry and theology. Appendix 1 is a close reading of one of the most luminous of Petrarch's songs (*Canzoniere*, song 126) in the light of all these concerns. Appendix 2 summarizes the parabola of Petrarch's public life.

What is it, then, if anything, that bridges the gap across the disparate but adjacent domains of Petrarch's imagination and, paradoxically, leaves them as separate entities? The argument *The Worlds of Petrarch* submits is that there may be objective, natural affinities, such as friendships or blood relations, linking individuals together, and the bonds between friends or even brothers are usually conversations and dialogues between minds: they are important but partial in that they bracket the body's existence. There are sympathies between proximate viewpoints (those, say, of the Augustinian Dionigi da Borgo San Sepolcro to whom the letter from Mount Ventoux was sent or those of Petrarch's brother, Gherardo, and the poet himself). There are subjective associations, produced by thinking, memory, or imagination, that allow us to cut through partitions within ourselves and between ourselves and others. For Petrarch there is, centrally, love, which, though viewed as anguish or "war" (which is the ultimate metaphor of division) and though painfully exclusive (and, at any rate, Petrarch never communicates with Laura), involves the whole of oneself and impels one to shatter the walls around oneself and discover within oneself new worlds and new, unsuspected states of the soul.

But dialogues, imagination, thought, memory, and even love, just as the other passions Petrarch probes (fear, shame, hate, grief—which are all clustered within the single universe of love), by themselves are not sufficient to guarantee any communication. Dialogues are metaphoric displacements of monologues, just as monologues are always dialogical for Petrarch, who never fails to represent the lacerations within the individual. The universe of love, more specifically, is made of conflicting pulls such as, for instance, pleasure and regret. As for the other passions, they have the power to divide the mind and to drive it back to a motionless center where one's solitary, separate, and broken self is again found. But these passions are all needed exactly because they are divisive. Any unification can occur on the precondition of existing divisions: the unity, as was stated earlier, can only be a unity of parts. That Petrarch fully grasps this insight is made manifest by his repeated assertions that the correlation of the various worlds is established by the rhetorician's will(power) and the poet's languages wherein memory, imagination, thought, love, and the passions are all implicated. The analysis of the relevant aspects in the poetry of the *Trionfi,* the *Canzoniere,* and other discursive texts shows Petrarch's sense of the power of poetry and rhetoric to join. A couple of examples from the *Canzoniere* will illustrate the point at hand.

The most flagrant example is found in the figure of Laura, who is for the lover, as only the beloved can be, a *terra incognita,* a self-contained, elusive figure removed from all factitious reality. The name of Laura, however, inspires in the poet-lover a host of coiled associations. Some of these associations—usually physical fragments, such as her skin, her face, her hair, her hand—belong to her, just as the description of an object belongs to the object, for the name, as much for Petrarch as for Dante, is an integral part of the knowledge that the thing designated by the name delivers. Other associations she provokes, however, are contiguous, metonymic extensions of the name: Apollo's laurel tree (*lauro*) and the chase of love (Daphne), the poet's laurel crown, the poetic themes of praise (*lode*) and reverence that the syllables of the name (*lo-re*) elicit (the word *laurus* comes from *laus*), the preciousness and timelessness of gold (*oro*), the transparency of the air (*aura*). Her name also evokes the beauty of the Avignonese land-

9

scape, the music of the flowing pure waters of the Sorgue River, the world of painting, the event of Christ's passion; it awakens the buried, secret resonances of the name of the weekday, Good Friday (*venerdì*, which is both the day of Christ's passion and literally the day of Venus), when the lover first saw her; her death eclipses the light of the world; the love for her inspires Petrarch's poetry; and, finally, his poetry monumentalizes both Laura and his self.

I am describing here metaphoric associations Petrarch lucidly deploys through acrostics and paranomasia (see sonnet 5 and its discussion in chapter 3) and through each and every poem of the *Canzoniere*. The sense of these associations, refracted through the name of Laura and determined by it, emerges only from the aesthetic simulation which is given by Petrarch's poetry. As a figment of the poet's imagination, "Laura" implicates many possible worlds, and it is the power of her name that evokes diverse experiences which are in themselves literally worlds apart and do not properly belong to her but are discovered by the poet's art. This is the essence of Petrarch's style, and one could extend this sort of textual investigation endlessly, from the word for love to the poet's own name, Petrarca, which is the eponym for this mode of writing up to at least the nineteenth century.

The persuasion that poetry has the power to gather together the separate, heterogeneous entities of experience or to join the past to the future leads Petrarch to envision poetry (which, in the wake of Dante, he views simultaneously in terms of music and rhetoric) as the foundation of political associations (this is the brunt of the myth of Orpheus discussed in chapter 6) and as a theological activity (which chapter 7 explores). But there is a countermovement to this myth of poetry's power to spellbind the listeners and create a univocal space of imaginary unity. A brief account of a sonnet from the *Canzoniere* clarifies the argument that chapters 3 and 6 advance in some detail.

> Voglia mi sprona, Amor mi guida et scorge,
> Piacer mi tira, Usanza mi trasporta,
> Speranza mi lusinga et riconforta
> et la man destra al cor già stanco porge;
>
> e 'l misero la prende, et non s'accorge
> di nostra cieca et disleale scorta:
> regnano i sensi, et la ragione è morta;
> de l'un vago desio l'altro risorge.

Vertute, Honor, Bellezza, atto gentile,
dolci parole ai bei rami m' àn giunto
ove soavemente il cor s'invesca.

Mille trecento ventisette, a punto
su l'ora prima, il dì sesto d'aprile,
nel laberinto intrai, né veggio ond'esca. (sonnet 211)

Desire spurs me, Love guides and escorts me, Pleasure draws me, Habit carries me away; Hope entices and encourages me and reaches out his hand to my weary heart, and my wretched heart grasps it and does not see how blind and treacherous this guide of ours is; the senses govern and reason is dead; and one yearning desire is born after another. Virtue, honor, beauty, gentle bearing, sweet words brought us to the lovely branches, that my heart may be sweetly enlimed. One thousand three hundred twenty seven, exactly at the first hour of the sixth day of April, I entered the labyrinth, nor do I see where I may get out of it.

The sonnet starts by describing what is called a *psychomachia*, the battle that Desire, Love, Pleasure, Habit, and Hope stage within the lover's soul (ll. 1–8). The map of the mind, which the *Secretum* draws more fully, is here given as the economy of the passions, as a cluster of personified impulses and desires endlessly springing from other desires. The virtues of Laura themselves—Virtue, Honor, Beauty, gentle bearing, and sweet words—have treacherously conspired with the passions to enthrall his heart (ll. 9–11). The battle, then, was lost from the start, and the last tercet records the time of the beginning of his obsessive love: April 6, 1327, the first hour of the day, is the indelible mark of the time of his self-loss and his love. That was, so states the climactic line of the sonnet, when "nel laberinto intrai, né veggio ond'esca" (l. 14), which Robert Durling translates as "I entered the labyrinth, nor do I see where I may get out of it."

Love's labyrinth, where there is no exit, where every door hides a new partition and every opening leads again and again into the heart of the maze, is for Petrarch his work of art, which he, like Daedalus, creates and in which he, like Daedalus, gets caught. But the labyrinth, which is the simultaneous emblem of parts and totality, also figures the work of art as a radically autonomous structure erected and sustained by its own laws rather than by an outside code which would make its plan decipherable; the labyrinth is the self. More than that, for Petrarch the final word of the sonnet, "esca" (get out of it) hides within itself its very opposite. "Esca" translates the Latin *hamus*, the bait of love, and traditionally it is the etymological origin of *amor*. The duality within a seemingly innocent word, its quality to say one thing and at the same time its very opposite, breaches the claim of selfsame identity and unity of poetic language. Doubleness and division lurk at the very heart of a word and of the self. At the center of the labyrinth, as Daedalus knew and as Petrarch knows, there is the monster of death.

Ever since he wrote the *Vita nuova*, Dante was questing for a form of visionary poetry that would bind together various strands of experience against the partitions and fragmentations engendered by critical, analytical thinking. The prose of the *Vita nuova* indicts the view of poetry in terms of formal, technical divisions, as if this sort of prosaic analysis could release mere simulacra of thought and partial (and hence false) glimmers of the whole. Petrarch, who views poetry as the act by which fame is acquired and death is conquered, never loses sight of the ultimate illusoriness and vanity of art, which, in fact, makes his idolatry hollow, a temptation which merely signals his ironic desire for some form of stability for his restless quest.

He understands the politics and the practice of power as few men of letters have (with the exception of Machiavelli, who duly acknowledges Petrarch at the end of his *Prince*). His endorsement of rhetoric, which at bottom is a theory of power (as theoreticians of rhetoric from Nietzsche to Foucault clearly grasp), unavoidably stumbles, however, against rhetoric's utter limit. It is not through a theory of argument, no more than it is through forms of power, that the unity he longs for can be achieved, for power stems from, feeds on, and foments division and arguments. Unity can be achieved (and this is the burden of chapter 7) by a radical turn, whereby love is understood as surrender, as the charity that he finds in the solitude of the contemplative heart. It can be achieved by prayer as the conversation between the soul and God. The aesthetics of prayer induces a reconsideration of the notion of the subject: by prayer—by abiding, that is, in a language which preexists oneself and is not determined by oneself and which, because of its incantatory and formulaic structure, one cannot call one's own— the petitioner questions and quests for the very source of his being.

In this figuration of Petrarch, one can glimpse the faces of the Renaissance and the torn fabric of modernity and of modernity's self-inscription within the cult of power. The powerful disintegrative impulses that characterize the Renaissance's discoveries—its critical and philological arts that dissolve unity (Valla), the idea that politics is an autonomous pursuit (Machiavelli) and that science is not accountable to theology (Galileo), the tragic contentiousness within the various theological visions which ought to have served as the ground for any possible order—will be countered in the Renaissance by visionaries and poets. The individual, scattered strands of experience, which Petrarch traces in the loom of his language, will be disentangled, rethought, and, at least provisionally, once again interlaced for modernity by the prodigious energy of Vico's poetic philosophy.

CHAPTER I

Antiquity and the New Arts

The convention of partitioning history according to distinguishable and discrete intellectual periods has not gone unchallenged in recent times.[1] Historiographic categories such as "Renaissance," "modernity," and "Middle Ages" continue to retain at least a nominal validity as terms of chronological demarcation (certainly useful for primers of literary history), but the historical specificity of each epoch, which in the nineteenth century could be defined with ease, is now hard to pinpoint. In 1870 Francesco De Sanctis published his *Storia della letteratura italiana,* which is shaped by the Hegelian belief in the organic, teleological process of history. The security of the Hegelian historiographic model, wherein contradictory individual phenomena can be manipulated into an overarching totality or significant unity, is in question from a variety of perspectives. Paradoxically, two radically contrasting premises about history usually end up agreeing in their dismissal of historical boundaries. These boundaries are arbitrary, it is said, because "human nature tends to remain much the same in all times." The judgment is underwritten by those who believe in the irreducible individuality of each spiritual and artistic experience.[2] But the major doubts about the legitimacy of traditional historical periodizations occur to scholars who, engaged as they are in interpretive practices, inevitably come to discover that data cannot be rigidly classified or epistemological breaks identified and to recognize the crudeness of the notion of originality and foundation in literary history. They discover, in short, that textual details do not always fit the generality of formulas established a priori and that canons of a culture repress or exclude what may contradict the myths of that culture.

These doubts have been recently reinforced by deconstructive modes of analysis, but they need not be thought of merely as the domain of deconstruction theory. Renaissance scholars, for instance, have long been aware of how blurred the dividing line between "medieval" and "Renaissance" culture is. They have wondered whether the concept "Renaissance" is, in the words of Erwin Panofsky, an accurate

Blurred dividing line

"self-definition" or a mere "self-deception," and they have probed the degree to which the uniqueness of the Italian Renaissance extends the Carolingian revival and the Ottonian resurgence of the tenth century.[3] The notion of "modernity" is certainly no less problematical. In an important study written in the 1970s, *The Legitimacy of the Modern Age*, Hans Blumenberg argues that modernity, a period that stretches broadly from the 1600s to the present, is a legitimate category of history in that it inaugurates a new configuration in the field of knowledge. The "epochal threshold" or reversal of direction from the core of theological dogmatics, which characterizes the historical process until the 1600s, is not embodied by Nicholas Cusanus, as Hans-Georg Gadamer maintains, but by Giordano Bruno's "heretical" casting of the plurality of worlds in an infinite cosmology.[4] Blumenberg never stops to consider "modernity" as a theoretical, persistently present question of positing a break from tradition if only to discover that modernity is forever inscribed in the archives of the past. Nor does he probe the self-evident aporia of any historicist philosophy that affirms the ceaseless mobility of the historical process and yet must arrest history's flow in order to impart a new direction to it. His aim, rather, is to counter Karl Lowith's assertion that the discourse of modernity is a secular retrieval of medieval themes. The legitimacy of the modern age, stated simply, resides in the scientific subversion of the authority of the canon as well as of the paradigms of knowledge rampant in the theological, medieval models of the economy of creation.

Medieval and Renaissance scholars could easily take to task Blumenberg's concept of a prolonged, unified Middle Ages as well as his version of an unscientific Middle Ages as the last in an endless series of myths that modernity keeps forging about the past in order to justify itself. If one were to look at the 1979 issue of *New Literary History* devoted to the "Alterity of the Middle Ages," one could perceive the fallacy of, say, Henry O. Taylor's *The Mediaeval Mind*, with its overt claim that the Middle Ages was a time of spiritual homogeneity.[5] One could also see the gulf yawning between the present state of medieval studies and that of the nineteenth century, when Gaston Paris at the Collège de France, Francisque Michel at Bordeaux, Léon Gautier, and, eventually, Joseph Bédier made the knowledge of the Middle Ages (in the double value of the genitive case) central to the curriculum. These savants could even object to the distortions as to what the Middle Ages were (and the list of perpetrators goes from Rabelais to Voltaire to Chateaubriand to Hugo) without themselves escaping other distortions they inevitably committed in the name of paleography, philology, and archaeology. The old myths about the Middle Ages linger tenaciously in new guises. Because the encyclopedia of Vincent of Beauvais, written toward the middle of the thirteenth century, in many ways derives from Isidore of Seville's *Etymologies*, written some seven centuries earlier, it is still assumed by medievalists that the inventory of knowledge remains unchanged.[6] That Vincent makes available to the general public the new Aristotle, Arabic writings on the sciences, and the Chartrians is not deemed sufficient to dispel the notion that knowledge in the Middle Ages is a perpetual anachronism, an immutable, closed-off space of superstitious beliefs. The impression of an immobile universe of knowledge is reinforced by the practice of biblical exegesis (notoriously conservative), which, in its quasi-mechanical repetitiveness, seeks to shelter the sovereignty of the Biblical Text from subversive encroachments. The infinitely selfsame message of biblical exegesis, of the Neoplatonic structures, and of forever-fixed scholastic arrangements of the totality of creation unavoidably project the Middle Ages as the parable of an untroubled utopia of the soul, of an otherness no longer accessible to us, of an "alterity," in short (the word, of course, is the matrix of allegory), that is both an alibi and a scandal to current intellectual concerns.

This powerful and alluring vision of an ordered world is a repression of history, of the contradictory voices punctuating the philosophical debates, the spiritual lacerations, or the political struggles of the thirteenth and fourteenth centuries. One would only have to mention the impact of Aristotle's *De anima* and its commentary by Averroës at the universities of Oxford and Paris in the thirteenth century; Marsilius's doctrine of law as coercive power (*potentia coactiva*), his determination of the ground of authority and popular sovereignty; or the crisis of biblical exegesis, which was the genuine bone of contention between St. Bernard of Clairvaux and Abelard.[7] Finally, one would have to mention the consciousness that poets such as Jean de Meun, Dante, Chaucer, and others have of the crisis investing the various forms of knowledge. Because of the steady interrogation of their own values and epistemological premises, these poets and philosophers question us at the moment in which we recognize the problematic status of the Middle Ages as a category of cognition.

Petrarch divides

I have no wish to cut through this swath of problems in an abstract manner. I shall focus on Petrarch, instead, because he consistently reflects, both in his prose meditations and in his poetry, on his own radical difference from the world of the past as well as his apartness from his own times. This private experience of apartness is the basis for the articulation of a larger historical rupture. It is Petrarch, as a matter of fact, who posits a clear-cut division between the Middle Ages and modernity as the historical time that supersedes and alters the achievements of what has come to be known as the "Dark Ages."[8] The phrase, which reappears in d'Alembert as "la nuit médiévale" to be opposed to "l'époque de lumière," had circulated even before Petrarch.[9] For Petrarch it designates the limits of vision—the limit of a culture that ignores the values of the classical world and that spans the time between the birth of Christ and his own age. In truth, Petrarch will also say that the advent of Christ marks "the end of the darkness and the night of error . . . the dawn of the true light." Yet the decline of Rome and the concomitant eclipse of classical antiquity has cast a thick shadow on man's earthly life.[10]

In and of itself, the desire to promote the rebirth of classical antiquity and its rich spiritual deposit cannot be said to start with Petrarch. The twelfth-century revival of classicism simply belies such a hypothetical claim. In Italy, on the other hand, the likes of Albertino Mussato, Lovato dei Lovati, Geremia da Montagnone, and Giovanni del Virgilio were involved in the early fourteenth century in salvaging what seemed to be the hopelessly defaced documents and texts of the pagan past. Few poets had understood, as much as Dante, the radical modernity of Vergil. Modernity, as a matter of fact, is a thematic strain in Dante's poetic thought. Guinizelli is acknowledged as the ranking poet in the *uso moderno*—a phrase that makes modernity another term for the ephemeral, for the predicament of temporality in which each experience will be unavoidably transcended by a succeeding one.[11] But Vergil's modernity is asserted as his power to enter and affect the concerns of the present. More generally, a mere listing of well-known titles—*Poetria nova, Logica nova, Vita nova*—or of the awareness of a new poetic style, the *stil nuovo*, shows that there is a rhetoric of the "new" which is systematically invoked for the accretion of knowledge or for stressing departures, whether real or not, from established practices.

We must, however, distinguish between the new as a fact and the

Christ = end of darkness
Decline of Rome → thick shadow

new as an idea or as a way of thinking. New facts and experiences are indisputable throughout the medieval centuries. The idea of the new, paradoxically, was introduced by Christianity's subversion of the most cherished myths of classicism, by the insertion, that is, into history of the story of redemption that was bound to perplex the exacting rigor of the natural philosophers. The paradox consists in the fact that the renewal of man's spiritual history entails the closure of history. As far as Petrarch goes, the laicization of culture, which he calls for, is an imaginative extension of the "dawn of light" ushered in by the Incarnation.

If there is any radicality in Petrarch's epistemological break from the Dark Ages, it will be found in the retrieval of antiquity not as an episodic, contingent event, but as a systematic undertaking, as a total personal enterprise that involves him in a fundamental rethinking of the whole canon. Even after making allowances for the genuine affection Boccaccio felt for Petrarch, one is struck by how deeply Boccaccio grasped the significance of Petrarch's role as he acknowledges that Petrarch alone among the figures of his times had reinstated "Apollo in his ancient sanctuary"; that he had "reinvested the muses, soiled by rusticity, with their ancient beauty," and "had rededicated to the Romans the Capitol."[12]

Contemporary critics of Petrarch, Petrarch's own claims notwithstanding, continue to consider him as a belated poet, painfully aware of the long shadow Dante casts on him; as a self-absorbed, narcissistic figure forever moaning over the impermanence in the world of time. This common perception of Petrarch's pathos, in point of fact, superimposes on Petrarch the fads of later Petrarchism and mistakes the pose of later poets for that of Petrarch himself, as if he were unaware that the ruptured sense he has of himself turns into the imaginary space where larger concerns are tested. But how exactly does Petrarch's insight into his own self affect his impulse to forge a new culture? In what way is this culture new?

There are many texts one could study in order to carry out such an exploration of how the figuration of a broken self issues into a sustained intellectual project. I shall look at a well-known letter from *The Familiares* (Letters on Familiar Matters) Petrarch wrote as a response to Giovanni Colonna, who bids him to write down the conversation they held one day while wandering through the ruins of Rome.[13] I should remark on how essential conversations, letters, and polemics (his hatreds are subtle but famous) are to Petrarch's style of thought. It is a style that needs the support of objective evidence, of different minds *turning together,* in conversation, as if the discovery of truth were inseparable from the ability to communicate. But Petrarch will never lapse into the illusions of what in modern times has come to be known as objectivist literature.

He begins his letter by evoking wistfully that wandering, "deambulabamus Rome soli," until the two of them sit among the Baths of Diocletian. The chief rhetorical move of the letter is to insist that he is unable to duplicate the intensity of the pathos felt that day: "Redde mihi illum locum, illud ocium, illam diem, illam attentationem tuam, illam ingenii mei venam. . . . Sed mutata sunt omnia; locus abest, dies abiit, ocium periit, pro facie tua mutas litteras aspicio" (Give me back that place, that idle mood, that day, that attention of yours, that particular vein of my talent. . . . But all things are changed; the place is not present, the day has passed, the idle mood has gone, and instead of your face I look upon silent words).[14] The anaphoric sequence, "illum . . . illud . . . illam," which makes poignant the impossibility of regaining the multifaceted moods of that day, stresses from the start the awareness of the gaps of time, the sense of disjunction between proximate temporal experiences, or, to put it most simply, the perpetual fragmentation in the ordinary texture of life.

The rhetorical structure of this paragraph aims at providing the revelation of time's fleeting essence: it introduces time as the principle of difference and as a devastation from which nothing is left untouched. But the metaphor of "wandering" ("deambulabamus") that opens the text forces us to considerations of the complementary problem of space. Wandering, let me say, is a favorite metaphor with Petrarch, for it brings to one focus the movement of the Augustinian unquiet heart and pure drifting. Many of his texts crystallize such ambivalent motion. "The Ascent of Mount Ventoux" is the record of a quest and gratuitous mountain climbing. *On His Own Ignorance* is written during a ride on the Po River, as if the tortuous flow of the river were a metaphor for the rambling of the mind. "Wandering," properly speaking, is neither a journey with a destination, nor is it quite an exile, for "home"—whether Platonic or biblical, a place of departure and arrival one longs for—is not the issue. To wander is a pure adventure in pursuit of the ghostly traces of time, a moving about which allows a worldview to emerge. This worldview combines the aimlessness, the utter dislocation of the sightseer as he confronts alien objects, which are themselves dislocated out of any intelligible framework, with the muteness of the ruins. The ruins, in turn, recall something else, but what is conjured up does not rise up as it once was. Because ruins suspend the principle of identity and show that the past is out of reach, they are the material signs of time as it effaces all signs, emblems of a difference made materially immanent. The shifting viewpoints in the two friends' perambulation, finally, yield the figuration of a noncommunicating world which stands in stark contrast to the conversational mood enveloping them.

This figuration puts Petrarch, as well as us, in the path of a revelation: the revelation of both time and space as ruptured both in themselves and from each other. But the fragmentariness of viewpoints, of time, space, and objects, also reveals the power of local, partial shapes. The principle of localization, I submit, is central to Petrarch's imagination: the source of the Sorgue River, the grass of Vaucluse, the Capitol in Rome, and not Paris, as the place where the crowning of the poet must occur, Avignon, the Roman forum, are privileged spots which show that for Petrarch there is a truth of the moment as well as the truth of a place. The irreducible *genius loci* lays a trap, ensnares the poet, and forces him to extract its secret essence.[15]

The thematic burden of the letter is the record of the (un)recognizable spots of Roman myth. Petrarch and Giovanni Colonna see, the letter says, where Evander's residence stood; they point out the cave of Cacus and the she-wolf that nursed Romulus and Remus. They remember the duel of the Horatii and Curiatii, the Tarpeian Rock, and the place of Caesar's triumph and death. They wander from the column of Trajan to Hadrian's tomb, to the palace of Nero and that of Augustus. Giovanni Colonna, on his part, takes special note of the Christianized pagan ruins—Trajan's bridge, which has taken the name of St. Peter; he points out the place where St. Peter was crucified, St. Lawrence grilled, and Constantine healed of his leprosy.

The dual perspective on history, pagan and Christian, shows that history is not a homogeneous totality or a monolith: there are in the same theater of history, on the contrary, divergent lines, diversified chronologies, and residual layers buried under or scattered over the ground: "As we walked over the shattered city, with the fragments of the ruins under our eyes, we talked about history, which we appeared to have divided between us in such a fashion that in modern history

20

! exploring ancient Rome

[*historiae novae*] you, and in ancient history [*historiae antiquae*] I, seemed to be more expert; and ancient were called those events which took place before the name of Christ was celebrated in Rome and adored by the Roman emperors, modern, however, the events from that time to the present."[16] In this penumbral world of graves and of time's dominion, history is an archaeological palimpsest whereby time turns into laminations of space. In a primary way, however, history is memory, the poetic recollection of the legends and the realities of Rome, whose ground is hallowed by its antiquities.

Petrarch's synoptic sketch of Rome is a profound alteration of medieval historiography on Rome.[17] The fall of Rome in 410 A.D. was more than the collapse of a city, for what had been shattered with that fall was the Vergilian myth of the eternity of Rome. The Fathers of the Church, from St. Jerome to St. Augustine, responded with shock at the news of the havoc wrought in the city of Rome. Vergil's prophecy in the *Aeneid*, "I give them [the Romans] dominion without end," had deluded men into believing in the stability of the earthly city. The fall of Rome, which exposes the fallacy of the Vergilian prediction, elicited contrasting assessments.[18]

In a way, the early Church apologists longed for the fall of the Roman Empire. The Book of Revelation, after all, had identified Rome with Babylon, while the Roman persecution of the Christians, it was felt, justified the Christians' harsh judgment against the empire. Irenaeus eagerly waits for the fall, as does Tertullian.[19] But for Lactantius the fall of Rome, which must inevitably take place, was identified with the imminent fall of the world:

> The fall and ruin of the world will shortly take place, although it seems that nothing of that kind is to be feared as long as the city of Rome stands intact. But when the capital of the world has fallen . . . who can doubt that the end will have arrived for the affairs of men and the whole world? It is that city which sustains all things. And the God of Heaven is to be entreated and implored—if indeed his laws and decrees can be delayed— lest sooner than we think that detestable tyrant should come who will undertake so great a deed and tear out that eye by the destruction of which the world itself is about to fall.

Such apocalyptic ruminations are echoed by St. Augustine in his *Sermon on the Ruin of the City* and by the Pseudo-Bede, who writes the famous lines, "Quamdiu stabit Coliseus stabit et Roma; quando cadet

Coliseus, cadet et Roma; quando cadet Roma, cadet et mundus" (As long as the Colosseum will stand, Rome will stand; when the Colosseum will fall, Rome will also fall; when Rome will fall, so will the world).[20]

That Petrarch is aware of this apocalyptic strain deduced from the fall of Rome is beyond question. The *canzone* on Rome, "Spirto gentil" (song 53) (Noble spirit), recalls the sepulchres of the ancient Romans who will be remembered, "se l'universo pria non si dissolve" (until the universe is dissolved). But in the letter to Giovanni Colonna, Petrarch puts himself at the end, at the point where history is already over and he is bewildered by the incommensurability of the fragments and their deathlike fixity. The pathos of his prose initially reminds the reader of St. Jerome's reaction on hearing, while in Bethlehem, the news of Rome's fall: "When the brightest light on the whole earth was extinguished, when the Roman empire was deprived of its head and when, to speak more correctly, the whole world perished in one city, then I was dumb with silence, I held my peace, . . . and my sorrow was stirred."[21] The initial response in Petrarch, who is not in the place of a new birth as Jerome was, can be called an *aesthetics* of ruins, for they are adumbrations of his own mortality. The time of reflection, which is the recollection of the promenade among the ruins, swerves from the apocalyptic visions of an Irenaeus, a Lactantius, or a Pseudo-Bede. He perceives discontinuities at the heart of the tradition, which someone like Dante would still view as a uniform reality; he recognizes the pastness of the past in the sense that the monuments of the past appear to him as taciturn shadows of a shattered historical discourse, obscure signs of the withdrawal of what men have made into the opaque surface of the ground. The archaeological findings, finally, excite the writer's imagination. By the imagination, which has the power to unify and totalize the parts of the broken world, the past takes shape in the mind of Petrarch. From the gloom of piled-up ruins, distinct shapes emerge, buildings are resurrected from the dust in which they lie and are rearranged in the rigorous topography of the eternal city.

This is not to say that Petrarch's reconstruction happens simply in his mind, as if the mind were a theater of chimeras and private phantasms. The ruins, which are narratives of lost realities, are not lifeless relics; rather, they are inexhaustible coils of memory, tumultuous signs rising up from the dark depths of time. Because in the very effacement of the columns the legend of time is indelibly inscribed, the relics draw him within their ghostly boundaries. Objects become subjects capable of summoning us into the enigma of their presence, prodigious points of force from which memories endlessly radiate. To miss the power of what amounts to Petrarch's poetics of objects and places would mean missing the sensuous signs of his desire.

In this authentic place of desolation and imaginative excitement, the *commonplaces* of Roman history arise. But there is more to it. Petrarch does not surrender to the forebodings of a general apocalypse, nor does he get absorbed in thoughts of personal annihilation. The text tells us that after discussing history, Petrarch and Giovanni Colonna turn their attention to problems of moral philosophy, the arts, and their authors and practitioners. He even writes that a book is needed in order to go over the origin of the figurative arts.[22] In *De remediis utriusque fortunae* (from chapter 34 to chapter 40), Petrarch discusses the origin of the liberal arts and of painting and sculpture. In the letter he seems to announce a speculative work on painting, sculpture, and architecture.

Here lies, in truth, the novelty of Petrarch's cultural project. This awareness of death, which he experiences in a variety of ways and from which he never quite frees himself, triggers a rethinking of the sense of tradition. He discovers, to be exact, that the canon of knowledge, like the plot of history, is not a sacrosanct, untouchable concept but a historical construction liable to change and subject to manipulations. The circle of knowledge he proposes excludes current scientific fashions; he jettisons the metaphysical baggage of the scholastics; he dismisses physics and dialectics and circumscribes the status of medicine. At the same time, he responds to the new musical theories and experiments of the fourteenth century, and he gives the pride of place to rhetoric, historiography, and the figurative arts. In theology he replaces Aquinas's abstractions with the detailed, steady self-analysis of St. Augustine's *Confessions* and the meditative strains of St. Bonaventure's *Itinerarium mentis in Deum.* In his poetics he contrives to place his voice in the interval between the real world and the elusive now of his consciousness. The real world remains, in all its obduracy, outside, but the poet carries within himself an internal world etched with discontinuous moments, varied places, sounds, memories, footprints, wanderings, murmurings, flights, and halts—the ephemeral profiles of his exorbitant experience.

What binds together the different aspects of this massive cultural shift is the conviction, as will be shown further in chapter 5, that history is, above all, the work of man's language and the construction of his imagination. Dante wrote with the knowledge, however ironic, that the poet could impart a moral direction to history; history, for him, was an objective, recognizable reality which his vision would shape. Petrarch, on the contrary, installs the intellectual as the agent of history, as the hero in the empire of culture. The sense of this move bears some clarification. The dense tangle of ruins comes alive only in the mind of the intellectual, who is a rhetorician, poet, moral philosopher, by virtue of his power to evoke history's sedimented memories, echo its myths, and wrest its voice from its sepulchral silence.

From this perspective it is clear why Petrarch, hemmed in by the crumbling images of history, internalizes the outside world. Philology and antiquarianism are his tools for retrieving and safeguarding the relics of the past, but the empire of knowledge is under the sovereignty of the imagination. As a book collector, antiquarian, and philologist, Petrarch is the custodian of memories. To internalize this world means that nothing is blotted out, because nothing can be blotted out if not at the risk of self-annihilation. In this internalization, finally, the self is not an isolated figure; Petrarch implicates, rather, the ghosts of the past and present in his consciousness, where there occur perpetual encounters of other minds, incongruous encounters, at that, across epochs—St. Augustine, Seneca, Cicero, and numberless other figures of his displacement of self.

A question, however, forces itself on us. Is there ever a principle of transcendent order, an objective norm, by which the world of history is imaginatively re-formed? Or does a political act, such as the making of the self as a public persona, depend purely on the subjective taste, the whim and self-interest, of the individual? To answer this crucial question, I shall look at the role the city of Avignon plays in Petrarch's discourse as it is registered in his *Liber sine nomine* and in two sonnets from his *Canzoniere*.

Petrarch's political judgment of Avignon's usurpation of what properly belongs to the history of the city of Rome is well known.[23] As the illegitimate see of the Popes, Avignon is variously the "golden labyrinth," "Babylon on the Rhone," a "den of thieves," the "woman clothed in scarlet," from Apocalypse 17. And the crimes Petrarch witnesses elicit in him a sinister catalogue of unnatural acts perpe-

Avignon

trated by the likes of Pasiphae, Semiramis, Nero, Domitian, and Nimrod. Playing, as he consistently does, with the Latin etymology of *Avignon* (*Avinio*), this is the city of drunken frenzy where the authority of God's laws and the laws of nature are perverted.[24]

The exposure of the curia's moral transgressions recalls the language of the Franciscan Spirituals (for example, Ubertino da Casale's description of the Church as "ecclesia carnalis"), Dante's arguments in *Monarchia* and his political letters, and Catherine of Siena's appeal to the Popes to return the Church to its proper place.[25] But Petrarch's sense of Avignon's political illegitimacy surfaces in the effort and subsequent failure of Cola di Rienzo's attempt to restore the Roman republic against the tyranny of the barons. In the crisis, Petrarch argues, the authority of the Church is weakened by its illegal practices, which are a flaunting mockery of the principles of Roman justice. When the tribune Cola di Rienzo is imprisoned, Petrarch writes: "Like a thief of the night or a traitor to his country, he pleads his cause from chains. And, what is never even denied to a sacrilegious person, he is deprived of the right to defend himself before the judges of the world and the magistrates of justice. . . . But Rome does not merit this, for in times past her citizens were untouchable and exempt from punishment by law."[26]

Both in *Liber sine nomine*, letter 4, and in the invective *Contra eum qui maledixit Italie* Petrarch maintains the impossibility of a *translatio* from Rome to Avignon. The legitimacy of Rome is grounded in the divine plan, for the Incarnation took place, he says echoing *Monarchia*, when Rome had established peace and justice on earth.[27] Emperors may wander, but the empire is "fixed and stable." The perpetuity of the empire, secondly, is guaranteed by Vergil's divine prophecy of a dominion without end granted to the Romans. Aware of St. Augustine's disapproval of this prophecy, Petrarch takes him to task, much as Dante had obliquely done.[28] Thirdly, in *Contra eum* Avignon is deemed illegitimate because the eternal city has not completely fallen: its walls and buildings are crumbling, but "gloria nominis immortalis est." The statement, which finds its extension in a rhetorical question such as "what else, then, is all history if not the praise of Rome?,"[29] draws history within the orbit of rhetoric, and Clio or Fama is its muse. In sum, Rome is the literal ground of any legitimacy. The claim rests on a theological rationale as well as on a rhetorical understanding of names as forces and topics of discourse.

Compares injustices on the popes / Church to the ideals of Roman Law

The resistance to the political *translation* from Rome to Avignon effaces the basis of metaphor, which is the Greek term for *translation* and which is a trope, as Quintilian writes, whereby "a noun or a verb is transferred from the place to which it properly belongs to another where there is either no literal term or the transferred is better than the literal."[30] The implicit contradiction between a political conviction and poetic metaphor casts poetry into an area of illegitimacy.

There is no palpable causality between the empirical experience of lawlessness in Avignon and Petrarch's rearrangement of the cultural paradigms of his times. Positive philological proofs are unavailable, yet it is of interest to note that exactly in Avignon Marsilius and Ockham elaborate heterodox doctrines on authority. Petrarch, a one-time student of law at Montpellier and Bologna, may have known all along what jurisprudence states, that laws are nothing but legal fictions. At any rate, over and against his harsh judgment of Papal Avignon, it is clear that Avignon, which had become a cosmopolitan intellectual crossroads, was a major catalyst in Petrarch's thought. In Avignon were to be found Nicholas Trivet, Marsilius of Padua, Pierre Bersuire, Ludwig van Kempen, Luca delle Penne, William of Ockham, Jean de Jandun, Convenevole da Prato, Philippe de Vitry, and Richard de Bury. More importantly, in Avignon Petrarch came to know the painter Simone Martini.[31] Painting was a truly novel art form in his time, an art which the "Dark Ages" had forgotten and modernity had brought back to light. What exactly is painting for Petrarch? And how does he stage a confrontation between painting and poetry in some of his texts?

The kinship between the two "sister arts"—as they are so often called—is a cliché of literary history. From Plato, who says that "the poet is like a painter," to Horace's notion of poetry's pictorialism contained in the dictum, "Ut pictura poesis erit. Non erit dissimilis poetica ars picturae," to Leonardo's assertion of the superiority of graphic over verbal expression, the focus falls on the insight that painting is mute poetry and poetry is a speaking picture.[32] Poets, in turn, have always deployed pictorial or figurative devices: Vergil's *ecphrasis* of Aeneas's shield, Guillaume de Lorris's sculptures in the garden of the *Roman de la rose*, Boccaccio's *Amorosa visione*, and Chaucer's *House of Fame* and many other texts exemplify the persistence of the technique. In the lyrical tradition of Provence and

Sicily one consistently finds the topos of the painted image of the beloved that the lover carries within his heart.

From this viewpoint, these poets entertain no suspicion about the illusionism of painting, embodied in the Platonic repudiation of painting as sheer deception and as a mimetic art listed among activities such as weaving and interior decoration. This suspicion of painting is voiced in the Middle Ages by Isidore of Seville, who in his *Etymologies* states that "*pictura* is the representation expressing the appearance of anything, which when it is beheld, makes the mind remember. *Pictura* is, moreover, pronounced almost *fictura*. For it is a feigned representation, not the truth. Hence it is also counterfeited, that is, it is smeared over with a fabricated color and possesses nothing of credibility or truth."[33]

What to Isidore is a counterfeit (color, he believes, is a sign of painting's unreality) is greeted by Dante and Boccaccio as the art of the new age.[34] Petrarch's involvement with painting goes beyond their excitement at the discovery of this visual art by Giotto. Petrarch owned a painting by Giotto, which he bequeaths to Francesco da Carrara; in the *Rerum familiarum libri* he links Giotto and Simone Martini along with Apelles and Phidias; and he alludes to paintings by Giotto and Simone that he had seen in Naples. Of the two, he favors Simone, whom he had met in Italy and saw again in Avignon during the years 1339–44, when painters such as Matteo Giovannetti and Thomas Daristot and Hugh Wilfred from England were brought in to work at the Palais des Papes.[35] But Petrarch's favor for Simone is also intellectual, for he belongs to the tradition of Agostino di Duccio and Byzantine miniaturists, a tradition that opposes the mimetic representation of reality that Giotto embodies. Boccaccio, writing of Giotto's aesthetics, praises the powerful illusion of reality he achieves, though he also understands how inscrutable the appearances in Giotto's realism are. Simone Martini's painting, on the other hand, places the natural objects and the phenomenal world away from their ordinary context in a transfigured space. This is, at least, what one can infer from the two sonnets Petrarch writes on Simone Martini's now-lost portrait of Laura.

> Per mirar Policleto a prova fiso
> con gli altri ch'ebber fama di quell'arte

mill'anni, non vedrian la minor parte
della beltà che m'ave il cor conquiso.

Ma certo il mio Simon fu in Paradiso
onde questa gentil donna si parte;
ivi la vide, et la ritrasse in carte
per far fede qua giù del suo bel viso.

L'opra fu ben di quelle che nel cielo
si ponno imaginar, non qui tra noi,
ove le membra fanno a l'alma velo.

Cortesia fe'; né la potea far poi
che fu disceso a provar caldo et gielo
et del mortal sentiron gli occhi suoi. (sonnet 77)

Even though Polycletus should for a thousand years compete in looking
with all the others who were famous in that art, they would never see the
smallest part of the beauty that has conquered my heart. But certainly my
Simone was in Paradise, whence comes this noble lady; there he saw her
and portrayed her on paper, to attest down here to her lovely face. The
work is one of those which can be imagined only in Heaven, not here
among us, where the body is a veil to the soul; it was a gracious act, nor
could he have done it after he came down to feel heat and cold and his
eyes took on mortality.

Quando giunse a Simon l'alto concetto
ch'a mio nome gli pose in man lo stile,
s'avesse dato a l'opera gentile
colla figura voce ed intelletto,

di sospir molti mi sgombrava il petto
che ciò ch'altri à più caro, a me fan vile.
Però che 'n vista ella si monstra humile
promettendomi pace ne l'aspetto.

Ma poi ch'io vengo a ragionar con lei,
benignamente assai par che m'ascolte:
se risponder savesse a' detti miei!

Pigmalion, quanto lodar ti dei
de l'imagine tua, se mille volte
n'avesti quel ch'i' sol una vorrei. (sonnet 78)

When Simon received the high idea which, for my sake, put his hand on
his stylus, if he had given to his noble work voice and intellect along with
form, he would have lightened my breast of many sighs that make what

others prize most vile to me. For in appearance she seems humble, and
her expression promises peace; then, when I come to speak to her, she
seems to listen most kindly: if she could only reply to my words!
Pygmalion, how glad you should be of your statue, since you received a
thousand times what I yearn to have just once.[36]

That the two sonnets are meant to be read together is made clear
by their common argument: Laura's painting by Simone Martini.
Textual details, such as "mill'anni" in sonnet 77 and "mille volte" in
sonnet 78, as well as the two symmetrical references to the sculptors
Polycletus and Pygmalion, respectively, certainly mark them apart
from the poetic sequence. On the face of it, there is even a thematic
progression in the two sonnets, which is also suggested by the mythic
resonances of the two sculptors. In sonnet 77 the focus falls on the
artistic process: Simone Martini is said to have been in Paradise to be
able to produce this portrait of Laura. The conceit behind the en-
comium of Simone is the praise of the incomparable beauty of the
model. In sonnet 78 the lover is not simply engaged in an aesthetic
contemplation of the icon, for a disruptive tension is introduced by the
lover's will to animate the figure and possess her. If Polycletus is the
emblem of a most excellent sculptor who has been surpassed by
Simone, Pygmalion is the sculptor who, according to Ovid's *Meta-
morphoses* and Jean de Meun's *Roman de la rose,* carved an ivory statue
of an unresponsive maid and is seized by a lovesickness for it until
Venus transforms the statue into a living woman.[37] A mythographer
such as Arnulf d'Orléans interprets the Ovidian fable as the allegory
of idolatry, as the narrative of the artist who loves the work of his own
hands as though it were a true woman.[38] The import of such an
allegorization is not immediately clear in the two Petrarchan sonnets.
At an explicit, literal level, in point of fact, the similes of the mythic
sculptors break down in the unfolding of the poetic argument: Poly-
cletus, the text says, could not find an adequate beauty for his art as
Simone did; Petrarch can never embrace, as Pygmalion did a thousand
times, Laura's living body.

This collapse of the analogies that the poet institutes is meant to
suggest, first of all, the otherworldly uniqueness of Laura's beauty and,
second, the anguish of the forever unrequited lover. It also suggests,
more generally, Petrarch's disjunctive consciousness dramatized over
the two sonnets. Thus, in sonnet 77 the painting transposes Laura into

an enigmatic, spatial dimension where an otherworldly vision is available. The distinction between the ordinary perception of reality and its aesthetic transfiguration is stressed by the repeated juxtaposition of terms of place: "ivi" (l. 7) is balanced by "qua giù" (l. 8); "nel cielo" (l. 9) by "qui tra noi" (l. 10). The spatial contrast crystallizes the sense of Simone's representation as a supreme visionary experience. The language of vision, as a matter of fact, punctuates the movement of the sonnet: the word, "mirar" (l. 1)—literally a gazing—introduces Polycletus's hypothetical contest; we are told that Polycletus and the other painters would never be able to see a portion of Laura's beauty (l. 3); the work of art could only have been imagined in Paradise and not by mortal eyes (ll. 9–11). The icon, in its visionariness, opens our eyes to the knowledge that images force us to look within them. If for Dante and the mystics a visionary experience comes forth as a real event, in sonnet 77 vision is an aesthetic construction, the effect of art. This aesthetic vision is suspended between two contradictory experiences of vision: beauty (l. 4) and faith (l. 8). A standard definition of beauty holds that beauty, which is a principle of form, is that which, being seen, pleases. The term, "fede," on the other hand, suggests that this painting is not a counterfeit or a *falsigraphia* but a *simia veri*, a faithful reproduction of Laura's beauty. Faith, however, is also the evidence of things unseen.[39] This buried resonance of the term questions the referentiality of the model and stresses the iconic value of the portrait.

Sonnet 78 undoes the pattern of signification of sonnet 77. The timeless, transfigured spatiality which painting simulates turns out in sonnet 78 to be illusory. The image of painting is mute and unresponsive to the lover's entreaties (ll. 9–11). The muteness of the image is the counterpart of its deceptive surface: Laura in appearance seems humble (l. 7); her expression promises peace (l. 8); she seems to listen most kindly (l. 10). Painting, to state it plainly, falls short of the expectations it stirs: its elision of voice and the immobility of the image reveal the portrait to be the mask of death. This quality describing the essence of the portrait means that to look at it is to be caught in the contemplation of death. But we are not to see here a version of the traditional rivalry between painting and poetry. Unlike painting, poetry speaks, but because it speaks it is under the sway of time. By the end of the two sonnets, then, an aporia sets in: painting and poetry are provisionally brought together, only to return, like noncommunicating vessels, to their originary disjunction.

In this contemplation of death emerging from the work of art, the poet, who is unlike Pygmalion, turns out to be like Narcissus. In the *Roman de la rose,* when Pygmalion discovers his own passion for the image he has carved, he compares his insane love to that of Narcissus, who loved "sa propre figure." Whereas he can touch and kiss his statue, Narcissus is more of a fool because he only has a shadow in the fountain as the object of his desire. Later in the narrative, when the statue turns into living flesh, Pygmalion does not know whether or not what he beholds is a sorcery, a "fantosme ou anemis." The maid, who earlier had been unresponsive to either his speech or his prayer (a motif that Petrarch explicitly picks up in sonnet 78), answers that she is no demon and no phantom shape.[40] By his question, however, Pygmalion uncovers the narcissistic quality of his fixation: like Narcissus, who is suspended in a self-fascination in the mirror of the water, Pygmalion is in pursuit of an *eidolon,* which is a Greek term for an image or phantom of his own mind.

To claim that Petrarch is like Narcissus entails some notable consequences. Like Narcissus, who gazes at his reflected image and discovers himself—discovers, that is, that he, too, is a shadow—Petrarch looks at Simone's painting of Laura and "sees" in it his own mute reflection. The painted image's fixity, one may add, seduces the lover into its boundaries of beauty, which, ironically, has the fixity of death. Second, to claim that Petrarch is like Narcissus, the figure who never coincides with itself and who mistakes the self for another, implies that desire has an imaginary structure in that it is forever a desire for a figure or a shadow that cannot be reached; that figure can be oneself, another being, or a phantasmic self-image, which, in the labyrinthine articulation of the imagination, are never identical with but never wholly different from each other. It is of interest, finally, that Petrarch can voice these insights about the self through the new art form of his own times, painting. Just as the figuration of Narcissus shows, there are no clear-cut boundaries between the self and the other, the outside and the inside, the old and the new. The boundaries Petrarch steadily posits between Avignon and Rome (or barbarians and Italians), which are emblems of his vision of political order, are blurred by his poetic practice.

From this standpoint, Petrarch can be viewed as "epochal," but on the condition that the term be taken in its etymological sense, from the Greek *epoché,* which means a halt and a suspension. Petrarch is "epochal" in the sense that his poetry marks a pause and occupies the interval where cognition and judgment hang and where events, which are separated from each other in actuality, are gathered in thought. What is truly epochal, then, is thinking, which is a fairly common word in Petrarch's diction and which designates the rambling of the mind or the pause of reflection. The essence of thinking for Petrarch, as his *canzone* "Di pensier in pensier" shows, can (and must) be divined from the etymological resonance of "pensier"—from the Latin *pendere,* which means to hang or to suspend. Thought is a suspension, the insertion of a break in the flow of history, the effort to arrest the unseizable flight of time.

This in-between time, which historically we call *medium aevum,* is the unavoidable, forever recurring time of audacious thought, which is what poetry is. In this in-between time, the poet retrieves images of the past and discovers that the achievements of modernity are always inscribed in the past; that the figures of the past have the power to unsettle the complacencies of the present. This in-between time, finally, is the time of contradiction in which an ideology of power (Rome over Avignon) is reasserted, and in which the imaginative, noncanonical, transgressive experience of Avignon turns out to be the beginning of a new poetic canon, which was to be known as Petrarchism.

Petrarchism

CHAPTER II

The Thought of Love

Petrarch's place in the intellectual history of modern times is secure. Historians of philosophy, from Francesco Fiorentino to Giovanni Gentile, from Ernest Cassirer to Eugenio Garin and Paul O. Kristeller, have consistently recognized Petrarch's role as "the initiator of Renaissance humanism."[1] The acknowledgment is no doubt fully deserved, especially in the light of Petrarch's commitment to the *studia humanitatis*, which subsumes his conviction that knowledge has to be defined narrowly as the pursuit of humanistic disciplines such as grammar, rhetoric, poetry, history, and moral philosophy. In keeping with the recognition of what amounts to Petrarch's cultural project, he has been studied for his ideas of history, his ethical theories, his epistemology, his politics, and, in literary circles, for his poetry.

However, because his ideas are never organized systematically, his thought has always been difficult to define. We are constantly reminded, by the poet's own admission, of the large and varied fields of knowledge he traversed, of the sundry books he collected and eagerly read. But the content of his thought, the sources of which have been elaborately documented by scholars over the years, has never quite crystallized into a clear shape. This elusiveness most certainly has to do with the fact that Petrarch himself was never appreciative of the conceptually rigorous architectonics made current by the systematic dialecticians (Aquinas and the masters of Oxford and Paris), who proceeded on the assumption that the validity of ideas depends on their being part of a coherent and stable rational structure. Petrarch's work, on the contrary, appears as a restless succession of self-reflexive postures, as an analytic of the moods of thought and autobiographical experiences, but without a clear design or definite intellectual order.

Yet, as I shall argue in this chapter, Petrarch's mind and works move steadily around one overarching question, which is neither purely theoretical nor simply experiential. This question can be called, with some provisions, his "philosophy," but it is best summarized, by breaking up the word's etymological components, as the thought of

Argue that there is intellectual order

love, as a reflection on the relationship between love and knowledge, and this question radically shapes his poetic-intellectual vision. One could indeed talk, as the historians of philosophy mentioned above have done and continue to do, with the exception of Giovanni Gentile who theorized the link between poetry and philosophy, of a philosophical bent in Petrarch's work, but one can legitimately do so only on two conditions. The first is to acknowledge that he alters the conventional definition of philosophy; the second is that the poetry of the *Canzoniere* be included as the powerful locus of Petrarch's most advanced spiritual speculations.

"Philosophy," writes Hugh of St. Victor at the start of his *Didascalicon*, "is the love and pursuit of Wisdom, and, in a certain way, a friendship with it."[2] He adds that from this Wisdom are born "truth of speculation and of thought ... and action." Petrarch's philosophy, in effect, may be construed as a critical reflection exactly on the links joining love and wisdom: prior to any wisdom, he maintains, there is thinking. Since my primary concern here is to chart the main lines of his thought, I will first clarify more sharply the design of my argument. I begin my discussion by evoking Petrarch's sense of philosophy as is debated in *On His Own Ignorance*.[3] Knowledge for Petrarch, as we shall see, is power, and he elaborates a myth of *cultura* that he largely draws from Prudentius. The two polemical tracts, the *Invective contra medicum* (Invective against a physician) and *Contra eum qui maledixit Italie* (Against a detractor of Italy), which I shall examine next, cast *cultura* as the historical prolongation of his philosophy of power, as the realm of shared meaning, as the constellations of ideas and significant memories of the community. Finally, I shall analyze what Petrarch means by the relationship he establishes between "thought" and "love." This is in many ways the original center of his lyrical reflections, and to this end I shall examine song 129 of the *Canzoniere*, "Di pensier in pensier" (From thought to thought), in which Petrarch explicitly raises the question of what thinking is and roots it in the power of love.

I do not claim that this concern gives a paramount "unity" to his thought, for, in effect, Petrarch's thinking and his ideas of love resist unity and are rooted in the consciousness of division and plurality. To emphasize a fact of common critical agreement, contradictory forces both outside and within himself mark the various dimensions of his experiences. We are all made quickly aware by even the hastiest

From thought to thought

thinking = love

perusal of his lexicon of his radical understanding of his existence as a tangle of conflicts, wars, and struggles. Accordingly, the stylistic oxymora of his poetry—the living death which is love, the contrary winds of his passion—have been duly recorded by critics as the emblem of the wounds scarring the inner realm of the poet's self.[4] The full title of his *Secretum* (*De secreto conflictu curarum mearum*); the *Invective contra medicum;* random lines from his poetry, such as sonnet 134 of the *Canzoniere* ("Pace non trovo, et non ho da far guerra" [I cannot find peace, and have nothing with which to make war]); the worn motif of love as war; the rhetoric of the *Trionfi;* the intellectual aggressiveness he displays in his polemical tracts against specific individuals, for example—all of these show Petrarch's clairvoyance into the permanent and fundamental experience of violence holding sway over one's own self and, beyond that, over history, where distinct individualities frankly oppose each other.

This insight into the reality of opposition as the principle of private and public living is a given of Petrarch's writings. It accounts for Petrarch's longings for peace from and as an alternate mode to the destructive impulses he observes with clinical precision within his own self and within the world of politics. The absolutely last word of the last poem of the *Canzoniere* is "pace" (peace), just as the political song 128 ends with a sorrowful threefold call to "pace, pace, pace." It would be too simple to dismiss the consciousness of conflict and the unrealizable call for peace as another acute form of Petrarch's ironies, of the ceaseless contradictions and ambiguities punctuating any single pronouncement he makes. In point of fact, in the metaphoric space between peace's desirability, in which he certainly believes, and in the conviction that the world of time is made up of divisions reside both his reflections on philosophical knowledge and his figuration of the myth of *cultura,* which I shall now summarily sketch.

His ideal of culture, a Latin myth which translates the Greek *philosophia* and which Petrarch revives from Prudentius's *Psychomachia,* traces a curvature of discourses triggered by the mobility of his mind as well as by his will to redefine the terms of the intellectual debates. In his project of definition of the debates, he accords great importance to what are called universal questions—such as truth, morality, faith—and he places them within the realm of contingency as if to reveal the discrepancies and contradictions that the principle of contingency will generate within the general pattern of abstract ideas.

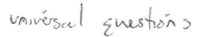

35

THE WORLDS OF PETRARCH

This means that a description of his thought is at the same time a
description of the broad intellectual horizon within which he moves.
It also means that a discussion of his ideas turns into what could be
called the cartography of his memories and passions.

A useful point of departure for catching a glimpse of the contours
of Petrarch's cultural project and its provisional crystallization is his
Epistle to Posterity, where we are told of his studies in the Avignonese
"exile" he calls home; his travels through France and Germany; his
plan to write the epic *Africa;* the competition between Paris and Rome
to give him the laurel crown; and his final years in Padua. This general
biographical narrative line is flanked by claims that he is versed in
poetry and in moral philosophy, in classical as well as sacred literature,
from that of St. Jerome, who thought of himself as a Ciceronian, to
that of St. Augustine. We also learn that he is interested in history,
"the study of ancient times," and that he considers Plato, not Aristotle,
the greatest of all philosophers; in short, Roman eloquence, Christian
dogma, and Platonic philosophy, as is commonly acknowledged, are
the boundaries of his thinking.[5]

His education + passions

How exactly these intellectual and spiritual perspectives the *Epis-
tle to Posterity* conjures up affect one another remains a genuine
problem (see Appendix 2). In fact, Petrarch cannot be said to belong to
a sharply defined school of thought. All too often, if anything, he
comes forth as a perplexed skeptic, a proselyte of the academy, who is
reluctant to state anything firmly and whose mind travels in both
directions ("in utramque partem") of any given issue.[6] In his "Self-
Portrait," in response to Francesco Bruni who had called him an
orator, historian, philosopher, poet, and theologian, Petrarch presents
himself as a *scholasticus,* a term Pliny had used for Suetonius (*Ep.*
1.24.4). The word, which is akin to *philologus,* a lover of learning,
defines not an adept of dogmatic Scholasticism; rather, and the irony
in the pointed deployment of the term is transparent, one who never
quits school and is always striving for a Truth which is difficult to
discover in the sphere of immanence.

Such a quest for truth, he says, so entangles him in errors that he
throws himself "into the embrace of doubt instead of truth."[7] Doubts
and suspicions about truth, which a rhetorical philosophy inherently
promotes, are ciphers of a desire (or nostalgia) for power. How-
ever uncertain he may be about the direction his mind should take
in personal moral decisions—an impasse which the *Secretum* fully

*In love w/ learning
recognized ignorance*

probes—it must be said that Petrarch understood that skeptical predicaments are to be resolved by the acknowledgment of authority and its power. Confronted with disagreements in historical narratives, he says in the *Epistle to Posterity,* he chooses sides by dint of the writer's authority.[8] There is an overt link between his methodical doubt about any epistemological question whatsoever and his assent to a view solely on the ground of verisimilitude of a narrative and of authority. The link lies in Petrarch's insight, as we shall see, into the complex strands joining together questions of power to questions of knowledge.

The text where Petrarch carries out a thorough critique of what constitutes knowledge is *On His Own Ignorance.* I shall discuss this polemical tract from a complementary angle later in chapter 5, and here I shall focus on what I take to be Petrarch's redefinition of the essence of philosophy. The tract, written against four young neo-Aristotelians who have accused him of ignorance, of lacking a rigorous knowledge of modern philosophy, and of being only an expert in empty eloquence, is addressed to a grammarian friend of Petrarch's, Donato. This recording of contingent details, which is a constant feature of Petrarch's style of thought, sheds light on his understanding of what can be termed intellectual experiences. Petrarch shapes his life relentlessly as a life of the mind in the full sense of the phrase: he is not a philosopher in the classical Aristotelian mold, the thinker who produces a systematic, architectonic order of thought. Thinking, on the contrary, is an act rooted in the depths of living, part of the ordinary texture of daily existence. Such an insight into thinking (which encourages the so-called autobiographical fallacy) and into the nature of knowledge is central to Petrarch's argument.

The drawing of knowledge within the bounds of one's lived experience allows Petrarch, as will be shown more extensively in chapter 5, to think of philosophy as ethics and history. I shall stress here that from this perspective of ethics and history he plunges into a history of philosophy as a history of intellectual violence and argument, bitter disputes and savage polemics. Whereas Petrarch is engaged in writing to his friend Donato, the four young neo-Aristotelians and the history of philosophy that he drafts force on us the conviction that there is no friendship or love of wisdom in traditional philosophical discourse. The inventory of violence the tract surveys ranges from Epicurus's hatred of Plato, Pythagoras, Aristotle, and Democritus, to the rivalry between Quintilian and Seneca. The inescapable conclusion is that there are dark passions, such as envy and grudges, forfeiting philosophy's ideal claims of love of wisdom, and they expose those claims as hollow.

This history of philosophy Petrarch sketches is also meant to dramatize Petrarch's sense that philosophical knowledge is not and cannot be construed as a repository of immutable, dogmatic opinions endorsed by the authority of the ancients. There is no unity of knowledge or consensus available in this history of these ideological arguments. Accordingly, Petrarch takes to task the view peddled by his young opponents that Aristotle is the sole philosopher. To dismantle this claim, eclectic opinions drawn from Plato, Cicero, the Stoics, Democritus, Aristotle, the Epicureans, and others are pulled together and critically confronted.

This anthology of philosophical fragments may strike one at first as Petrarch's vain ostentation of his own erudition in the face of those who deny that he has any knowledge. More fundamentally, this display of self, which Petrarch understands in its full political force, is also a way of dramatizing how the plural, partial elaborations of the sundry philosophical systems are shifty, self-contradictory, and, in one word, historical. Truth, one might say, the truth elaborated by the philosophers, is the daughter of time in the sense that it forever carries with it the marks of irreducible contingency. The contingency of thought, to say it in a slightly different form, effectively equates history and philosophy.

This outline of philosophy as a savage, chaotic universe of deliberate a priori dissidence largely resonates, I submit, with Prudentius's representation of *cultura* in his allegorical *Psychomachia*. Prudentius understands Cultura as the repository of pagan and secular values, as the "worship of the old gods," a "veterum cultura deorum" which is opposed to Fides (ll. 21–30).[9] His allegorical-spiritual epic, which is patterned on the *Aeneid*, essentially relates the ruthless battle between Fides and Cultura, and their antagonism is the epitome of man's two-sided nature, which in turn accounts for the constant vicissitudes of the soul's struggle and for the conflicting passions in the darkness of the human heart. The war between vices and virtues, between darkness and light, between pagan knowledge and Christian faith, will only stop for Prudentius when Faith, queen of the virtues, reaches the throne of divine Wisdom.

There is hardly a trace of Prudentius's allegorical machinery either in Petrarch's *On His Own Ignorance* or in the *psychomachia* of the *Canzoniere*. Yet the brunt of *On His Own Ignorance*, as in the *Psychomachia*, is to map the discrepancy between faith and secular knowledge. Petrarch's severe indictment of the philosophers who oppose him and who question his moral authority and good name comes to a focus in the representation of the tension existing between faith and knowledge, revelation and philosophy, and he proceeds to explore their relation. In effect, the proposition that knowledge is historical and never absolute leads Petrarch to ground his quest for certainties in the domain of faith. His procedure is here somewhat oblique. The metaphor which best conveys Petrarch's understanding of experience, both intellectual and existential, is that of the Po River. The metaphor is suggested to him by the circumstantial fact that he is writing to his friend Donato in a barge while crossing the river. Its stormy waves are the figure for the "whirlpool of human affairs," just as the friendship of the grammarian is a more reliable, solid bond than that of the four contentious Aristotelians. Consistently with this insight into the precariousness of life and unreliability of the logicians, Petrarch mounts a critique of Aristotle's ideas about happiness from the perspective of faith and immortality, which the Stagirite neglects in his system of ethics (p. 78).

The path of faith in the divinity and in the providential structure of the cosmos becomes the principle of valorization in Petrarch's reflection. Traces of such a criterion of judgment show in his recording of Cicero's opposition to Epicurus, for instance, or, more generally, in his focus on the perpetual controversy of the philosophical schools as to whether the cosmos is "a product of chance or of necessity or of Divine Reason and Intellect" (p. 81). The perspective of religious faith is the core of Petrarch's critique of the value of philosophy. His sympathies, predictably enough, go in the direction of the efforts of the Chartrians, such as Chalcidius, who seek to reconcile the creation myth available in Genesis with the myth of the *Timaeus*, while he opposes Democritus's and Epicurus's atomistic conceptions of the universe. Their conceptions effectively ratify the natural phenomena as a dis-integrated reality of antagonistic forces. Yet the philosophers' disagreements over the questions which are the foundation of all knowledge force him to claim what he calls, and what the Cusan will call, *docta ignorantia*.

[handwritten margin notes: "faith v philosophy will / will to think |reason| ratian"]

Such an ignorance, epitomized by Socrates' dictum, "This one thing I know, that I know nothing" (p. 126), is to be seen as a philosophical skepticism. This skepticism about abstract knowledge allows Petrarch to argue for and justify the value of eloquence or rhetoric, which the young Aristotelians find inessential to philosophical knowledge. Petrarch's reasoning is here straightforward. If the structure of the world remains inaccessible to a reflective investigation, then what counts is the reality of one's existence, history, and moral choices. Eloquence, the art of Cicero, is not for Petrarch pure ornamentation; rather, it is the discipline of history and of the commonplaces of memory. It crystallizes the deeper sediments of language and brings them to life; it constitutes, more exactly, the domain of history and choice by virtue of its being the art of persuasion (p. 61). Eloquence, one can add, embodies Petrarch's knowledge that one must cast a spell on those who hear; in short, it is the recognition of the force and power of language and of self to reach and capture the recesses of the will of the listener.

Retrospectively one easily grasps Petrarch's valorization of the will (the locus of choices) over the thought of the philosophers and its nebulous epistemological core; one can also grasp the rationale for viewing faith as superior to philosophy, and, finally, one understands Petrarch's sense of intellectual power, the power of eloquence to animate one's world. What is not clear in this tract, however, is the sense of the forces that set thought in motion, or, to say it differently, how thinking is related to the will. There is a well-known history to this question, and it bears a brief summary.

It is an all-too-accepted view that rhetoric and the rationalist philosophy of the latter-day disciples of Aristotle appear to be separated in *On His Own Ignorance,* as they are in Plato. For Socrates, at least in the *Gorgias,* rhetoric is not a medium for true knowledge; it is, rather, a cleverness at winning arguments by trickery. Cicero criticizes the divorce Plato (through Socrates) establishes in the *Gorgias* between the science of wise thinking and that of elegant speaking, because to him this severance represents an absurd division between the tongue and the brain.[10] Plato's radical critique of rhetoric is considerably attenuated in the *Phaedrus,* where Socrates acknowledges that there is little difference between dialectic, or the discovery of truth, and rhetoric, or the persuasive exposition of truth. For Petrarch, rhetoric is the privileged path to knowledge.

The claim is already present in *On His Own Ignorance*. But Petrarch goes into a full-fledged defense of the primacy of rhetoric in another polemical tract he writes, *Invective contra medicum*, a collection of four books written from 1352 to 1355 against an anonymous physician who felt offended by a letter Petrarch had sent to Pope Clement VI to warn him about the impostures and malpractice of doctors attending him during his illness.[11] The argument, however, quickly turns into a reflection on the relation between rhetoric and medicine within the framework of the traditional debates between the liberal and mechanical arts.[12]

The outline of the reasoning, in spite of its digressions, personal insults hurled at the opponent, and crowd-pleasing postures, unfolds according to an essentially binary principle of structure. From the viewpoint of the physician, as one infers from Petrarch's account, rhetoric is associated with the useless, the vague, and the obscure. Medicine, on the other hand, wears the aspect of a reliable and necessary science. Predictably enough, Petrarch vehemently contests the physician's claim as nothing less than a subversion of the order of knowledge, and he seeks to reestablish a hierarchy of the arts whereby the seven mechanical arts (fabric making, commerce, agriculture, hunting, medicine, armaments, and theatrics) correspond and are subordinated to the arts of the trivium and quadrivium (grammar, rhetoric, logic, arithmetic, music, geometry, and astronomy).[13]

In this neat demarcation of the spheres of knowledge, Petrarch, then, envisions two separate and unequal realms: a superior realm of speculation and discourse, which is under the aegis of rhetoric, and a lower realm of empirical realism within which medicine plays a useful role of material means to a transcendent spiritual end. No possible relation or conversation exists between these two realms. As a matter of fact, Petrarch's "interlocutor" systematically seems to miss or misstate the real intent of Petrarch's remarks, and Petrarch's mockery of the physician's intellectual pretensions is a *specimen* of abusiveness as a weapon in argument. What is more, by the end of book 3, on the strength of Vergil's comment in the *Aeneid* (12.397), he consigns medicine to the region of silence (p. 938). Petrarch's point is clear: in a context such as this, where existence is thought to be shaped by language, the realm of discourse belongs to the rhetorician and poet.

The impulse to write *On His Own Ignorance,* as has been shown, comes from the philosophers' own spirit of division and contentiousness to which Petrarch juxtaposes the gentleness and benevolence of the conversation between friends, Donato and himself, as the concrete practice of philosophical theories. In the *Invective*, however, Petrarch himself practices what he decries in *On His Own Ignorance*. Unlike rhetoric and poetry, which are unbounded in their extensiveness, medicine stumbles against the limitations of a mechanical art, and, so Petrarch asserts, it is not a science of moral philosophy. If anything, it is a philosophy of nature, and because of the value with which it invests the body, it is called the art of Averroës. The physician, like Averroës, is made to wear the complexion of a skeptic who denies the existence of the immortal soul and raises the division between body and soul to a metaphysical principle. Over and against the world of matter, which is the province of medicine, Petrarch pits the world of poetry and aggressively defends its prestige (book 3).

Recasting conventional arguments from Plato's *Republic* and Boethius's *De consolatione philosophiae*, Petrarch maintains, as Boccaccio will maintain in his *De genealogia deorum gentilium*, that there is no constitutive, inherent quarrel between poetry and philosophy. The quarrel, on the contrary, involves obscene, morally licentious poets and philosophy. By this strategy Petrarch upholds both the morality and inclusiveness of poetry, which to him is part of all the liberal arts and is the original language of theology. Finally, the world of poetry, in opposition to the tyranny of nature and of the body, is the sphere of freedom, and the emblem of this freedom, one infers, is the license poets are empowered to take with language.

Yet immediately after staking these claims about poetry's power to open up possible passages to new worlds of experience one carries within oneself, the tract shifts its focus and turns into a praise of solitude (book 4). There is a phrase in one of Petrarch's letters (*Fam.* 8.7) that emblematically condenses Petrarch's perception of man's loneliness on earth: "Sumus, frater, sumus . . . vere soli" (We are, brother, we are really alone). In a way, solitude is valorized as a condition of happiness because it allows one to shun "iniquitas et contradictio in civitate, et labor in medio eius, et iniustitia, et non deficiens de plateis eius usura, et dolus" (*Invective*, p. 948) (iniquity and dissent among citizens, the labor of living among them, injustice, usury, which never leaves the city-squares, and deception). If life in the city is a troubling existence marked by dissent and violations of one's own world, solitude is the condition in which the autonomy and delimitation of self occur. The juxtaposition, which suggests the paradigm of the Epicurean sage, is too simple to hold for Petrarch. Because solitude, here evoked as his *desideratum* against the turbulence and contradictions of communal life, is a central category of Petrarch's thought and poetry, I must qualify its value. *De vita solitaria*, which calls for a divesting of oneself, one's illusions and desires, in order to sink (or rise) into the realm of pure spiritual perfection, will be discussed in chapter 7. But even a quick look at a sonnet, "Solo et pensoso" (Alone and filled with care) (*Canzoniere*, sonnet 35), reveals the complex sense of Petrarch's imagination of solitude.

> Solo et pensoso i più deserti campi
> vo mesurando a passi tardi et lenti,
> et gli occhi porto per fuggire intenti
> ove vestigio human l'arena stampi.
>
> Altro schermo non trovo che mi scampi
> dal manifesto accorger de le genti,
> perchè negli atti d'allegrezza spenti
> di fuor si legge com'io dentro avampi:
>
> sì ch'io mi credo omai che monti et piagge
> et fiumi et selve sappian di che tempre
> sia la mia vita, ch'è celata altrui.
>
> Ma pur sì aspre vie nè sì selvagge
> cercar non so ch'Amor non venga sempre
> ragionando con meco, et io co llui.

Alone and filled with care, I go measuring the most deserted fields with steps delaying and slow, and I keep my eyes alert so as to flee from where any human footprint marks the sand. No other shield do I find to protect me from people's open knowing, for in my bearing, in which all happiness is extinguished, anyone can read from without how I am aflame within. So that I believe by now that mountains and shores and rivers and woods know the temper of my life, which is hidden from other persons; but still I cannot seek paths so hard or so savage that Love does not always come along discoursing with me and I with him.[14]

In this sonnet the lover seeks to draw a circle of solitude around himself, wherein he finds the inexorable conversations going on in his mind. The exclusion of others, which is also a delimitation of self, would restore him—this is the overt thematic thrust of the poem—to his innermost thoughts and would shelter his interior self from the outside world. If the primary moral impetus of the *Canzoniere,* as will be seen in chapter 6, is to construct a theater of memory and of shame (see the opening sonnet), to make an object of oneself and a spectacle of one's vanity for others to see, in sonnet 35 Petrarch seeks to escape the gaze of others, for in fact it reveals him in his absolute transparency. But solitude, which an age-old motif refers to as "beata solitudo, sola beatitudo," in this sonnet is not merely the blissful state of avoidance of others as a preamble to reaching the depths of oneself. On the contrary, it gives rise to a number of crucial questions which steadily engage Petrarch's attention.

The triple alliteration ("*solo* . . . pen*so-so*") in the opening couple of adjectives suggests a continuity between the state of loneliness and pensiveness, as if solitude generates thoughtfulness (and thoughtfulness solitude), and it makes solitude the realm of private, inviolable thoughts. These thoughts are self-contradictory. In the search for solitude, the inner self appears self-defining: he refuses to be an object of public curiosity and perception and takes refuge in the innermost, authentic, and hidden realm of his mind. By the retrieval of this private and internal space of his own thoughts, his love is affirmed as itself an authentic experience without any essential bonds to anything else around him. In his solitary wanderings the lover seeks to conceal from others the signs of the secret love he envelops within himself. But the secret is not containable within the space of the self, and it flows into the woods, streams, slopes, and banks so that they know the temper of the lover's life, which he keeps hidden from other persons.

The retreat from the public world into the landscape of nature signals the lover's will to regain his mastery. Whereas the intimacy of his thoughts and passion is threatened by the glance of others who reduce him to a spectacle, the natural world only reflects his state of mind. The *speculum naturae* (which is intimated by the language of sight running throughout this text)[15] is the conceit whereby the lover, who seeks the loneliness of the countryside, is integrated within the landscape. The mirroring of the self in nature does not mark, however, a state of repose in the illusion of a regained unity between man and nature. While he roams over the countryside, his inner self is aflame with a chaotic passion he cannot control ("di fuor si legge com'io dentro avampi" [1. 8]), and he can never escape what he most wants to avoid, the tyranny of Love's discourse. Nonetheless, the lover's presence in the countryside arranges the external space, and his own gaze is the privileged viewpoint or principle of organization of the sundry entities of nature which know and respond to his love anguish. The lover's solitary distress places him under the crushing dominion of Love's discourse (which, manifestly, is the very poetry Petrarch disseminates and authorizes); but his solitude invests him with the power to control his and our perception of the scenery. Solitude is more than an experience whereby one retrieves an authentic state for the self. The analysis of "Solo et pensoso" shows, in fact, that the contradictions Petrarch decries within the social world are inscribed within his own self.

Much as the reflective mode of the *Canzoniere* discovers tensions within the lover's soul and signals the presence of the despotic power of Love and of writing, the *Invective contra medicum* discovers contradictions as the distinctive, permanent structure of social life. By admitting to intellectual disagreements within the history of philosophy or between himself and the physician, Petrarch acknowledges the existence of a possible viewpoint that transcends one's own and breaks the circle of solipsism. The validity of his own viewpoint, which is to say the validity of the cultural paradigm he seeks to impose, depends on his rhetorical power to persuade, master, or silence the opponent.

Petrarch's lucid consciousness of power as the decisive question of culture is made apparent by a metaphor he deploys in the *Invective*. At the very start of the polemic, it is called a "certamen" (p. 819), indeed a polemic. But the word, with its resonances from the domains of poetic contests, gymnastics, the gladiators' battles in the circus, and so on, touches the essential point. No doubt, its first explicit meaning is to convey Petrarch's sense of the frivolousness, of the inconsequential quality of his polemical undertaking and of the unworthiness of his opponent. Implicitly, the metaphor removes questions of power belonging to the dark regions of experience from it and makes it part of a playful exchange. But, at the same time, the metaphor also suggests that the determination of cultural values (the place of medicine and rhetoric in the scheme of knowledge) cannot be merely reached by the consensus of intelligences; rather, it is decided as a contest of colliding viewpoints.

The vision of philosophy as contention in *On His Own Ignorance* and of *cultura* as power play in the *Invective* is forcefully reformulated in *Contra eum qui maledixit Italie*. Petrarch addresses the tract, which he wrote late in his life (1373), to Hugutio of Thiene who had shown him a polemical text by a friar, John of Hesdin. The friar had objected to a letter sent by Petrarch to Pope Urban V (*Seniles* 9.1) exhorting him to move the Holy See from Avignon back to Rome and had upheld Avignon's rights to replace Rome.

The debate carries Petrarch to draft an inventory of the history between Rome and France, from the conquest of Gaul by Julius Caesar, to the Roman foundation of Paris, to Bernard of Clairvaux's critique of the Roman court in his *De consideratione,* to an intellectual history of France (with proper acknowledgments of the value of Alan of Lille) and of Italy.

In a sense, the tract shows the inevitable modern collapse of the unity of the "medieval" world into national and competitive fragments.[16] The obverse side, however, of the cultural particularisms that the tract exemplifies is the assertion of the universality of the culture of Rome. More than that, Petrarch's lifelong uprootedness and cosmopolitanism help us to qualify his position—and chapter 5 will return to this question—as the pursuit of an empire of culture grounded in the unchallenged stability and universality of Rome.

Philosophy and its political extension, the world of *cultura,* disclose the centrality of rhetoric, of the power of expression, to create and impose symbolic systems of value. But Petrarch does not probe in his own philosophical and polemical tracts how rhetoric becomes epistemology. In order to grasp his sense of how thought and will are yoked together, how the force of thought and the force of the will are conceived together, we must turn to song 129 of the *Canzoniere.*

> Di pensier in pensier, di monte in monte
> mi guida Amor, ch'ogni segnato calle
> provo contrario a la tranquilla vita.
> Se 'n solitaria piaggia rivo o fonte
> se 'nfra duo poggi siede ombrosa valle,
> ivi s'acqueta l'alma sbigottita;
>   et come Amor l'envita
> or ride or piange or teme or s'assecura,
> e 'l volto, che lei segue ov'ella il mena,
> si turba et rasserena
> et in un esser picciol tempo dura:
> onde a la vista uom di tal vita esperto
> diria: "Questo arde et di suo stato è incerto."
>
> Per alti monti et per selve aspre trovo
> qualche riposo; ogni abitato loco

è nemico mortal degli occhi miei.
    A ciascun passo nasce un penser novo
de la mia donna, che sovente in gioco
gira 'l tormento ch'i' porto per lei;
        et a pena vorrei
cangiar questo mio viver dolce amaro,
ch'i' dico: "Forse anco ti serva Amore
ad un tempo migliore:
forse a te stesso vile, altrui se'caro":
et in questa trapasso sospirando:
"Or porrebbe esser ver? or come? or quando?"

Ove porge ombra un pino alto od un colle
talor m'arresto, et pur nel primo sasso
disegno co la mente il suo bel viso.
    Poi ch'a me torno, trovo il petto molle
de la pietate, et alor dico: "Ahi lasso,
dove se' giunto? et onde se' diviso?"
    Ma mentre tener fiso
posso al primo pensier la mente vaga,
et mirar lei et obliar me stesso,
sento Amor sì da presso
che del suo proprio error l'alma s'appaga;
in tante parti et sì bella la veggio
che se l'error durasse, altro non cheggio.

    I' l'ò più volte (or chi fia che mi 'l creda?)
ne l'acqua chiara et sopra l'erba verde
veduto viva, et nel troncon d'un faggio
    e 'n bianca nube, sì fatta che Leda
avria ben detto che sua figlia perde
come stella che 'l sol copre col raggio;
        et quanto in più selvaggio
loco mi trovo e 'n più deserto lido,
tanto più bella il mio pensier l'adombra.
Poi quando il vero sgombra
quel dolce error, pur lì medesmo assido
me freddo, pietra morta in pietra viva,
in guisa d'uom che pensi et pianga et scriva.

    Ove d'alta montagna ombra non tocchi.
verso 'l maggiore e'l più espedito giogo
tirar mi suol un desiderio intenso.
    Indi i miei danni a misurar con gli occhi

comincio, e 'ntanto lagrimando sfogo
di dolorosa nebbia il cor condenso,
      alor ch'i' miro et penso
quanta aria dal bel viso mi diparte
che sempre m'è sì presso et sì lontano.
Poscia fra me pian piano:
"Che sai tu, lasso? forse in quella parte
or di tua lontananza si sospira."
Et in questo penser l'alma respira.

      Canzone, oltra quell'alpe,
là dove il ciel è più sereno et lieto,
mi rivedrai sovr' un ruscel corrente
ove l'aura si sente
d'un fresco et odorifero laureto;
ivi è 'l mio cor et quella che 'l m'invola:
qui veder poi l'imagine mia sola.

From thought to thought, from mountain to mountain Love guides me: for I find every trodden path to be contrary to a tranquil life. If there is on some solitary slope a river or spring, or between two peaks a shady valley, there my frightened soul is quieted; and, as Love leads it on, now it laughs, now weeps, now fears, now is confident: and my face, which follows wherever my soul leads, is clouded and made clear again, and remains but a short time in any one state; and at the sight anyone who had experienced such a life would say: "This man is burning with love and his state is uncertain."

Among high mountains and through harsh woods I find some rest; every inhabited place is a mortal enemy of my eyes. With every step is born a new thought of my lady, which often turns to pleasure the torment that I bear for her; and I would hardly wish to change this bitter, sweet life of mine, for I say: "Perhaps Love keeps you for a better time; perhaps, though vile to yourself, you are dear to someone else." And I go over to this thought, sighing: "Now could it be true? But how? But when?"

Where a tall pine or a hillside extends shade, there I sometimes stop, and in the first stone I see I portray her lovely face with my mind. When I come back to myself, I find my breast wet with pity and then I say: "Alas, where have you come to, from what are you separated?" But as long as I can hold my yearning mind fixed on the first thought, and look at her and forget myself, I feel Love so close by that my soul is satisfied by its own deception; in so many places and so beautiful I see her, that, if the deception should last, I ask for no more.

Song about the conjunction between Love + Thinking

I have many times (now who will believe me?) seen her alive in the clear water and on the green grass and in the trunk of a beech tree and in a white cloud, so beautiful that Leda would have said that her daughter faded like a star covered by the sun's ray; and in whatever wildest place and most deserted shore I find myself, so much the more beautiful does my thought shadow her forth. Then, when the truth dispels that sweet deception, right there in the same place I sit down, cold, a dead stone on the living rock, like a man who thinks and weeps and writes.

Where the shadow of some other mountain does not reach, toward the highest and freest peak an intense desire is wont to draw me. Thence I begin to measure my losses with my eyes, and then I weeping unburden my heart of the sorrowful cloud gathered in it, when I see and think how much air separates me from the lovely face that is always so near to me and so distant. Then to myself softly: "What do you know, wretch? Perhaps off there someone is sighing now because of your absence." And in this thought my soul breathes more easily.

Song, beyond those Alps, where the sky is more clear and happy, you shall see me again beside a running stream, where the breeze from a fresh and fragrant laurel can be felt: there is my heart, and she who steals it from me; here you can see only my image.[17]

The argument of the poem is distance, and in a primary way it tells the lover's distance from his beloved. As a matter of fact, the motif of "lontananza" (l. 64) allows us to place the song in the lyrical tradition of the Provençal *amor de lonh*, the yearning, from the perspective of a *terra longinqua* to mention another version of the same myth, for the object of one's desires. In this poem the lover is returning to Vaucluse, and in the landscape of shady valleys, sunless cliffs, hollows, and escarpments, which Petrarch conjures up, he retrieves in his imagination the memory of Laura.

There is, thus, another journey, which mirrors the one in the physical world, and this is an interior journey over the vast spaces of the mind, where Laura's traces are indelible. From this point of view, the poem can be said to retrace the pattern elaborated by St. Bonaventure in his *Itinerarium mentis*, which is the paradigm of the mind's quest for divine illumination *extra nos, intra nos,* and *supra nos.* But for all the echoes of Bonaventure's tripartite movement of the soul (the itinerant poet goes into the outside world, retreats into his thoughts, and climbs over high mountains), the poem dramatizes how motion turns into an impasse, how the mind, in its random mobility, gets

P is in love w/ the Mind

Journey's within the mind

caught by its own phantasms. More than a spiritual ascesis, this inner journey records the lover's interior distance, a self divided from itself.

The *envoi* yokes together the double distance, just as much as the first line of the poem announces the double journey. The line, "Di pensier in pensier, di monte in monte," figures interiority as the mirror of exteriority, the journey within as a reflection of the journey without. The *envoi*, on the other hand, recalls the place beyond the Alps, Vaucluse, where Laura is and where, in keeping with a well-known conceit of the troubadoric convention, the poet's heart also is, while in the present space the poet occupies, the Italian landscape, one can see only his image. Paradoxically, the lover's physical displacement does not coincide with the dislocation within the self. What Petrarch figures, on the contrary, is the existence of a relation between the landscape and the self, and this relation has to be understood as simultaneously a mirroring between self and landscape and a disjunction between them.

The conjunction of the journey within and the journey without suggests that the mind is also a space marked with continuities, discontinuities, proximities, and juxtapositions that are not clearly mapped. The poem, in a fundamental way, seeks to probe the mind's depths, chart its boundaries, places, and limits, and discover its powers. The idea of power, in fact, is of paramount concern. The opening line, "Di pensier in pensier, di monte in monte"—with its double iteration—graphically conveys the reflective mood of the poem. But thinking is neither self-originating nor is it seen as the firm, substantial ground for the lover's musings. On the contrary, in their aimless wandering, thoughts have no precise direction and are in themselves inert. The power that moves them is love.

It is possible to suggest that Petrarch is essentially a poet of the thought of love. The statement has to be understood in a particular way to mean that he discovers the *event* of thought. The event of thought means not that thought is necessarily triggered by a material fact; the event is imaginary and this in turn suggests that thought is at one with the imagination. Unlike the philosophers, who operate on the principle that there is a natural, spontaneous love of knowledge, he reflects on the erotics of thought, on love's instigation of thought, so that thought is an occurrence or outcome of the phantasms of love's compulsions. It would even be possible, let me say parenthetically, to bring within the broad orbit of a strong Petrarchism (as opposed to the mannerisms of the European Renaissance crystallization of the Petrarchan love discourse) the "thought metaphors" in texts such as Milton's *Il Penseroso* or Leopardi's *Pensier dominante*. A sonnet such as "Solo et pensoso," as has been shown, joins together thinking and solitude in order to dramatize how self-reflection can be best achieved. The sonnet also dramatizes the conjunction between love and thinking, which is the thematic center of song 129.

As the run-on second line makes clear, "mi guida Amor, ch'ogni segnato calle," the mind's thoughts are under the despotic dominion of Love. More than that, love in this poem is not an object of thought; rather, thinking is rooted in love. One thinks, not as the Averroists believe, by the expulsion of love or other contingencies from thought, but under the compulsion of love. There is a fundamental difference even from the stilnovists, such as Dante and Guinizelli, in Petrarch's conception. These poets of the "sweet new style" figure a hierarchical, ordered continuity between love and knowledge. Petrarch's poem, by contrast, is articulated at the point of intersection between love and thinking (the two words "amore" and "pensier" appear in the first three stanzas, always at some distance from each other, while in the last two stanzas the word for love is eclipsed, and "pensier" is used by itself as if it were the only term left to give unity to the text).

The metaphoric link between the two constitutive words of "philosophy"—love and thought—sheds some light on the relation existing between them in Petrarch's poem. If love is a force, a powerful presence guiding the self, the word "pensier" resonates with an entirely different sense. In a passage of the *Confessions* (10.11), which Petrarch knows very well and even quotes in his "Ascent of Mount Ventoux," St. Augustine expatiates on the spacious palaces of memory, its vast fields and deeper recesses. The word "cogitation," St. Augustine says, is linked to memory; *cogo* and *cogito*, respectively, "collect" and "recollect," are related to each other, for what is remembered or gathered is what is thought upon. To say it differently, for St. Augustine, and a whole Augustinian tradition, to think is to remember.[18] Petrarch is mindful of the Augustinian idea of the temporality of thought, as we shall see later. But the primary resonance of "pensier" is the one suggested by its Latin etymology. Etymologically, as was suggested in the previous chapter, the word comes from the Latin *pendere* and it

means a suspension and a halt, the pause of reflection of the mind
beset by love's tyranny.

The poem draws what can be called the phenomenology of the
mind in love. The mind, controlled by love, is restless; thoughts
appear and are rapidly swept away. There is a clinical term for the
uncontrolled shifts of the mind; they are known as *perturbationes*, and
they describe the vertiginous spiral of lovesickness with its steady
oscillations of laughter, tears, fear, and false security (l. 8). The alter-
ations of the mind come to a focus in Petrarch's text through the series
of oxymora, such as "dolce amaro" (l. 21). In historical terms, the
account of the "mente vaga" (l. 34) echoes the language of *Donna me
prega* by Cavalcanti or even the language of the physician Dino del
Garbo's commentary on that song and, generally, of Bernard of Gor-
don, who in his *Lilium medicinae,* first published at Montpellier,
writes of love as a cerebral sickness.[19] These perturbations are also for
Petrarch the turbulence of the weather, the atmospherics of the heart,
as it were, with the soul variously clouded and made clear (l. 10), and
the heaviness of the heart ("di dolorosa nebbia il cor condenso" [l. 58])
finding relief when the lover breathes the clear air of the summit.

If the physicians believe that a change of weather cures the malady
of love, for Petrarch the relief is a self-willed deception, a sweet error,
which is forever short-lived. Love, in effect, is the exteriority of
thought, or, to put it differently, thought (that of the philosophers or
physicians) seeks to limit the power of love. Petrarch, by contrast,
acknowledges that love dwells, as it were, outside of thought, and he
proceeds to map the relation between love and thought. The fourth
stanza, in fact, focuses on the mind's obsessions. We are plunged into
the depth of the imagination, in the dark region of phantasms, ghostly
shadows, and labile dreams.

Throughout the poem, the lover is attracted to the "ombrosa
valle" (l. 5) or the shade cast by a hillside or a tall pine (l. 27). Shade is
not the privation of light; it is the hidden light. In a way, it is as if the
pure light of judgment were intolerable to him. But the "ombrosa
valle" is a bleak reminder of the valley of the shadow of death, which is
where the obsession of love provisionally leads the lover. In the fourth
stanza, the lover imagines to have seen Laura (who is never directly
mentioned) alive in the clear water, on the grass, and in the trunk of a
beech tree.

This love madness, which provisionally erases the judgment of

THE THOUGHT OF LOVE

reason, is, in effect, a sign of love's power. The power of love consists precisely in this: it brings the self, however divided or alienated from itself it may be, back to itself (there is always a narcissism in Petrarchan love) by revealing its limits and its subjection to death and unreason. When the impression that the ghostly memories have taken a life of their own vanishes, when the pure imaginings without any moorings in reality disappear, the subject discovers another version of his subjection: he sits, we are told, like a dead stone on the living rock (l. 51). The phrase "pietra viva" translates, I submit, "lapis vivus," from the *Aeneid* (l. 166), which, because of its association with the living cornerstone (1 Peter 2.4), became very popular in Christian iconography.[20] For Petrarch, the phrase carries no intimation of peace or sacred awe; rather, it describes his death in life as well as the reconsignment of the self to himself, for there on that stone he is like a man who thinks and weeps and writes (l. 52).

The three verbs, which recall thinking, the passions (weeping), and writing, call attention to their mutual implication in Petrarch's poem. There is a disjunction, as I have shown, in the representation of each term: love is unbounded; thoughts are rooted in love, and in their random occurrence, they pursue love in the attempt to mark love's limits, to grasp its significance; the subject is subjectivated and dislocated both from the beloved and from itself. But each self-disjointed term is interlocked with the other.

What joins them together is writing or, to use the language from *On His Own Ignorance*, rhetoric. In *On His Own Ignorance* eloquence is posited as essential to philosophy and to the persuasions of the will. In the poem, on the other hand, language is seen, first, as potentially disjoined from the lover's imagination ("now who will believe me?," the poet asks [l. 40]). More than that, language comes forth both as a personal, irreducible perspective—that which one can call a Petrarchan style—and as an entity that does not belong to anyone, is itself outside of the control of the self. The *envoi* of the song, wherein the poet sends it off on its way where the breeze (the "aura") of the fresh and fragrant laurel can be felt (ll. 69–70), recognizes the property of language to be the metaphor between the dislocated self and the outside world where the object of love is forever out of reach. In a general way, it can also be said that the citational structure of Petrarch's language, which in song 129 ranges from Ovid to Vergil to Lucan and Dante, shows poetic language to be not the locus of solitary recollections but, on the contrary, the repository of the commonplaces of language as well as the memory theater of inventions, topics, and myths which tradition has endlessly forged.

Petrarch is well known as the poet of time and of the precariousness of man in time, and he is also known as the poet whose voice articulates the infinite migrations of desire. But, as this chapter has shown, there is at least another side to this poet—that of the humanist who thinks about space, the dislocations of self, the places of love, the spaces of the mind, the palace of memory, the topics of rhetoric. In a poem such as "Di pensier in pensier," Petrarch maps the concerns of the humanist who, later in his life, will write *On His Own Ignorance* but with a difference that is to be attributed, no doubt, to his lucidity as a poet. In the poem, paradoxically, Petrarch shows that he is at his most philosophical when writing poetry because as he confronts the practice and process of poetic language, he discovers the historical reality of language as the voice of desire as well as the place of a common memory.

What establishes a relation among the heterogeneous elements scattered throughout song 129—a divided self, a faraway and still unnamed Laura, multiple and variable thoughts, phantasms, the landscapes of Vaucluse and Italy, the present tense, and the deluded imagining that there may yet be a serene, pacified future for the lover (ll. 22–23)—is exactly language. Language, as I have shown, appears in the song as the doubleness of memory, the subjective memory of the self in its temporality and imagination: memory as the archive of history, the place where time has turned into space, and where figures of thought and figures of the will are joined by an irreducible complementarity and are indistinguishable from each other.

Because of this doubleness of memory (as both time and space), the psychologism and will, which comprise the phenomenology of love in the poem, or its rhetoric, turn into epistemology. But what sets all these terms in motion, what changes the spatial, fixed relations into mobile entities, is love. Few poets have caught, as much as Petrarch has, love's disabling power. And even fewer poets have represented, as Petrarch has represented, the insight into love as simultaneously passion and force.

This idea of love as force certainly echoes the Augustinian formula of the *pondus amoris*, love as the pull of gravity, as well as the stilnovists' sense of love as *virtù*, which redeems and redirects the

poetic Language

energies of love as passion. I submit, however, that there is another strand in Petrarch's complex figuration: the idea of impetus, which comes to him from the physics of the Stoics. A text that strikes me as a partial model that Petrarch deploys for his tract *On His Own Ignorance* is Seneca's *De providentia*, in which he rejects, much as Petrarch does, the Epicurean notion of the blind turbulence of natural phenomena, the principle of fortuitous impulse that effects the concourse and dispersal of the heavenly bodies. Opposed to these elements of Epicurean materialism there is for Seneca the conviction, which Petrarch shares, of an ordered creation, of a kinship between the immortality of the human soul and God.

In the song, just as in most poems of the *Canzoniere*, love brings about a provisional self-forgetfulness, induces self-analysis, threatens the order of the mind, is outside of all thoughts, and becomes the object of all thoughts. This understanding of the passion, clearly, is far removed from the Stoic ethics of apathy, which is rightly conceived as patience in suffering or as indifference to perturbations. The importance of the ethical universe of the Stoics for Petrarch remains, as we shall see in chapter 4, central. What matters most here is to stress the Stoic principle of an all-pervasive pneumatic power, a divine substance that is the vital source binding together and animating the world within and the world without and that allows the transformation of phantasms and simulacra into sensible representations. In the light of this Stoic problematics, finally, one can see how for Petrarch, within the heterogeneity of love and thought, the power of love accounts for the force of thought, how love turns into the principle of intellectual action.

To gauge the link between these two ideas of force, I should like to refer briefly to Petrarch's *Secretum*.[21] The dialogue between the fictive Augustine and Petrarch takes place in the presence of Truth, who is a silent witness to the exchange between the two interlocutors. Truth, then, is not the point one arrives at as a consequence of the confrontation of two perspectives; Truth, rather, is here the given or the evidence, the precondition, as it were, of the exchange. At the same time, her silence intimates what one can call the powerlessness of Truth, who cannot defend herself except by lapsing into rhetorical arguments that would dis-figure her *evidence*. More than that, Truth, in her silence, which is a scandal to the garrulousness of Augustine and Petrarch, transcends and encompasses the viewpoints of the two

In The Presence of Truth

55

Soul

speakers; truth's silence provides a sort of "categorical imperative" that guides the speakers' words; it grounds their particular perceptions in the transparency of Truth's light. But her silence also suggests something more decisive and radical about Petrarch's figuration of Truth. That we should find Truth's depths of silence *strange* or unfathomable is implied by the fact that she is patterned after medieval allegorical figures (Boethius's Philosophia and Alan of Lille's Natura) who profusely voice their speculations and moral lessons. Unlike them, the silence of Petrarch's figuration of Truth conveys the idea that truth is not to be found in the finite horizon of words, and univocal statements, propositions uttered by Petrarch, no more than they are to be found in the absolute, traditional proclamations of the philosophers. Truth, rather, lies in the process of hermeneutical self-discovery Petrarch has undertaken.

At the center of this confessional disclosure of self, Petrarch reviews the problem of the structure of the soul. The text, in fact, can be called a *psychomachia,* and in book 2 Augustine, after reviewing the deadly sins that hold sway over Petrarch's life, focuses on the powers of the soul: "Why do you sigh? What was it, do you suppose, that caused all these problems? Your soul, of course, which was ashamed to obey the laws of its own nature and thought that it was a slave only because it had not broken the chains that held it. Even now it drags you along like a runaway horse and unless you rein yourself in, you will rush to your destruction" (p. 74).

St. Augustine, who believes, like Plato, in spiritual perfection as a harmony and balance within the soul, presents in this passage a picture of virtue as the horseman's skill to hold at bay the runaway, wild steed of the soul's chariot. From his standpoint of the blessed, who grasp the justice of the cosmos, Reason's control of the passions safeguards the soul from utter destruction, and he imparts this lesson to the recalcitrant Petrarch. Deploying arguments taken from the Stoics, St. Augustine even reminds Petrarch of "the promise of the Stoics, who vow they will pull out the diseases of the soul by the root" (p. 80). But Petrarch, as Bortolo Martinelli points out, argues, against the Stoics, that vices and virtues have the same root and that the effort to extirpate the vice inevitably entails the eradication of the virtues.

At the conclusion of the dialogue, Petrarch acknowledges that there are two chains holding him in spiritual bondage, love and glory. Augustine urges him to abandon these worldly preoccupations, but

Petrarch cannot but refuse to comply with the saint's request. In an overt polemic with the historical Augustine, he asserts the value of contingent projects. What is notable, however, is the admission that the two chains stem from the same root, that the love passion is the fold, while glory, the passion that forces Petrarch into the outside world, is the explication or exteriority of the interior dimension.

This is to say that Petrarch, the poet/humanist who marks the limits of thought in its pursuit of love, brings love and thought into a new relation, which is neither that of the Aristotelians of the Averroistic or Thomist persuasion, nor is it exclusively that of the stilnovistic poets. By interlocking love and thinking as complementary terms, Petrarch puts into relief the force of thought. Thought as an event, necessarily figured by material facts, is not a substance or an accident or a process, but it occurs in the imaginary. To say it differently, it is poetry, which for Petrarch can only be poetry of love, that makes thinking once again possible: love does violence to the mind and forces the lover to reflection; poetry's obliqueness submits the clarity of the philosophical discourse to the interrogation by the shadows of the imagination. From the standpoint of this insight, which both depends on and exceeds the imaginative elaborations of his predecessors, we can explore and chart Petrarch's bold rethinking of the tradition, which coincides with the project to refound the culture of his critical times. This project is essentially grounded in his ideas of the "individual," and the next two chapters will probe the ceaseless, contrapuntal pattern of negation and assertion with which Petrarch evokes and represents his understanding of the self.

CHAPTER III

The *Canzoniere* and the Language of the Self

It would be difficult to exaggerate the importance of the poet's selfhood in the *Canzoniere*;[1] one might even say that few other poets are as tenaciously intent as Petrarch on making the self the locus of singular and significant experiences and so obsessively bent on registering its variable moods. Critics have long spoken of Petrarch's humanism and modernity precisely in terms of his discovery of the centrality of the self: this self appears, as they have acknowledged, fragmented, wounded in his will;[2] or, as the poet himself writes, alluding to his moral drama, "et veggio il meglio et al peggior m'appiglio" (sonnet 264, l. 136).

The status of the moral dilemma, which is suggested by this line and which demonstrably punctuates the *Canzoniere,* is by no means clear in the economy of the text. There are critics who have dismissed the value of the moral language or, a priori, reduced it to a symbolic function, a formal element in the aesthetics of pure poetry that Petrarch, as a Mallarmé *avant la lettre,* entertained as his fundamental project.[3] One might object, however, that there seems to be a sense in which Petrarch would certainly want us to believe in the authenticity and exemplary character of his moral experience. The very first sonnet of the *Canzoniere* comes forth as a palinode, a deliberate self-staging, in which the poet, on the face of it, speaks with a voice of moral authority, the voice of a public self who finally confesses his past errors and disavows them.

With a few exceptions,[4] critics have been alert to the extended ironies that disrupt the notion that the *Canzoniere* is the poetic narrative of a conversion, the moral account, that is, of the experience of a poet who has finally reached the vantage point from which a structure of intelligibility can be imposed on the temporal fragmentation of the self. The first palinodic sonnet, for instance, recalls the last *canzone* to the Virgin. The implied link between beginning and end gives the poetic sequence a circular structure which challenges the possibility of renewal and leads the reader to suspect that the moral claim is the ambiguous expedient by which the poet attempts to constitute his own self as an "authority."

Faced with these poetic and moral ambiguities (of which the recurrent pattern of antitheses and the oxymora are transparent stylistic emblems), other critics read the *Canzoniere* as the account of the poet's deeply divided mind, caught in the fallen world of nature, unable or unwilling to reach grace, and seeking an aesthetic redemption. The *Canzoniere* is thus viewed as a narcissistic and idolatrous[5] construct because it tells the story of a poet who loves the work of his own hands and manufactures his own grace. The "fama" or the laurel tree which Petrarch relentlessly seeks is seen as the humanistic and idolatrous simulacrum of Christian eternity.

All of these critical perspectives share the sense that the poetic text is the ground for the constitution of the self; it may be a moral, idolatrous, or aesthetic self, but it is one that occupies an unquestionable centrality in his poetic discourse. The poet, it would seem, is certainly involved in a world of mortality and time, but poetry is the act which reduces his shifting, fragmented existence into manageable disguises of order and unity. Gianfranco Contini refers to the *Canzoniere* as precisely the attempt to unify experience;[6] and, by a deliberately formulaic turn of phrase, he defines it as the place where "romantic" oscillations and moods are disciplined by a counterpoint of formal "classical" order.[7] On the other hand, when the fragmentary character of the text is stressed, critics will account for it by a curious but common extratextual detour rather than by an analysis of the poetic mechanism at work. Making use of an essentially Petrarchan scheme of historical periodization, they place Petrarch at the center, at the critical crossroads where a medieval view of the cosmos, sustained by principles of hierarchy and order, gives way to the new humanistic age which he heralded and forged.[8] In this new age, there is no certainty in a Logos that may gather together the shattered pieces of experience, and traditional perspectives of moral order have lost their vital applicability.

Yet Petrarch seems to call into question in the *Canzoniere,* as I plan to show in the following pages, precisely the myth of the center and of the centrality of the self. My exegetical effort will be directed not so much toward contradicting previous critical views as toward redefining terms such as the self, its unity and presence, in what might be called Petrarch's poetics of fragmentation. My point of departure will be a close examination of a few poems in which the paradigm of the self is made much of (the myths of Narcissus and Actaeon particularly). Memory, imagination, and desire, the terms within which the poet's act of self-making is carried out, appear to be ambiguous instruments of the poetic project. The second part of this chapter will explore Petrarch's sense of this ambiguity, his intuition that the constitutive ambiguity of poetic language blurs any explicit thematic formulation. It is undeniable, for instance, that at an explicit thematic level, Petrarch oscillates between idolatry and conversion. Idolatry and conversion, however, are both postures by which he attempts to charge the elusive and deluding nature of language with a substantiality that language can never achieve. The ambiguities of the *Canzoniere* are of a moral order only in a secondary sense. This does not mean that they can be dismissed as simple accessories to the poetic nucleus, as Adelia Noferi suggests;[9] they are secondary because they depend on the knowledge that the self, in the mirror of self-reflection—as he is the object of his own thoughts—can never coincide with his own specular images.

Along with my concern to show the insufficiency of thematic criticism, I also wish to suggest some traits of Petrarch's lyrical voice. I ought to remark at the outset that the conventional judgment on his lyric is still well within the bounds of De Sanctis's evaluation:[10] when Petrarch is not too deliberate and indulgently self-conscious, as is occasionally the case, he is considered a truly lyrical poet. The lyric emerges as the conventional privileged form of literary discourse because it is the representation of the will and the direct and spontaneous expression of the self; Laura may be absent, but the voice of the poet is always present to relieve the grief because, as Petrarch himself has it, "cantando il duol si disacerba" (song 23, l. 4) (singing, pain becomes less bitter).

Sonnet 90 has conventionally been read as a specimen of genuine lyrical self-suppression. In it, Laura's past beauty—as Noferi argues in her extensive analysis—is recovered and transfigured in the "absolute space"[11] that the poem manages to evoke:

> Erano i capei d'oro a l'aura sparsi
> che 'n mille dolci nodi gli avolgea,

e il vago lume oltre misura ardea
di quei begli occhi, ch'or ne son sì scarsi;

e il viso di pietosi color farsi,
non so se vero o falso mi parea:
i'che l'esca amorosa al petto avea,
qual meraviglia se di subito arsi?

Non era l'andar suo cosa mortale,
ma d'angelica forma; et le parole
sonavan altro, che pur voce umana.

Uno spirto celeste, un vivo sole
fu quel ch'i' vidi: et se non fosse or tale,
piaga per allentar d'arco non sana.

Her golden hair was loosed to the breeze, which turned it in a thousand
sweet knots, and the lovely light burned without measure in her eyes,
which are now so stingy of it; and it seemed to me (I know not whether
truly or falsely) her face took on the color of pity: I who had the tinder of
love in my breast, what wonder is it if I suddenly caught fire? Her walk
was not that of a mortal thing but of some angelic form, and her words
sounded different from a merely human voice: a celestial spirit, a living
sun was what I saw, and if she were not such now, a wound is not healed
by the loosening of the bow.

The sonnet is articulated, quite clearly, on a temporal antithesis, the
then of the vision and the present ravages of time on Laura; the
antithesis introduces and stresses the persistence of the poet's memory
and his love. The poet's memory, in a real sense, is the privileged
metaphor; by it, the sonnet seems to move toward transcending the
flow of time, toward preserving inviolate—by the aesthetic transfigu-
ration—the image of Laura. At the same time, memory is the meta-
phor which engenders the poet's stability and gives continuity to his
own temporal experience. Now, as then, the concluding phrase im-
plies, the wound produced by the arrows of love in the poet goes on
bleeding.

We must look more closely at the poem, however, to discover the
complications of this explicit thematic thrust. The metaphor of the
"esca amorosa" (l. 7) by which the lover is trapped in the snares of love
literally describes the tinder that sets the fire, but it also means a decoy,
and as such it is strongly reminiscent of a central element in the

Memory

61

repertory of amorous rhetoric: Andreas Capellanus's definition of love. In *De arte honeste amandi,* partly following the etymology canonized by Isidore of Seville,[12] Andreas derives the word *amor* from *hamus,*[13] because by it man is "hooked," chained by desire. The metaphor he uses is that of the shrewd fisherman who uses bait to catch fish,[14] or, as a fourteenth-century Italian translation of *de arte* renders it, "colui che ama, dalli uncini della concupiscenza é preso e disidera di prendere l'altro col suo amo, siccome il pescatore savio s'ingegna coll'eschette di trarre li pesci" (he who loves is captured by the hooks of concupiscence and he desires to catch the other with his bait, just as the wise fisherman devises to catch fish with his baits).[15] Andreas's chains are chains of cupidity; Petrarch, on the contrary, suspends the erotic charge of the allusion within a distinctly stilnovistic rhetoric.

As has been widely acknowledged,[16] the sonnet echoes both Dante's "Tanto gentile" (So gentle) and Guinizelli's "Io voglio del ver" (I want truly). The stilnovists, to be sure, burden the appearance of the lady with a sense of moral illumination, but Petrarch rescues their language from definite moral overtones and deploys it so as to transfigure the image of Laura within a magic timelessness. We should not see in the conflation of the courtly motif and stilnovistic resonances simply an instance of Petrarch's dualism, his ambiguous view of the lady who is partly "donna angelicata" (the woman as angel), partly object of erotic desire. Much as for Dante in "Tanto gentile," for Petrarch the celebration of Laura's otherworldly beauty is the pretext for raising what is perhaps the fundamental question of the sonnet, the meaning of appearance.

The metaphor of appearance is introduced in the opening two lines of the sonnet. It has been suggested that these lines are patterned on Vergil's description of the vision of Venus in the *Aeneid* ("dederat-que comam diffundere ventis")[17] and the Ovidian myth of Daphne ("et levis impulsos retro dabat aura capillos").[18] But these reminiscences, I would submit, cluster about a closer parallel which occurs in Ovid's description of Diana in the *Metamorphoses.* The goddess, attended by her nymphs, prepares to bathe; one nymph takes the bow, another the robe, the defter of them "*sparsos* per colla *capillos conligit in nodum,*"[19] a line which is verbally echoed by and woven into Petrarch's "erano i *capei* d'oro a l'aura *sparsi* / che 'n mille dolci *nodi* gli *avolgea.*" Characteristically, Petrarch draws what Ovid describes as the action of the nymph on Diana (and the differences between the two of them) into a solipsistic and self-reflexive circle: it is the "aura" which ties Laura's hair in a thousand curls. Ovid's myth, as we shall see later on, deals largely with Actaeon's glance that violates the nakedness of Diana as he looks into that which should remain invisible and is subsequently transformed into a stag.

Like the stilnovistic allusion, the Ovidian echoes celebrate Laura's epiphany as a visionary experience bordering on the phantasmic; but, paradoxically, she is absent from the sonnet. The pun "l'aura" (l. 1) is both the stylized *senhal* for Laura and the sign of her elusiveness. This elusiveness occurs at the heart of the vision: she appears, in a real sense, by being invisible, as "uno spirto celeste, un vivo sole" (l. 12), emblems that imply transparency or light which in its excess dazzles and blinds. Her very face, like the sound of her words, is defined ambiguously, "non so se vero o falso mi parea" (l. 6). The deceptiveness depends, no doubt, on the divine and human attributes of the image. But more is implied. For Petrarch, the very nature of the appearance of the image is for it to be unsettling, with its contours blurred.

By the act of memory, the poet tries to give Laura's apparition a stabilized and fixed presence that may redeem and abolish time; but the image cannot be deciphered. More importantly, the act of memory dislodges the poet into a disorienting space where the reality of Laura's decline ("begli occhi, ch'*or* ne son sì scarsi" [l. 4]) is suspended into an hypothesis. The concluding lines of the sonnet, "et se non fosse *or* tale / piaga per allentar d'arco non sana" (ll. 13–14), by their hypothetical structure, throw into doubt the reality of the present time. The poet's memory then, far from being simply a stabilizing metaphor, manifests itself both as the illusory act of the mind to establish a temporal continuity and as the fiction which threatens the poet's sense of time and his stance.

But the poet is threatened in a more radical way. The vision of Laura which binds his will and from which there is no escaping is obliquely cast in terms of a specifically poetic danger, namely, the danger of losing the poetic voice. In Dante's "Tanto gentile," at the appearance of Beatrice, "ogni lingua deven tremando muta" (every tongue trembling becomes mute), and, as in Guinizelli's "Io voglio del ver," the poet can only praise the lady's virtues. In the Ovidian tale, on the other hand, Actaeon sees Diana and loses his voice: "Nunc tibi me posito visam velamine narres / si poteris narrare licet."[20] His loss of voice is the consequence of his moral transgression. For Petrarch, by these oblique allusions, what seems to be a spontaneous experience of lyrical self-expression is ironically reversed into an awareness of a poetic crisis that depends on the unsettling nature of the imaginary experience.

In the only sonnet where the myth of Narcissus is explicitly re-called, Petrarch explores precisely the dangers of the imaginary expe-rience. Paradoxically, the myth (which in the *Secretum* becomes the explicit point of reference for describing Petrarch's self-fascination) is here applied to Laura, not to the poet-lover; sonnet 45, in fact, focuses on her as she sees herself reflected in the mirror and is absorbed in a narcissistic self-love.

> Il mio adversario in cui veder solete
> gli occhi vostri che Amor e'l cielo honora,
> colle non sue bellezze v'innamora
> più che 'n guisa mortal soavi et liete.
>
> Per consiglio di lui, donna, m'avete
> scacciato del mio dolce albergo fora:
> misero exilio, avegna ch'i' non fôra
> d'abitar degno ove voi sola siete.
>
> Ma s'io v'era con saldi chiovi fisso,
> non dovea specchio farvi per mio danno,
> a voi stessa piacendo, aspra et superba.
>
> Certo se vi rimembra di Narcisso,
> questo et quel corso ad un termino vanno,
> benchè di sì bel fior sia indegna l'erba.

My adversary in whom you are wont to see your eyes, which Love and Heaven honor, enamors you with beauties not his but sweet and happy beyond mortal guise. By his counsel, Lady, you have driven me out of my sweet dwelling: miserable exile! even though I may not be worthy to dwell where you alone are. But if I had been nailed there firmly, a mirror should not have made you, because you pleased yourself, harsh and proud to my harm. Certainly, if you remember Narcissus, this and that course lead to one goal—although the grass is unworthy of so lovely a flower.

The mirror has seduced Laura and is thus the rival of the lover; described in terms of negativity and emptiness at the beginning of the poem ("colle non sue bellezze" [l. 3]), it acquires in the second stanza a

dangers of imagination

definite substantiality as it insidiously charms Laura to cast the lover into exile.[21] Discreetly, the mirror is alluded to as a kind of *losengier*.[22] In the poetry of both trouvères and troubadours, the *losengier* is the deceiving and inimical talebearer who insinuates himself into the lady's graces, flatters her, and displaces the true lover. In the troubadoric love drama, the *losengier* plays the role of the voyeur whose eyes violate any secrecy; for Petrarch, it becomes a purely imaginary and fictive self-projection. Like a *losengier*, the mirror flatters and separates the lover from Laura, and by a dramatic twist, Petrarch exposes the narcissistic basis of troubadour poetry as he shows that the blandishments of the *losengier* are a mere self-gratifying reflection leading to harshness and self-love (l. 11).

The sonnet ends with an allusion to Narcissus and his death. Laura is in the presence of her own image, and the poet reminds her, locked in her erotic self-reification, that the coincidence of self and self's image is nothing less than Narcissus's experience of death. The allusion to the Ovidian myth of Narcissus is more than a simple metaphoric correlation or a reference of merely historical interest: by recalling the story from the *Metamorphoses*, Petrarch undertakes a reading which is startlingly profound.

Narcissus, in Ovid's story, can live only if he will never know himself—such was the promise of the gods. The youth dies at the fountain when he has known himself, when he has seen, that is to say, his own image and has discovered its emptiness. He sees first the emptiness of the shadow he loves ("*nihil* habet ista *sui*"[23] is the lament, and Petrarch seems to echo it in the phrase "non sue bellezze") and then discovers that he is that empty shadow: "iste ego sum."[24] The conceptual implication of the story is clear: whatever authentic self-knowledge is possible, it is equivalent to death. Or, what amounts to the same thing, death is the knowledge of one's own vanity.

The idolatrous self-love of Narcissus is the tragedy of self-knowledge, the unbearable experience of facing one's own finitude. At the same time, the imaginary self-representation emerges as the locus of death. But Petrarch alludes to Narcissus and moves well beyond the moment of his death. The metaphor of the metamorphosis, on which he insists in the last three lines of the sonnet, implies that the coincidence between the self and its image is illusory. It also spells out the fact that Narcissus after death is displaced into a radical otherness: as he is metamorphosed into a flower, the flower is caught in the world of temporality and impermanence where it will live by continuously dying. Metamorphosis is for Petrarch the metaphor of spatial and temporal dislocation, the hint that no form is ever stable and that every form is always moving toward still other forms.

The analogy between Narcissus and Laura, which is the burden of the last tercet, carries with it the implication that Laura, too, is threatened with the same displacement that Narcissus experienced. Yet the last line, "benchè di sì bel fior sia indegna l'erba," subverts the analogy. We should perhaps remark that we are dealing here with a common rhetorical feature of Petrarch's poetry, one which was most fruitfully picked up, for instance, by Leopardi. An analogy is set up between two terms, but the movement of the poem finally denies the posited correspondence. Leopardi deploys this technique constantly: in "Canto notturno d'un pastore errante dell'Asia" (Night song of a shepherd wandering through Asia), to give one example, a resemblance between the moon and the shepherd, "somiglia alla tua vita / la vita del pastore" (your life resembles the life of the shepherd), is established. The articulation of the poem, however, shows the analogy to be the poet's wistful impulse to find significant bonds between the self and what the self is not. The analogy is finally demystified, and its terms return to their original disjunction.

In Petrarch's sonnet, the collapse of the analogy between Narcissus and Laura seems, on the surface, to function as a mildly hyperbolic device to insinuate the notion of Laura's singularity and the praise of her beauty. The seemingly conventional and innocuous tribute hides, however, a less reassuring and less bland meaning. It does not do violence to the text to read the distinction of Laura from Narcissus as a suggestion that Laura will be displaced like Narcissus, but unlike him, she will belong literally nowhere: she will be a purely imaginary flower and will exist in the nonplace of the imagination. The detail of the unworthiness of the grass to bear and contain Laura subtly alludes to the poet's own unworthiness "avegna ch'i' non fôra / d'abitar *degno* ove voi sola siete" (ll. 7–8). The dislocation is total: Narcissus is a flower, Laura is in the utopian domain of the imaginary, the poet is in his exile. Petrarch, as we know, gives thematic weight to the question of exile: the lover is always distant, always somewhere else, forever seeking the time and space of his encounter with Laura. Distance, in this sense, is essential to desire, for it allows desire to exist as perennial tension. But dislocation exceeds the thematic notion of loss of space and involves, as we shall see presently, the very conditions of figurative language.

In both the sonnets that we have examined, the image elicited by memory or reflected by the mirror, far from being a stable and idolatrous sign for the self, endangers the sense of selfhood. In sonnet 45, as Laura is provisionally related to Narcissus, the poet is Echo, an emblem of the disembodied voice alluding to its own hollowness. The myth of Actaeon, which reappears in a short poem (madrigal 52), goes even further and exemplifies the dislocation of the poetic voice as an involuntary experience.

> Non al suo amante più Diana piacque,
> quando per tal ventura tutta ignuda
> la vide in mezzo de la gelide acque,
>
> ch'a me la pastorella alpestra et cruda
> posta a bagnar un leggiadretto velo,
>
> che a l'aura il vago e biondo capel chiuda,
> tal che mi fece, or quand'egli arde il cielo
> tutto tremar d'un amoroso gielo.

> Not so much did Diana please her lover when, by a similar chance, he saw her all naked amid the icy waters, as did the cruel mountain shepherdess please me, set to wash a pretty veil that keeps her lovely blond head from the breeze; so that she made me, even now when the sky is burning, all tremble with a chill of love.

The madrigal has a deceptive pastoral simplicity: ostensibly it is built on a comparison between Actaeon's pleasure at seeing Diana bathing naked and the poet's own pleasure at seeing a shepherdess washing a veil which will tie Laura's hair. Unified by metaphors of bathing (Diana's ablutions and the veil's being washed), rhyme, and internal assonances ("quando . . . biondo . . . quand'egli"), the madrigal attempts to capture a sense of harmonious pastoral order and moves toward the conventional cliché of the final line, the antithesis of ice and fire.

The myth of Diana is once again recalled, but this time from Actaeon's point of view. Actaeon is like the poet, and, in effect, he is the metaphor for the poet, the voyeur who sees unseen Diana's nakedness and transgresses the bounds of the sacred space that must remain inaccessible to him. As Petrarch alludes to the myth, however, he simultaneously eludes it. The strategy of the transition from Actaeon to the poet's experience is remarkable: it is as if in the empty space that separates the two tercets, Petrarch turns his eyes away and blinds himself to the possibility of violation.

A chain of metaphoric dislocations from the erotic scene of Diana is thus set in motion. Whereas Actaeon sees the naked Diana, who in Ovid's language was "posito visam velamine," Petrarch picks up the veil and covers that nakedness. The sequence of images, the shepherdess who washes the veil that will tie the hair of Laura (herself, once again, alluded to and eluded by the pun "l'aura") bears a tenuous relation to the myth. There is no necessary link between the two experiences: Petrarch domesticates the scene as he evokes Actaeon's encounter. The diminutives "pastorella" and "leggiadretto" conjure up a pastoral world (and the madrigal is the poetic form of the pastoral) which shelters the self from the tragic possibilities of the myth, what in song 23 is referred to as a veritable loss of one's own image (ll. 155ff.).

The final phrase of the madrigal, "tutto tremar d'un amoroso gielo," ostensibly makes the self the endpoint of the sequence of dislocations and suggests how the poem moves toward the constitution of the self as a center of perception. But the phrase circles back to the opening description of Diana "*tutta* ignuda / . . . in mezzo de le *gelide* acque." If the analogy between Actaeon and the poet collapses as the poet does not look at the goddess, he now insinuates that he is like Diana. The shift of perspective is hardly surprising in Petrarch's poetry: he often casts himself, as is well known, in the role of Apollo and, in the same breath, casts Laura as the sun. The shift implies that the categories of subject and object are precarious and reversible. More fundamentally, the shift insinuates a doubleness at the moment in which the selfhood is constituted: Petrarch is at the same time both Actaeon and Diana, but he is also neither, a double, like the two foci of an ellipsis always implicating each other and always apart.

It is in this space of the elliptical movement that the metaphoric circulation of Petrarch's poetry is woven. In all three poems so far considered in this chapter, at the moment of resolution each poem changes its direction and returns on itself to some other textual point insofar as its thematic sense is reversed and other hidden perspectives emerge. These perspectives are by no means hidden, they are rather the surface of the text in the sense that for Petrarch the text is always by necessity the surface. The prominent figure in madrigal 52 is precisely the veil which Diana has put aside and Petrarch stretches over her nakedness. The veil, the metaphor that makes the difference between the experience of Actaeon and that of the poet, is involuntary. The phrase "per tal ventura" (l. 2)—which directly echoes Ovid's sense of the fortuitousness of Actaeon's vision of Diana ("at bene si quaeras, *fortunae* crimen illo, non scelus invenies")[25] carries a special force in the madrigal. It is the contingency of the encounter, the involuntary experience that Petrarch stresses. We know that he frequently validates the involuntary events: in sonnet 3, for instance, he becomes a *captivus amoris* when he is "senza sospetto . . . del tutto disarmato" (confident . . . altogether disarmed).[26] The willed efforts generate illusory epiphanies, while the involuntary encounters are essential and significant. In a general sense, this is Petrarch's critique of the inadequacy of the will, the ironic awareness that his love quest is doomed to fail. More particularly, the phrase "per tal ventura" implies that the emergence of the veil lies beyond his will, that the dislocation which his own metaphors figure is involuntary. The poet's deliberate attempt to construct the self, to set up analogies by which the self is constituted, is obfuscated by the veil. But what does it mean to say that the veil is involuntary and what does the veil—a term deeply charged with allegorical resonances[27]—mask? We must look closely at song 125 where Petrarch grounds his notion of the self and its elusiveness within the larger questions of language and desire.

> Se 'l pensier che mi strugge,
> com'è pungente et saldo,
> così vestisse d'un color conforme,
>   forse tal m'arde et fugge,
> ch'avria parte del caldo,
> et desteriasi Amor là dov'or dorme;
>   men solitarie l'orme
> foran de' miei pie' lassi
> per campagne et per colli,
> men gli occhi ad ognor molli,
> ardendo lei che come un ghiaccio stassi,
> et non lascia in me dramma
> che non sia foco et fiamma.
>
>   Però ch'Amor mi sforza
> et di saver mi spoglia,
> parlo in rime aspre et di dolcezze ignude:
>   Ma non sempre a la scorza

ramo, né in fior, né 'n foglia,
mostra di for sua natural vertude.
    Miri ciò che 'l cor chiude,
Amor et que' begli occhi,
ove si siede a l'ombra.
Se 'l dolor che si sgombra
avèn che 'n pianto o in lamentar trabocchi,
l'un a me noce, et l'altro
altrui, ch'io non lo scaltro.

    Dolci rime leggiadre
che nel primiero assalto
d'Amor usai, quand'io non ebbi altr'arme,
    chi verrà mai che squadre
questo mi cor di smalto
ch'almen, com'io solea, possa sfogarme?
    Ch'aver dentro a lui parme
un che madonna sempre
depinge et de lei parla:
a voler poi ritrarla,
per me non basto; et par ch'io me ne stempre.
Lasso!, così m'è scorso
lo mio dolce soccorso.

    Come fanciul ch'a pena
volge la lingua et snoda,
che dir non sa, ma 'l più tacer gli è noia,
    così 'l desir mi mena
a dire; et vo' che m'oda
la dolce mia nemica anzi ch'io moia.
    Se forse ogni sua gioia
nel suo bel viso è solo,
et di tutt'altro è schiva,
odil tu, verde riva,
e presta a' miei sospir sì largo volo,
che sempre si ridica
come tu m'eri amica.

    Ben sai che sì bel piede
non toccò terra unquancho
come quel dì che già segnata fosti;
    onde il cor lasso riede,
col tormentoso fianco,
a partir teco i lor pensier nascosti.

Così avestù riposti
de' be' vestigi sparsi
anchor tra' fiori et l'erba,
che la mia vita acerba,
lagrimando, trovasse ove acquetarsi!
Ma come pò s'appaga
l'alma dubbiosa et vaga.

Ovunque gli occhi volgo
trovo un dolce sereno
pensando: qui percosse il vago lume.
Qualunque herba o fior colgo
credo che nel terreno
aggia radice, ov'ella ebbe in costume
gir fra le piagge e 'l fiume,
et talor farsi un seggio
fresco, fiorito et verde.
Così nulla sen perde;
et più certezza averne fora il peggio.
Spirto beato, quale
se', quando altrui fai tale?

O poverella mia, come se' rozza!
Credo che tel conoschi:
rimanti in questi boschi.

If the care that torments me, as it is sharp and dense, so were clothed in a conformable color, perhaps one burns me and flees who would have part of the heat, and Love would awaken where now he is sleeping; less solitary would be the prints of my weary feet through fields and across hills, my eyes less wet always: if she were aflame who now stands like ice and leaves not a dram in me that is not fire and flame. Since Love forces me and strips me of all skill, I speak in harsh rhymes naked of sweetness; but not always does a branch show forth its natural virtue in flower or in leaf. Let Love and those lovely eyes, where he is sitting in the shade, look on what my heart has shut up in itself. If my sorrow which unburdens itself happens to overflow in weeping or lamenting, the one pains me and the other pains someone else, for I do not polish it. Sweet graceful rhymes that I used in the first assault of Love, when I had no other arms: who will ever come who can shatter the stone about my heart, so that at least I can pour myself forth as I used to do? For it seems to me that I have someone within who always portrays my lady and speaks of her: I am not sufficient to describe her by myself, and I come untuned because of it; alas so has my sweet comfort fled! Like a child who can hardly move and untangle his tongue, who is not able to speak but hates to be silent any longer, thus desire leads me to speak, and I wish my sweet enemy to hear me before I die. If, perhaps, she takes joy only in her lovely face and flees everything else, do you, green shore, hear it and lend to my sighs so wide a flight that it be always remembered that you were kind to me. You know well that so beautiful a foot never touched the earth as on that day when you were marked by hers, wherefore my weary heart comes back with my tormented flanks to share with you their hidden cares. Would you had hidden away some lovely footprints still among the flowers and grass, that my bitter life might weeping find a place to become calm! But my fearful, yearning soul satisfies itself as best it can. Wherever I turn my eyes, I find a sweet brightness, thinking: "Here fell the bright light of her eyes." Whatever grass or flower I gather, I believe that it is rooted in the ground where she was wont to walk through the meadows beside the river, and sometimes to make herself a seat, fresh, flowering, and green. Thus no part is omitted and to know more exactly would be a loss. Blessed spirit, what are you if you make another become such? O poor little song, how inelegant you are! I think you know it: stay in these woods.

The poet starts by recalling his exile from Laura: cast in the form of a *planctus,* the poem dramatizes the poet's lonely wanderings (ll. 5–7) in an open and unbounded landscape as a veritable quest that culminates in the last stanza (ll. 66–78). Laura is nowhere in the poem, and the quest, in effect, is not for Laura but for her vestiges (ll. 60–63), which might allay the restlessness of the lover's heart. The landscape does not preserve her vestiges, and the poet recoils into a deliberate self-mystification: he acknowledges as illusory the space, the "qui" of her presence, for "come pò s'appaga / l'alma dubbiosa et vaga" (ll. 64–65).

This quest for the signs of Laura, which ends by exposing the self-mystification as the presence of a nothingness, masks and hides another more painful and insoluble quest, the poet's quest for poetic language, for the signs that might be adequate to the poet's inner thoughts and that may awaken Laura's love from its slumber (ll. 3–5). Seen in this perspective, the *canzone* is a veritable grammar of styles, an inventory of poetic possibilities. The two stylistic poles within which Petrarch moves, the "rime aspre et di dolcezze ignude" (l. 16) and the "dolci rime leggiadre / che nel primiero assalto / d'Amor usai" (ll. 27–29), are definite echoes from the *canzone* in the fourth treatise of the *Convivio,* "Le dolci rime d'amor ch'io solia" (The sweet rhymes of love that I used). In this allegorical poem in which Dante raises the question of the origin and nature of authority, he leaves behind the "dolci rime" and promises to use "rima aspr'e sottile" (harsh and sharp rhyme) as stylistic correlatives adequate to philosophical speculation. Petrarch inverts the terms: possessed by the "rime aspre" which he would leave behind, he recalls the "dolci rime" of the past.[28] We shall see later the crucial importance of Petrarch's allusion to the allegorical poem of the *Convivio*, for it is part of a more complex cultural-poetic polemic that Petrarch undertakes against Dante.

The first stanza, for instance, "et non lascia in me *dramma* / che non sia foco et *fiamma*" (ll. 12–13), ends with a rhyme scheme that partially picks up the rhyme scheme employed by Dante in the earthly Paradise: "men che *dramma* / di sangue m'è rimaso che non tremi; / conosco i segni dell'antica *fiamma*" (*Purgatorio* 30.46–48) (Not a drop of blood is left in me that does not tremble; I recognize the signs of the ancient flame). For Dante this is the juncture where Vergil disappears and the poet finally meets Beatrice. The irony of the allusion is transparent: the dramatic point at which Dante reaches Beatrice in the pastoral world of Eden marks the beginning of Petrarch's own quest for Laura, whom he will find only in the illusory garden of the mind. But the irony goes further than this. Dante abandons Vergil, and the translation of the Vergilian line which results ("agnosco veteris vestigia flammae" [*Aeneid* 4.23] [I recognize the vestiges of the ancient flame]) is a veritable metaphor which stresses Dante's poetic autonomy from his guide. The line that in its original context describes the suicidal and annihilating love of Dido is turned against Vergil to dramatize the pilgrim's and the poet's spiritual resurrection. Petrarch will also attempt to, and effectively does, free himself from the specter of Dante.

Song 125 is replete with other allusions to the *rime petrose* (stony rhymes).[29] Most notably, the lines "chi verrà mai che squadre / questo mi cor di smalto" (ll. 30–31) are a direct paraphrase of two lines in "Così nel mio parlar voglio esser aspro" (I want to be harsh in my speech): "fender per mezzo / lo core a la crudele che il mio squatra" (ll. 53–54) (split the heart of the cruel woman who cuts mine to pieces). Even the rhyme scheme, "scorza . . . forza" (ll. 25–26), in "Così nel mio parlar" is inverted as "sforza . . . scorza" (ll. 14–17) in Petrarch's canzone.

What purpose do these reminiscences from "Così nel mio parlar" serve in the economy of Petrarch's poem? Dante's song describes both his love for the so-called Donna Pietra as an experience of spiritual degradation which threatens to transform the lover into a stone and his attempt to write in a style which is commensurate with the harshness of his own erotic fall:

Non trovo scudo ch'ella non mi spezzi
né loco che dal suo viso m'asconda:
che come fior di fronda,
così de la mia mente tien la cima.

. . . . .

e il peso che m'affonda
è tal che non potrebbe adequar rima. (ll. 14–17, 20–21)

I do not find a shield that she does not shatter, nor a place to hide from her face; for like a flower on its stalk so does she hold the crest of my mind . . . and the weight that sinks me is such that no verse would suffice to describe it.[30]

This love occupies "de la mia mente . . . la cima"; the phrase actually translates the technical *apex mentis* and implies the absolute corruption of the intellect or, since *mens* is the faculty of intellectual vision, the darkening of reason by the sight of the Medusa.[31]

The first two lines of the stanza enact precisely an allusion to the myth of the Medusa threatening the unshielded lover who is, in turn, cast as an unsuccessful Perseus. More importantly, the dramatic process of the stanza hinges on the coherently related allusion to the Medusa and the poet's misdirected love defined as a weight that pulls the lover downward (ll. 20–21). Dante uses an unequivocally Augustinian doctrine of love. Love, for Augustine, is a metaphoric pull of gravity, the inner weight that urges the soul to seek its own place. This doctrine, known as *pondus amoris,* is illustrated by the natural movement of stone and fire. The fire designates the spiritual ascent; the stone, the erotic fall.[32] Augustine's metaphors are recalled by Dante: the "peso che m'affonda" is the downward *pondus* of the stone, the Donna Pietra–Medusa who reduces the lover into a stone.

Petrarch certainly accepts this view of desire as the metaphor of dislocation: the exile of the lover dramatizes precisely his displacement. Yet, by coupling the "rime aspre" of the philosophical poem with the "parlar . . . aspro" of "Così nel mio parlar" where the dark eros abrogates the power of the intellect, he draws attention to the contradictions of Dante's theory of poetic styles. Petrarch achieves this by using Augustine's theory of language against Dante.

If the first two stanzas of song 125 are charged with allusions to Dante, the third stanza is the turning point away from Dante to Augustine's theory of language and desire.

> Come fanciul ch'a pena
> volge la lingua et snoda,
> che dir non sa, ma 'l più tacer gli è noia,
> così 'l desir mi mena
> a dire . . . (ll. 40–44)

The explicit claim that language is rooted in desire is cast in the terminology of Augustine's *Confessions*. This spiritual autobiography, which is in a fundamental way a quest for language and the Word, focuses on the *paideia* of a rhetorician and "salesman of words" who, through complex intellectual temptations, gives up the duplicity of rhetoric and turns to the Logos made flesh. Augustine begins by recounting his childhood, the *infantia* (which should be taken with its full etymological sense of speechlessness), and elaborates his theory of signs and language. Language and desire are inextricably bound together: as Augustine will find out in his reading of the Vergilian Dido,[33] language engenders desire, and it originates in desire: "Quis me commemorat peccatum infantiae meae—quonian nemo mundus a peccato coram te, nec infans, cuius est unius diei vita super terram—quis me commemorat? . . . Quid ergo tunc peccabam? . . . Vidi ergo et expertus sum zelantem parvulum: *nondum loquebatur* et intuebatur pallidus amaro aspectu conlactaneum suum. . . . Nonne ab infantia huc pergens in pueritiam? non enim eram *infans, qui non farer,* sed etiam puer loquens eram."[34] The fairly close verbal echoes in Petrarch's text ("fanciul . . . che dir non sa" paraphrases both "nondum loquebatur" and "infans, qui non farer") disclose his assimilation of the heart of Augustine's linguistic concept. The child who cannot speak and cannot be still is the metaphor by which both Augustine and Petrarch make desire the foundation of language. Yet desire, properly speaking, cannot be a foundation, for desire is a pure privation, a lack generated by man's fallen state. Words and signs are generated from this lack and are hollow dislocations of it: the poet persistently attempts to achieve a formal adequation to desire and persistently fails because desire, in its uninterrupted movement toward totality, exceeds any formal adequation. For Petrarch, language is the allegory of desire, a veil, not because it hides a moral meaning but because it always says something else.

In the light of this, we can perhaps grasp the reasons for the presence of technical metaphors drawn from the repertory of the language of allegory. The thrust of "Se 'l pensier che mi strugge" is to find a language that "vestisse d'un color conforme" (l. 3) the lover's inner thoughts. The implication is that style is exterior to the truth, a veil for the inner feelings. If the term "color," furthermore, transparently alludes to the *colores rhetorici,* "vestisse" designates an allegorical *involucrum.* St. Paul refers to the body as a "cloth" for the soul, and Vulgate translates the clothing by "induere."[35] Macrobius, for his part, uses "vestire" as a conventional metaphor to indicate the cover of allegory.[36] Even more cogently, in the lines "Ma non sempre a la scorza / ramo, né in fior, né 'n foglia / mostra di for sua natural vertude" (ll. 17–19), the word "scorza" translates the technical *cortex,* the bark which in the language of allegory hides and obscures the meaning, the *medulla* within.

The series of oblique allusions to allegory could be extended,[37] but it is the allusion to Dante's allegorical *canzone* from the *Convivio* that seems especially pertinent. To Dante's seeming belief that language may reach a genuine philosophical knowledge, Petrarch opposes a vision in which the mind is first stifled by love and then, at the end of the poem, chooses to delude itself. To Dante's faith in the mimetic possibilities of language, Petrarch opposes the notion of a radical inadequacy of language. If allegory for Dante (as Petrarch read him) is the envelope of hidden truth and an instrument of knowledge, for Petrarch it is constitutive of language and marks the distance between desire and its signs.

Dante's conception of the allegory of poets in the *Convivio,* in spite of the lacunae in the text, is much more complex than Petrarch makes it out to be, as I will show in chapter 7. We must rather stress the necessity of the veil of allegory and the self-mystification in Petrarch's *canzone:* they are metaphors of a desire which cannot be named. The inadequacy of language is not merely a topos of authorial modesty, as the canons of rhetoric explain it; it suggests, rather, the poet's ironic awareness that there is not a proper name for desire. We must not, however, minimize the fact that desire for Petrarch has a name, bears indeed the proper name of Laura:

Quando io movo i sospiri a chiamar voi
e 'l nome che nel cor mi scrisse Amore,
LAUdando s'incomincia udir di fore
il suon dei primi dolci accenti suoi.

Vostro stato REal, che 'ncontro poi,
raddoppia a l'alta impresa il mio valore;
ma: TAci, grida il fin che farle honore
è d'altri homeri soma che da' tuoi.

Così LAUdare e REverire insegna
la voce stessa, pur ch'altri vi chiami,
O d'ogni reverenza et d'honor degna:

se non che forse Apollo si disdegna
ch'a parlar dei suoi sempre verdi rami
lingua morTAl presumptuosa vegna. (sonnet 5)

When I move my sighs to call you and the name that Love wrote on my heart, the sound of its first sweet accents is heard without in LAU-ds. Your RE-gal state, which I meet next, redoubles my strength for the high enterprise; but "TA-lk no more!" cries the ending, "for to do her honor is a burden for other shoulders than yours." Thus the word itself teaches LAU-d and RE-verence, whenever anyone calls you, O Lady worthy of all reverence and honor; except that perhaps Apollo is incensed that any mor-TA-l tongue should come presumptuous to speak of his eternally green boughs.

The existence of a proper name implies the possibility that language has a proper sense, a univocal, literal referent that localizes and fixes upon itself the infinite disarticulations of desire. The name of Laura seems to function precisely in this way: the syllables of "Laureta" are dispersed[38] through the text (ll. 3, 5, 7, 9, 14), and, by the dispersion, they sustain the movement of the poem and serve as a fulcrum to organize and orient the space of the sonnet. Her name is "proper" in another sense: it contains and hides within its syllables the great themes of love poetry—praise and reverence. It might be said, actually, that the sonnet, with its stress on praise and Apollo's pursuit of Daphne, dramatizes the etymological possibilities of the word *laurus*. Isidore of Seville, for instance, explains that "laurus a verbo laudis dicta. . . . Hanc arborem Graeci *dafnen* vocant quod numquam deponat viriditatem" (The laurel is so called from the word for praise. . . . The Greeks call this tree *daphne* because it never loses its green color).[39] Just as for Isidore etymology is the metaphor for a direct and necessary link between word and referent, it is Petrarch's fiction that a "proper" relationship exists between the master-word and its textual disseminations.

But the anagram ironizes the explicit thematic burden of the poem. It implies that words have no preestablished stability, for, by virtue of the anagram, letters can be extrapolated and reassembled at will—and words become generative of all possible other words. The linear sequence of the text is abolished, and the text loses its quality of being an ordering of signs, each fixed, distinct, and self-containedly referential. The property of the name is threatened by the duplication of the name "Laureta" into "Laurea" (ll. 9, 12). In a way, the sonnet is about the process of duplication. The vision of the real Laura doubles the poet's virtue (l. 6), and the writing of the poem repeats the words of the inner dictator. In these two cases, the doubling is meant to assert the correspondence between language and reality. But as the name Laura is duplicated in "Laurea," the duplication endangers the unity of the proper name and subverts the possibility that the voice of love is bound to a univocal, stable sign. The allusion to Apollo in the final tercet, while it draws attention to the poetic act, discloses the symbolic reciprocity—long acknowledged—of "Laura" and "lauro." This Petrarchan conceit (which is multiplied in other variants such as "l'aura," "auro," and so on) shows that desire is always cloaked under false names, that each name is a mask for the restless instability of desire.

Petrarch's idolatry, his so-called narcissism, the palinodic poems—all are willed attempts to fix the endless migrations of desire in a stable form. The impulse for totality and unity is involuntarily blurred by the awareness of the nature of language and desire. Language *betrays* desire, both in the sense that it reveals desire, is its spy, and because language bears an essential otherness to the desire that generates it. At the same time, in the universe of desire, totality is never possible: desire knows only shreds and fragments, even if plenitude is its ever elusive mirage. The *Canzoniere* is, to be sure, the attempt to restore the pieces, to give an illusory unity to the fragments. The 366 poems (the days of the year plus one) simulate the eternal calendar of love, a symbolic order imposed on the fragmentation of time, but the fragments remain as such, "rime sparse." The point is that the unity of the work is the unity *of* fragments *in* fragments. Not even each fragment, each individual poem, may be said to possess a unity: each poem attempts to begin anew,[40] to be an autonomous and self-enclosed totality, but it inevitably ends up repeating what has already been tried before and leads to other contiguous poems. The poetic sequence is governed by recurrent motifs, such as the phoenix, the sun, the cycle of seasons, metamorphoses, and the like. These motifs, which are in turn metaphors of recurrence constantly alluding to their own instability, disclose the principle of repetition which is at work in the *Canzoniere*. Through them, the totality and unity of the text are given as a movement of forms which are discontinuous, which repeat themselves and fall upon themselves.

It is the metaphor of the labyrinth (explicitly recalled in sonnet 211, discussed in the Introduction, and sonnet 224) that best describes the *Canzoniere:* it designates a monadic structure in which the parts are a series of communicating vessels simultaneously proximate and disjointed and in which each partition leads to and separates from another. The metaphor is particularly apt because it also suggests the poet's experience of being locked in a cosmos of his own creation from which there are no exits (as sonnet 89 dramatizes) and where the only thing left for the poet is to call and make his voice resonate.[41]

Petrarch, as we well know, gives a deliberately melocentric structure to his poetry: the very first sonnet, to which I shall return later in this book, opens with the famous appeal, "Voi ch'ascoltate in rime sparse il suono" (You who hear in scattered rhymes the sound). The sound would seem to constitute, in the poet's general experience of negativity, the irreducible residue of his presence, the domain where the poet's selfhood takes shelter. But the melocentrism of the first sonnet is ironic both because it obscures the moral meaning of the palinode and, more fundamentally, because the sound is hollow, an empty sign which points to its own insubstantiality. In a real sense, the paradigms of the poet's voice are Echo and Orpheus: Echo, the maiden who loves Narcissus and whose love is not returned, is damned to repeat sounds and exist as pure voice, while her body by the mercy of the gods is changed to stone. Orpheus, the poet who wishes to seduce death and recover Eurydice by his song, loses Eurydice. Their voices, like Petrarch's, speak their losses and are veritable allegories of a presence which the self, caught in the riddle of language, can never recover.

CHAPTER IV

Ethics of Self

right v. wrong

Whenever a polemic or some other specific occasion—such as a letter to one of his correspondents—would call upon him to set forth his ideas about the scope and value of philosophy, Petrarch hardly ever hedged. The proper domain of philosophical investigation, he maintains without wavering, is ethics. The rubric does not simply designate the reasonable discourse on and construction of abstract rules of moral conduct. Petrarch believes, *not just* rather, that ethics plays a central role in the scheme of knowledge by virtue of its power to establish concrete norms whereby the fabric of life and of self can be kept from unraveling at the seams.

For ethics to be effective, Petrarch repeatedly warns, there must be an explicit recognition that the moral virtues cannot be merely a subject of limitless invention, theoretical debates, or abstract speculation on the general shape of reality. At its most general, ethics joins together theory and practice. But at its core ethics is a theory of relations—both individual and political. Because for Petrarch the foundation of our practices, values, and beliefs is to be found in the self, most of his works begin with and are steadily bound up with the assumption that the individual inner self is the primary source of all possible concerns. This means that what is logically fundamental in Petrarch's ethical thought is the relation of the self to oneself.

The double conviction that all questions of value are rooted in the self and that thought and will must be yoked together underlies and defines the force of Petrarch's polemic against Aristotle's *Nicomachean Ethics*, which is the primary concern of a text such as *On His Own Ignorance*. I shall examine this work from a different angle in the next chapter. I will recall here that *On His Own Ignorance* records an encounter with four young Aristotelians who have come to challenge the quality and depth of Petrarch's knowledge. Under the action of the impassioned controversy, Petrarch does not hesitate to confront head-on the flaws of Aristotle's moral vision as well as the cracks in the four disciples' understanding of knowledge. The nature of knowledge figures prominently in the polemic:

self v. oneself

On his own ignorance — critical of Aristotle [handwritten annotation]

Sometimes I smiled and asked how on earth Aristotle could have known something for which there is no reason and which cannot be proved by experience. They were amazed and felt angry at me in silence. They looked at me as though I were a blasphemer to require anything beyond his authority in order to believe it. Thus we clearly ceased to be philosophers and eager lovers of wisdom and became Aristotelians, or, more correctly, Pythagoreans. They revived the ridiculous habit of allowing no further question if "he" had said so. "He," as Cicero tells us, "was Pythagoras." I certainly believe that Aristotle was a great man who knew much, but he was human and could well be ignorant of some things, even of a great many things.

I should say more if those who are as much friends of truth as they are of sects permitted. By God, I am convinced and I have no doubt that "he went astray," as the saying goes, "the whole length of the way," not only in what is of little weight, where an error is unimportant and by no means dangerous, but in matters of the greatest consequence, and precisely in those regarding supreme salvation. Of happiness he has indeed said a good deal in the beginning and at the end of his *Ethics*. However, I will dare say—and my censors may shout as loud as they please—he knew so absolutely nothing of true happiness that any pious old woman, any faithful fisherman, shepherd or peasant is—I will not say more subtle but happier in recognizing it. I am therefore all the more astonished that some of our Latin authors have so much admired that Aristotelian treatise as to consider it almost a crime to speak of happiness after him and that they have borne witness of this even in writing. (p. 74)

The passage unequivocally highlights the absurdity in the dogmatic and scholastic claim of the "philosopher's" unquestioned, timeless, and immutable *auctoritas*. The zealous disciples' act of faith in the philosopher's *ipse dixit* turns into a negation of the essence of knowledge, for the assumption that all has already been authoritatively and definitively said elides time and short-circuits the very possibility of knowledge's growth in time. Genuine knowledge for Petrarch, on the contrary, is time-bound, and it consists in the recognition of the infinitely open possibilities of one's own contingent experience. To say it in a slightly different and clearer way: in order to be truly valuable, knowledge must be an open-ended adventure over the multiple paths of the experience of lived reality.

But the above quotation from *On His Own Ignorance* presents another issue. The juxtaposition of the *sermo humilis* of the pious woman, fisherman, shepherd, or peasant and, on the other hand, the finely spun language of the philosophers foreshadows Petrarch's sustained insight into the relationship between ethics and rhetorical style, to which I shall repeatedly return in the course of this chapter. It also prepares Petrarch's sense of the limits of Aristotle's understanding of ethics, which is overtly the burden of *On His Own Ignorance.*

Somewhat later in the treatise Petrarch will admit that he has read all of Aristotle's moral books and that he agrees with Aristotle's premise to his *Nicomachean Ethics* that "we learn this part of philosophy not with the purpose of gaining knowledge but of becoming better" (p. 103). He doubts, however, that Aristotle delivers on that promise. The Stagirite's penetrating insight into the moral aims of life is unquestioned, but "it is one thing to know and another to love; one thing to understand, another to will" (ibid.). The assumption of the antinomy between love and intellect, action and discourse, leads Petrarch to valorize the will over the intellect in questions of moral choices. His point is that words become reality and one learns to be better only through the persuasion of the will, which is the specific universe of rhetoric. Petrarch does not develop the traditional links between rhetoric and ethics. He proceeds, instead, to confront the limits of Aristotelian ethics. The ultimate goal of life does not lie in virtue, which is where the philosophers such as Aristotle locate it. The ultimate goal is immortality and faith, and virtue is only a way leading to that place (p. 105).

The consciousness of the discrepancy between philosophical virtue and Christian beatitude brings Petrarch to focus on and dramatize the presence of the discordant strains of his moral-intellectual tradition. As a general principle Petrarch consistently refuses to acquiesce in the belief in a harmonious, unifying synthesis of contrary intellectual forces. In *On His Own Ignorance* he perpetuates the oppositions by contrasting Aristotle's inability to urge the love of virtue and the hatred of vice (p. 103) with the power to move the will toward "the beauty of virtue," which is displayed in the texts of Cicero, Seneca, and Horace (p. 104). Petrarch chooses to follow them over and against the intellectualism of the pure philosophers.

These questions about knowledge show that knowledge is never simply a matter of abstract epistemological configurations. On the contrary, claims of knowledge are themselves inherently ethical claims. Petrarch deploys no argument to articulate this insight, but the link between knowledge and ethics is entailed by the logic of the text.

ultimate goal

Philosophy, he states, never delivers pure knowledge. At the same time, toward the end of the treatise, Socrates, the sovereign figure of philosophical irony, is singled out for his assertion that he knows nothing. Socrates' ignorance, which is explicitly Petrarch's own model of knowledge, is to be understood as a philosophical skepticism, as a skepticism toward philosophy's pretentious, dogmatic, and authoritarian assertions.

From Socrates' ironic perspective, ignorance is tantamount to the consciousness of the permanent incompleteness of one's knowledge, and this consciousness defines for Petrarch the only responsible philosophical way of being in the world and of coming to terms with the world's inexhaustible marvels and enigmas. In their radical bifurcation, Aristotelian knowledge and Socratic ignorance imply two contrary modes of establishing a moral relation between self and world. Whereas the Aristotelians are always in danger of being crushed down by the self-flattering view of their own knowledge and are aggressively intolerant of dissent, Socratic irony provides the horizon wherein the definitiveness of knowledge and the pride of philosophy vanish. Yet for all the ethical differences implied by these two versions of the philosophical life, both models subordinate man's will to the tyranny of absolute consciousness, and neither induces love for the beauty of virtue. It is the task of rhetoric to set the will in motion.

Because morality's foundation is in the will and in the passions (love of virtue and hatred of vice) and because he is interested in the way in which ethics alters the contours of a life, Petrarch's conception of ethics requires at the outset an existential description of the warring forces and passions that shape his own subjective existence. Practically all of Petrarch's texts, from the *Canzoniere* to the *Secretum* to the *Familiares* to even the *Trionfi,* are rooted in the analysis of the self and its opaque spiritual folds in the conviction that what gives meaning and value to experience in one's own self.

From this standpoint, his thought is marked by a double feature. On the one hand, the self is divided, subjected to constraints of time and place, and the will is paralyzed. But this side of Petrarch, as scholars have so often argued, has a counterpart to it. Petrarch also presents the self as the absolutely responsible subject of his own existential choices and as the source from which flows all objectivity. Accordingly, especially in the *Canzoniere,* he steadily seeks to grasp the obscure essence of the self in a sort of purified utter solitude, of a

Petrarch's view of the self — double feature

self stripped of the world of material objects and bracketed within a range of timeless concerns.

This view of the self as the source of all values, as the subject cast in a world of objects that revolve around him and of which he is the virtual center, is the traditional view of Petrarch as the epochal figure of modernity who exercises his mastery over that world of objects. As the preceding chapter has shown, Petrarch does not have such a naive idea of the substantiality of self, of the self as its own firm foundation, nor does he strictly adhere to such a radical stripping of self. The fragmentation and solitude of self, as I shall argue here, are the reverse side of a self as a knot of roots inextricably bound in a bundle of contradictory relations.

The doubleness in Petrarch's representation of the self should not be dismissed as mere inconsistency. Petrarch works steadily through ironic juxtapositions: he tenaciously stages contradictions, contemplates the contrary pulls and splinters of his soul, proposes decisive shifts, lapses repeatedly into customary impasses. These rhetorical strategies that he deploys in the construction of his texts must be considered as a whole, for it is together, in the unity formed by their fragmentary and contradictory forces, that they convey the relentless, unremitting rhythm of Petrarch's imagination.

Textual examples arguing for the necessity of such an all-encompassing procedure in the reading of Petrarch abound. Take the letter that relates the ascent of Mount Ventoux (*Fam.* 4.1), which scholars have recently probed in great detail. If one were to take the letter by itself, without any concern for the series of letters that follow it (4.2–8), one would miss Petrarch's compelling sense of how his spiritual world is composed of disparate regions; how seemingly separate experiences constitute the vast latitude of the many worlds he inhabits, and how he figures his heterogeneous association of interests as the unity and design of a series.

What is it that joins together this specific segment of the *Familiares?* These early letters of book 4 of the *Familiares* are letters Petrarch sent to different correspondents who stand for different versions of himself: to the Augustinian Dionigi da Borgo San Sepolcro, to the philosopher and king Robert of Sicily, to Cardinal Giovanni Colonna, and to Barbato da Sulmona. Whereas the first letter deals with the poet's ascent of Mount Ventoux, the others are a series of reflections on the poet's ascent of the Capitoline Hill, where he is to get the laurel crown. Four different correspondents, two opposed spiritual experiences, two contrary stories of moral failure and poetic "success" (which has, as it turns out, its own vanity), more or less correlated between them, constitute a series neither haphazardly nor by an overt principle of causality. What joins them together is Petrarch's will or, to say it differently, the rhetorical organization of the narrative.

We know that for Petrarch writing is a way of life, not simply in the sense that he mythomaniacally poeticizes his life, seeks to extract his life's secret essence and keep it from sinking into oblivion. Writing is also for him a daily labor and a social occupation whereby he plays the role of a self-appointed custodian of private and public memories. It will not do, thus, to ask where exactly lies Petrarch's "real" self; whether the idea of the poet's existential solitude is authentic or not; whether the poetic persona he constructs is at odds with the genuine religious impulses and needs present in the innermost realm of his self; or whether the ethical and social bonds he displays (for family, friends, his place of origin, his work, and so on) are superimposed postures or roles masking the solitary inner space of his subjectivity. All of these parts—the seemingly spurious and contrived as well as the seemingly authentic—are necessary elements of the jagged map of the self.

The uniqueness of Petrarch's insight into the self, to recapitulate the argument above and prepare its fuller development here, is that the self is not a unified whole; rather, it is made up of displaced, independent parts (the figurations of temporal and spatial disjunctions have shown this much), and no real distinction can be drawn between the complications of the interior dimensions of self and the various external worlds where the subject finds itself. The constitution of the self is splintered into so many parts that the reader wonders how it is possible for this subject, caught in an inner fragmentation and stuck in the impassable depths of his subjectivity, to relate to himself as well as to others. How is it possible for Petrarch to gain knowledge of the experiences of other selves? Is he not, rather, doomed to be mired in the predicament of the skeptics he adumbrates in the figure of Socrates? To answer these queries and to suggest the novelty of Petrarch's formulation of the question of the ethics of the self, I shall look at some letters from the *Familiares* and the *Trionfi*.

The *Rerum familiarum libri*, no doubt, constitute a unified text, much as one can speak of an epic, with its countless digressions, innumerable plots, counterpoints, and subplots, as a unified text. The

85

series of twenty-four books of letters addressed to the living and the dead transparently evokes the subdivisions of the Homeric epics that Petrarch had recently come across in the translation of Leonzio Pilato. Like the epic, which seeks to contain the totality of an experience only to end up giving a portion of it, Petrarch's letters, fictionally addressed to a heterogeneous variety of correspondents who do not necessarily communicate with one another, seek to retrieve Petrarch's own private life until the year 1366. The unifying element of the *Familiares,* thus, is Petrarch's composite idea of self, of the power the self exerts on oneself, and the letters are hybrid, discontinuous chapters of an ongoing autobiography which necessarily escapes any possible totalization.

But the formal model and the rhetorical implications of the epistolary genre, however, are discussed by Petrarch in the opening letter (*Fam.* 1.1), which forms an apt preamble to the structure of the whole work. Written to Ludwig Van Kempen, who is his Socrates, the letter begins with a general reflection on the hollow nature of time. Whatever the text gives, it gives through elliptical fragments, for this is the fundamental formal condition of letter writing. Writer and reader of the letter are necessarily worlds apart, elsewhere from each other in both time and space. The letter wills to bridge the gap and cover the ground between two absent figures, but the juncture it creates is feeble. For, notwithstanding the encounter between two selves that it brings about, the letter steadily exposes the absolute distance in time and in space between writing and reading. A letter presents itself as a provisional, brief crossing over the emptiness of time and its interminable flight. Eventually Petrarch will say that letter writing is a mechanism devised to relieve tediousness (*Fam.* 16.14). But to stress the idea that the letters are written against a background of time's gaps and dispersal and that they are posthumous fragments surviving by chance time's devastation, Petrarch refers to the year 1348, the year of the plague, as the dramatic beginning of the collection. If this is the aesthetics of Petrarch's letter writing, the empirical model came to him from the practice of the *ars dictaminis,*[1] in which humanists such as Lovato dei Lovati and Albertino Mussato had been engaged, as well as, the opening letter goes on to say, from the examples of Epicurus, Cicero, and Seneca. Like Cicero and Seneca, who, respectively, put domestic news and moral considerations in their letters, Petrarch combines personal anecdotes with philosophical considerations, such as his critique of the dialecticians in Britain, news about his health, occasional dreams, accounts of his eating and sleeping habits (*Fam.* 19.16), the plain pleasures of daily living, the routine of daily chores, his walks, his restless travels all over Europe, his birth in exile which allows him to claim at times that he is a citizen of the world, his steady self examinations, the moral advice he dispenses to kings and friends.

Seneca writes to his friend Lucilius. Cicero writes to Atticus, to Brutus, and to his brother and son. Petrarch writes for the benefit of the chosen few, the friends and soul mates who, whether they are alive or dead, never talk back but are conjured up as silent witnesses of the spectacle of a private self. Because friends, he says, are versions of oneself,[2] they take for him (and he for himself through them) the dimensions his imagination can muster, and he comes across as the real creator of an imaginary world. The explicit term of comparison between self and friends is Ulysses and his wanderings: friends are multiple places of the mind, stations of an epic journey of the self, with the self as the object of the restless quest.

The subject matter of the letters, which I have just traced in a most general way, changes according to each imaginary interlocutor and ranges over many topics. But some recurring themes are quickly recognizable: some are letters of consolation for the death of friends styled after Seneca's; many letters relate, on the other hand, an austere economy of abstinence, restraint of the appetite for power, moderation in banqueting, as he recalls sumptuous suppers with foreign viands and choice wines (*Fam.* 2.11) to which he contrasts the roughness of his home and fare. Self-sufficiency and control of self become the principles of moral consciousness, the rule of conduct that can direct one on the path of virtue.

Before being a question of politics and relation to others, as the rubrics of ethics have it, ethics—let me restate the point—is a question of self's relation to itself. Yet in the radical solitude of oneself one discovers the unavoidably social dimension of oneself. This insight shapes the set of simultaneously psychological and public injunctions to avoid penury and wealth; to shun envy and wrath; to pursue health, which is understood as the composition of contrary elements (*Fam.* 16.11).[3] Other letters of Petrarch evoke the practice of an idealized simple life in terms of the conventional contrast between *rus* and *urbs*: rusticity is equated with relief from anxiety and tranquillity of mind (*Fam.* 6.3), with the happy hours spent in his shady garden enjoying

87

the peacefulness of the place. City life, on the other hand, is linked with infected air (*Fam.* 17.3), unstable fortune, and civic turbulence. No doubt, the general thrust of these letters is to exemplify the self's removal from all extremes in pursuit of what Horace calls the *aurea mediocritas* (see letter to Guido Sette, *Fam.* 19.16).

The series of letters sent to Guido Sette, the archdeacon of Genoa (*Fam.* 17.3–5), brings to a clear focus Petrarch's concerns and can be construed as the compendium of his moral vision. Because Guido Sette, who is an idealized version of Petrarch himself, is slow in coming to visit the poet in his solitude of Vaucluse, Petrarch wonders whether he has forgotten the importance of friendship and is busy "accumulating wealth and possessions" (*Fam.* 17.4). The remark introduces a generalized reflection on the relationship between desires and needs and bemoans the fate of rich men who "admire grandiose and useless things" and yearn in their greedy minds "for mountains of gold and rivers of silver." The pursuit of wealth is a degraded pursuit of utopia, of the fabulous Land of Cocaygne, which is stridently countered by the assertion, with which the letter begins, that "nowhere on earth is life peaceful."

> In one place there is war, in another a peace sadder than war; in one place there is infected air, in another an even more fatal infected morality; in one place there is desolate famine, in another a flowing abundance more dangerous than famine; in one place there is wretched slavery, in another an insolent freedom arose than slavery; in one place there is thirst and a desert region, in another a widespread raging of rivers; finally in one place there is heat, in another cold; in one place attacks by beasts, in another the deceits of men; in one place a vast and horrible solitude, in another a rough and troublesome crowd. Thus the spot that we seek is nowhere. What are we to do? Depart more swiftly from this life? That is not allowed for any reason; it is not permissible. Let Anneus Seneca remain silent, for Cicero's opinion is better: "Both you," he says, "and all pious men must keep your soul the body's custody, nor must you leave human life against the will of Him who gave it to you." Noble words and equally noble the reason when he adds, "lest you seem to flee the duty imposed on humanity by God." (*Fam.* 17.4)

There is no general good to be found anywhere on earth. All is swallowed in irreconcilable extremities. This bleak reflection on the unevenness of the human condition (which is also a sign of Petrarch's anti-utopianism) develops in two directions. On the one hand, Petrarch addresses the contingent defeat suffered by the city of Genoa. On the other hand, the letter recommends, in the wake of the psalmist, patience in action; it advises, in the wake of Cicero, the cultivation of justice, for it is on the wings "of good work" that "we can climb to the our native land in Heaven." These moral prescriptions have their foundation in the belief in the radical instability of the world: "Nothing remains the same for long," Petrarch writes, "nothing ends as it began; everything passes, time flows on, years fly by, the days hasten on, the hours fly on; the sun pursues its vaulted path, the moon daily changes and is always other than it was, never beholding her brother with the same eye." These steady fluctuations and shifts of the season and of the natural world envelop the history of man, who changes according to places and times as well as fortune. Together they intimate that all that is human is held within the unshakable grip of death. There is no triumph for man's achievements. The defeat suffered by Genoa actually is the synecdochical defeat suffered by the human lot. In this perspective, self-assertion is false and Christian humility holds sway. The letter also confronts the predicament within which all moral norms are locked. To what extent must one love the "world," which is so inhospitable, and yet only within it can the self define itself. Petrarch's answer is that we should live "with our minds in heaven and our bodies on earth in moderation, in patience, in humility, and that we compensate for the wretchedness of place with peace of mind" (*Fam.* 17.4).

What emerges from the quickest synopsis of *Familiares* 17.4 and all of the *Familiares* is the adoption of an ethical scheme that is akin to the ethos of the Roman Stoics, though it is not entirely reducible to it. *Familiares* 17.4 mounts a critique of the Stoic ideal of suicide for its claim of ownership over a life one has received from the outside. But in general the Stoic tradition for Petrarch is chiefly embodied by Seneca, whose moral authority is frequently cited (see *Fam.* 6.1), and by Cicero's *De officiis,* which was the most widely read Latin book of ethics in medieval schools.[4] Petrarch is certainly eclectic in the way in which he absorbs specific and general moral principles from Aristotle and the peripatetics, the Epicureans (whom he also attacks; see *Fam.* 2.2), Cicero, and the Christian moralists. These various ethical traditions share a number of general principles, such as the definition of virtue as the mean, the conviction that the virtues come into being with the cultivation of good natural dispositions, or, more specifically, even the value of soberness as a remedy to the perturbations brought by excesses of the appetites.

Two successive letters to Guido Sette (*Fam.* 17.4, 5) focus on the psychological effect of Genoa's defeat (which is the pretext for the earlier letter) and on the praise of rural life. On the other hand, the series of letters Petrarch sends to Mainardo Accursio (*Fam.* 8.3–5) exemplify his deployment of the multiple strands of the moral tradition. *Familiares* 8.3, for instance, reflects more openly on the importance of place in the poet's life. It is at the mouth of the Sorgue River, he says, that he starts his *Africa* and completes his *Bucolicum carmen*. But Vaucluse is also a desirable residence, especially in the summertime: the peacefulness of the mountains, its clear streams, and the woods would help free him "from the weariness of the passions of the city." The passage on the serene landscape of Provence is interlaced with citations from Seneca, Horace, and Aristotle: "As Aristotle says, 'Nature by itself is insufficient for indulging in speculation; this requires a healthy body, food and other necessities'" (ibid.). *Familiares* 8.4, on the other hand, focuses on Petrarch's own eating habits. He takes delight in country food, and he agrees, he says, with Epicurus, "only in his position regarding light nourishment, for he placed the apex of his much-praised pleasure in his garden and in his vegetables." But he does not reject sumptuous meals, provided that he has them rarely and at adequate intervals from one another. These reflections on diet introduce the ideal of moderation for a better life by quoting Vergil, Seneca, and Cicero.

The idea shaping the *Familiares,* that ethics is fundamentally a question of self-government or self-control and that the self becomes the exemplary model for the larger world, is refracted and represented in a variety of aspects. The scope the letters give to ethics is large: it appears as a politics of self, as dietetics, as an inner economics, as etiquette or stylistics, and what I would call thanatetics (as the conduct of self before death, as it emerges from the letters of "Senecan" consolation). All these various aspects belong to and can be brought within the parameters of Stoic ethics.

The Stoic ideal of a harmonious, rational natural order containing the disruptions of the passions presides over the whole series of letters. Dietetics, the idea that the simplest foods are generally the strongest, that the foods obtained from the earth or from animals without killing them shelter the individual from the turbid exhalations that overshadow the soul,[5] figures large, as I have suggested above, in Petrarch's letters. These precepts were no doubt available to him from medical literature, but they are a keystone of the Stoic standard of moral conduct that is simultaneously embodied by principles of moderation and propriety: "To eat too much is wrong; to eat too fast is wrong; so it is to take too much pleasure in food, to prefer the sweet to the wholesome. . . . Another fault is to let meals interfere with business. In all these points we should look chiefly to health."

The moral prescriptions of the Stoics extend to what one would call the economics of the self. These principles include topics such as praise of poverty and contempt for wealth, which, in truth, most philosophical schools share. They also focus, just as Petrarch does, on the idea of corruption of self brought about by the luxuries of city life, the pursuit of which unnaturally absorbs the totality of one's daily occupations. The happy man, says Seneca in *Epistola* 94, gives up the complicated ceremonies of city life and chooses to live calmly in the healthy open air of the country, for in the country the household will be ruled by the virtues of temperance and justice. There is one particular concern among the Stoics that must have had some impact on Petrarch himself: the analysis of restlessness. Petrarch diagnoses it as the disease of his soul, and the diagnosis echoes both Horace's *Epodes* (1.11.25–27) and Seneca's view of restlessness as a grief of the mind.

Even the aesthetic questions of fashion and etiquette and generally style are part of the ethical discipline, whereby foppish clothes, indulgence in perfumes, elaborate hairdressing are all contemptible vices that violate the purity and balance of nature. These precepts find a counter in a series of consolatory suggestions as to how the mind can withstand the trials of fortune and the cruel afflictions that are brought on man by the death of friends, by exile, and by poverty. Yet the suggestions to follow nature's laws in ruling over oneself, which to a certain degree are the underpinnings of Petrarch's moral vision and possible life-style in the *Familiares,* do not really explain how they affect Petrarch's own self as a writer.

I do not wish to suggest that Petrarch elaborates some version of a Stoic poetics (the properties of which are sound, harmony, decorum, and so on), such as the poetics one can extrapolate from Lucan's epic and Seneca's tragedies.[6] Although he may well be doing this, my point is that questions of style and composition—paramount to the writer's craft—are crucial to the present understanding of the self, and they embody what I would call an ethics of writing. That Petrarch should turn so obsessively to these seemingly technical discussions about writing is to be expected from such a self-conscious writer as he is. His sense of technical and aesthetic rigor reveals the extent to which for him the proper care for language, like the proper care of the mind and of the body, can never be neglected.[7] This self-consciousness about the mechanics of writing—which for Petrarch is always more than a question of techniques—emerges from the opening letter of the *Familiares*.

We have already seen that this letter reflects on the traditions of letter writing and letter collections. It also expatiates both on the plain, unfamiliar style of the epistolary genre he is about to undertake and on his adoption of multiple stylistic stances because of the variety of his correspondents:

> The strong man must be addressed in one way, the spiritless one in another, the old man who has discharged his life's duties in another, and in still another manner the person puffed up with good fortune, the victim of adversity in another, and finally in yet another manner must be addressed the man of letters renowned for his talents, and the ignoramus who would not understand anything you said if you spoke in even a slightly polished fashion. Infinite are the differences between men nor are their minds any more alike than the shapes of their foreheads. And as one particular sort of food not only does not appeal to different stomachs but does not even appeal to a single one, so it is impossible to nourish a single mind at all times with the same style. . . . These difficulties compelled me to be very inconsistent, but I have in part escaped the censure of hostile critics by availing myself of the benefits of fire. (*Fam.* 1.1)

The reader should presumably be struck by the sincerity and confessional quality of all these *familiar* letters to be sent to correspondents who are friends and are like the reader, to whom the writer opens up to reveal himself and with whom he wills to share both his most withheld secrets and the rituals of his daily life.

To be sure, Petrarch does not claim to be sincere, but the effect of the confessional style—the aim of which is sincerity—is achieved in the passage above by the acknowledgment that his own style will have to adapt to the different subject matters as well as to the shifting state of mind and to the different stations of his interlocutors. Petrarch does not claim sincerity because he knows that sincerity is intrinsically a false idea. For by being "sincere" one makes oneself a transparent, fixed object for others, and, thereby, one denies the temporal fluidity of one's own existence. Rather, the point of the passage is that the truth about himself is inseparable from the styles and fictions Petrarch will deploy to create a persona for his readers.

The memorable term from the opening sonnet of the *Canzoniere*, the "vario stile" (l. 5) (varied style), which the poet employs for his lyrical fragments, signals the fundamental role style plays in Petrarch's poetry. The repetition of sounds, the glitter of the adjectives, the precious blending of noun and epithet, the rhythm, the question marks, and so on, which are some of the traits of the Petrarchan style, constitute the irreducible, subtle cadence of his authorial voice. It can be said that his style is the mark of his unmistakable and yet myste-rious individuality, the quality of Petrarchan music, which was to be inimitable and yet was destined to be infinitely imitated for centuries. In short, his style is the personal, limpid tonality imparted on the opaque murmurs and commonplaces of common speech. And yet few writers are as aware as Petrarch that one's style is borrowed, that it is complicated with endless variations that reach us from beyond our individual horizons; that one's voice resonates with either impercepti-ble or unidentifiable messages buried deep within the historical folds of language.

In *Familiares* I.8, written to Tommaso da Messina, Petrarch con-fronts the twin question of literary originality and imitation. The letter is itself so artfully constructed through a dazzling repertory of citations as to dramatize the stylistic strategies by which the illusion of originality is achieved. Seneca's advice on invention is first acknowl-edged: "His loftiest advice about invention is to imitate the bees which through an astonishing process produce wax and honey from the flowers they leave behind." Macrobius in his *Saturnalia,* Petrarch goes on to report, repeats the sense and the very words of Seneca, yet by his practice he seemed to disapprove the Senecan advice. The process of literary composition is then extensively described, and at this point I quote Petrarch's lucid analysis:

> How can I say that something another wrote is not mine, when Epicurus' opinion, as recorded by Seneca himself, is that anything said well by anyone is our own? Macrobius must therefore not be blamed because he not only reported but actually transcribed a large part of one letter in the proem of his work. The same thing has sometimes happened to me and to other greater writers as well. This much however I affirm, that it is a

> sign of greater elegance and skill for us, in imitation of the bees, to produce in our own words thoughts borrowed from others. To repeat, let us write neither in the style of one or another writer, but in a style uniquely ours although gathered from a variety of sources. The writer is happier who does not, like the bees, collect a number of scattered things, but instead, after the example of certain not much larger worms from whose bodies silk is produced, prefers to produce his own thoughts and speech—provided that the sense is serious and true and that his style is ornate. But in truth, this talent is given to none or to very few, so that we should patiently bear the lot of our personal talents, and not envy those above us, disdain those below us, or annoy our equals. (*Fam.* 1.8)

The mechanism of imitation comes forth as a unique transmutation of what is radically secondhand.[8] The incessant repetition and variation of what has already been said is certainly a way of gathering the scraps of the past and passing them on in new and unpredictable combinations. The process best describes the movement of tradition that Petrarch steadily charts. But this repetition is to be understood both as the desire to begin anew and as the discovery that one is inexorably part of a shared language preexisting oneself. The unavoidable duplication of other voices and textual fragments must appear to be a laborious production or reproduction so that the legitimacy of one's own voice may be reconstituted.[9]

The idea that the self is the echo of many intercommunicating voices is explicitly dramatized even in the *Canzoniere*. Poem 70, which I quote here in its entirety, focuses exactly on the complex constitution of the poet's voice:

> Lasso me, ch'io non so in qual parte pieghi
> la speme, ch'è tradita omai più volte.
> Che se non è chi con pietà m'ascolte,
> perch'è sparger al ciel sì spessi preghi?
> Ma s'egli aven ch'ancor non mi si nieghi
> finir anzi 'l mio fine
> queste voci meschine,
> non gravi al mio signor perch'io il ripreghi
> di dir libero un dì tra l'erba e i fiori:
> "Drez et rayson es qu'ieu ciant em demori."
>
> Ragion è ben ch'alcuna volta io canti
> però ch'ò sospirato sì gran tempo

che mai non incomincio assai per tempo
per adequar col riso i dolor tanti.
Et s'io potesse far ch'agli occhi santi
porgesse alcun diletto
qualche dolce mio detto,
o me beato sopra gli altri amanti!
Ma più quand'io dirò senza mentire:
"Donna mi priegha, per ch'io voglio dire."

Vaghi pensier che così passo passo
scorto m'avete a ragionar tant'alto:
vedete che Madonna à 'l cor di smalto,
sì forte che per me dentro nol passo.
Ella non degna di mirar sì basso
che di nostre parole
curi, che 'l ciel non vole,
al qual pur contrastando i' son già lasso;
onde come nel cor m'induro e 'naspro,
"Così nel mio parlar voglio esser aspro."

Che parlo? o dove sono? e chi m'inganna
altri ch'io stesso e 'l desir soverchio?
Già s'i' trascorro il ciel di cerchio in cerchio
nessun pianeta a pianger mi condanna;
se mortal velo il mio veder appanna
che colpa è de le stelle
o de le cose belle?
Meco si sta chi dì et notte m'affanna,
poi che del suo piacer mi fè gir grave
"La dolce vista e 'l bel guardo soave."

Tutte le cose di che 'l mondo è adorno
uscir buon de man del mastro eterno,
ma me che così adentro non discerno
abbaglia il bel che mi si mostra intorno;
et s' al vero splendor giamai ritorno
l'occhio non pò star fermo,
così l'à fatto infermo
pur la sua propria colpa, et non quel giorno
ch'i' volsi in ver l'angelica beltade
"Nel dolce tempo de la prima etade."

Alas, I do not know where to turn the hope that has been by now betrayed many times. For if there is no one who will listen to me with pity, why scatter prayers to the heavens so thickly? But, if it happens that I am not denied the ending of these pitiful sounds before my death, let it not displease my lord that I beg him again to let me say freely one day among the grass and flowers: "It is right and just that I sing and be joyful."

It is just that at some time I sing, since I have sighed for so long a time that I shall never begin soon enough to make my smiling equal so many sorrows. And if I could make some sweet saying of mine, give some delight to those holy eyes, oh me blessed above other lovers. But most when I can say without lying: "A lady begs me; therefore I wish to speak."

Yearning thoughts, which thus step by step have led me to such high speech: you see that my lady has a heart of such a hard stone that I cannot by myself pass within it. She does not deign to look so low as to care about our words; for the heavens do not wish it, and resisting them I am already weary; therefore as in my heart I become hard and bitter: "So in my speech I wish to be harsh."

What am I saying? or where am I? and who deceives me but myself and my excessive desire? Nay, if I run through the sky from sphere to sphere, no planet condemns me to weeping. If a mortal veil dulls my sight, what fault is it of the stars or of beautiful things? With me dwells one who night and day troubles me, since she made me go heavy with the pleasure of: "The sweet sight of her and her lovely soft glance."

All things with which the world is beauteous came forth good from the hand of the eternal Workman: but I, who do not discern so far within, am dazzled by the beauty that I see about me, and if I ever return to the true splendor, my eye cannot stay still, it is so weakened by its very own fault, and not by that day when I turned toward that angelic beauty: "In the sweet time of my first age."

The poem crystallizes Petrarch's classical experience: the drama of a disoriented self, of a self who does not know what he says or where exactly he is as the passion for Laura lays hold of the mind. In direct contrast to the self-uncertainty the lover feels, the poem features the self's anguished fixity on the thought of a distant Laura, and her silent distance makes the poem self-answerable, for it lucidly expects no response from her and is caught within itself. The first stanza directly confronts the text's own self-enclosure with no one listening to the poet's appeals. The poem, in short, constitutes its own imaginative world, and there is an absolute discontinuity between the poet's language and Laura. Within this imaginative realm, which is also the realm of the constancy of his passion, the end coincides with the beginning and the beginning coincides with the end (the poem begins with the thought of the end and ends with the nostalgic evocation of the sweet time of youth when the passion began). This radical reversibility of time that the poem figures means that the past never ceases to be present in the mind and it is in turn lengthened into the future.

Although the lover cannot determine the flow of time—no more than he can determine the events of the past—he does not desire to escape from time. There is not even the abdication of the will in the drama the poem charts. Unlike determinists who blame the stars for the human lot and in the process annihilate the possibility of moral choice, the lover has chosen his destiny as he neither wants nor can efface the thought of Laura. Actually the poem ends both with the statement that the poet cannot fathom the depths of God's abyss and with the complementary vindication of the dazzling beauty of the world, the beauty of Laura possessing him.

In thematic terms, the song is chiefly a poetic gesture evoking and renewing love's and poetry's beginnings. But the poem also contains a counterstatement to its overt theme. The last line of each stanza, as is known, is a quotation, a direct transposition, respectively, from Provençal poetry, from Cavalcanti, from Dante's *rime petrose*, from Cino da Pistoia, and, finally, from Petrarch himself. The final self-citation—it can be argued—is the endpoint of the poem's own literary history, and, at the same time, it is the source from which the movement of the lyrical tradition that the poem recalls is made intelligible.

These literary quotations, which Petrarch appropriates and around which he organizes each stanza, also reveal that his own experience is refracted through many other voices. The procedure primarily undercuts the myth of the poet's solitude: the poet may indeed be alone, but his loneliness is, paradoxically, crowded with the memories and echoes of multiple other poetic voices. By this strategy, Petrarch brings to light what in the *Familiares* he had probed as a question of style: that one's own poetry speaks from the depths of a shared language, that the self is literally the persona through whom the fragments of the past resound. Unsurprisingly, the artifice of interwoven citations through which the poet speaks and which speak through him is deployed in a poem that explicitly describes the poet's predicament about what he says (stanza 4). Style, which is one's own and is simultaneously borrowed, is the radical emblem of Petrarch's understanding of self: both are simultaneously made of alien voices and both turn into sources of values.

It can be said that this Petrarchan figuration of self is the locus of contradictory pulls crossing one another: in it there is Cavalcanti and there is Dante; there is Cino da Pistoia and there is Seneca; Provençal poetry and St. Augustine; St. Paul and Ovid; there is an orator, a historian, a poet, and a moralist. In this solitary space of the mind, which resonates with the fragmented heterogeneity of history, each voice is alien to and warring with the other. But no discordant single voice is repressed. On the contrary, Petrarch's "invention" of individuality has to be understood primarily as the acknowledgment of the value of the individual fragments composing the whole. What keeps these disparate pieces together is the rigor of style as both rhetoric and ethics; what establishes the ever-shifting relations among entities that are forever on the verge of flying asunder are the imagination, the moods, and the provisional viewpoint from which one sees and understands the world.

Petrarch steadily seeks to establish an ordered, hierarchical relation among the self's multiple regions of experience. How is the unifying viewpoint on a series of disparate and overlapping realms of experience established? His writings on the contemplative tradition, as we shall see in the final chapter of this study, attempt to give a religious foundation to secular culture. The briefest analysis of the *Trionfi*, a text which maps exactly both the various stages of an imaginative journey of self-discovery and the question of perspective, will show Petrarch's response to this question.[10]

The poem, which Petrarch wrote and revised over a period of more than thirty years, seems to be unfinished and has the appearance of what Ezio Raimondi rightly calls a "work in progress."[11] This radically unfinished, fragmentary quality has incited scholars to speculate as to the new design Petrarch sought for his thought: his steady revisions, in fact, suggest that he meant to have the *Trionfi* mark a qualitative leap into a new realm of thought, a quest for modes which are both categories of the mind and generalized, objective structures existing outside the will of the self. The importance this poem had for Petrarch is apparent from its general construction: it is the recapitulation or conflation of the major themes of his concerns. Under the guise of a traditional medieval dream-vision (such as the dream shaping the unfolding of the *Roman de la rose* or the procession at the top of Dante's *Purgatorio*), Petrarch presents a series of visions or triumphs: the triumph of love opens the series, and it is superseded by the triumph of chastity, which, in turn, is followed by the triumph of death. The triumph of death is followed by the triumphs of fame, time, and eternity. The sequence, which at least on the surface is a linear progression, constitutes a vast allegorical spectacle, yet Petrarch is not merely imitating the abstract allegorizations of, say, Prudentius's *Psychomachia,* wherein vices and virtues are intertwined in a cosmic battle. Rather, in the wake of Dante's own visionary allegory, Petrarch reflects on the crossing between the realm of vision and the realm of language. And in a way which is radically Petrarch's own, the poem is shaped by the crucial decision to make these triumphs part of his mind, of a dreaming self, as if the self alone could be the ground of its own partial truths. By pulling together the themes of his lifelong quest, it is as if Petrarch seeks finally to overcome the ravages of isolated, relative experiences and give them intelligibility and a unified shape. In a primary way, the *Trionfi* intends to restore the coherent order of the world as a hierarchical arrangement of values from love to the divinity in a linear and progressive movement.

The radical novelty of this poetic structure lies in the fact, then, that these themes or regions of experience—love, chastity, death, fame, time, and eternity—are subjective *existentialia,* and yet they transcend the boundaries of the self. For these themes, which are the grammatical subject of each poetic unit, are at once categories or laws of our common existence through which self and other recognize each other. The meaning of each of these components depends on oneself, for, indeed, it is Petrarch's own self that imaginatively unitizes these paradigms of the human experience. Yet together—love and time (which are both subjective experiences and transcendent forces), chastity (which is to be understood as the ethics of self-containment), fame (which is the self in history), death, and eternity—they are timeless principles, utterly private and yet shared experiences which constitute the self, determine the sense of oneself, and preside over the whole of life.

How are the various sections of the poem joined together? And how does the poet attain a global understanding of self and world? The two questions are two sides of the same coin. On the face of it, the mechanism linking the serial chain of visions is simple. Each experience is a fragment, a partial shred of experience contrasted to the other—love to chastity; chastity to death; death to fame; fame to time; time to eternity. None of them, in isolation, grasps the whole movement of experience and exhausts it. But as each element diverges from the other, each is also a vessel communicating with and leading to the other, just as love leads to and implicates chastity or as time implicates eternity. In this structure, more poignantly, no experience can really be understood outside the relation it has with the other divergent or complementary experiences. Eternity, for instance, is the perspective that alters the significance of the elements of the series, from time to fame and to death. Love, born of time, changes the meaning of time and of death; fame redefines time and death; death, in turn, alters the meaning and value of love, just as chastity gives love's deeper truth. By interlocking these fragments, like episodes of the life of the self, Petrarch, in short, has constructed a network of multiple resonances, a constellation of figures whereby the truth of each entity is to be found both within itself and within the successive members of the series.

What is it that unifies the series? What unifies the parts of oneself from falling asunder? What is the relation between self and other? Is it eros or chance, as happens in an epicurean universe? For Petrarch, it is improper to speak of unity, for there is only a polemical relation which is constituted by two radically disjunct and yet linked strategies. The first is the dream, the second is the shifting viewpoint of the dreamer. Within the economy of the dream all relations appear arbitrary, without the sanction of reason and will. The associations within a dream are associations of pure contingency, and they exist outside the law of willed causality. The epistemology of the dream is guaranteed only on the condition that the dream turns into a rhetorical construct, which Petrarch calls allegory. What determines the meaning of the allegory is the viewpoint of the dreamer.

Romantic literary theorists dismiss allegory as a rational, abstract conjunction, as an arbitrary superimposition of alien sense on the literal burden of a text. For Petrarch, allegory is a visionary form and it designates the intersection between the arbitrariness of the dream and the moral will to translate the oneiric imaginings into the intelligible shape of poetic language. Vision, as a matter of fact, is the explicit metaphor sustaining the poem (it is a dream-vision), and the anaphora of "vidi" (I saw), in its multiple variations, scans the procession of the chariots.

In a way, the poem tells the story of the poet who, led by an unnamed guide, is the disengaged spectator of the unfolding drama of the world's concerns. His mind is not entirely delivered from care and is still agitated by passions, the force of which, however, keeps decreasing as the mind grows in wisdom. In this educational journey of the self, the dreamer's viewpoint keeps changing, as if no single field of experience (love, time, death, fame, and so on) could contain and freeze the inexhaustible movement of his mind. Like desire, which keeps endlessly shifting from one object to the other, the mind encompasses ever-widening circles of thought. Petrarch is the poet of the mind's spirals and of its dialectical growth until it plunges into the contemplation of eternity, which is figured as the abyss where the ruins of time, love, death, and fame vanish. From his shifty and purified standpoint, the spectacle of the world is consistently reduced to a mere catalogue of events and objects for the self.[12]

Bound to the triumphal chariot of Love, for instance, are figures from the Bible, from fables and romances, from Pyramus to David, from Myrrha to Iseult. The catalogue, which is an epic device, is a rhetorical strategy that seeks to represent the elusive totality of experience: it is a synecdoche for that totality and unveils the fragmentary constitution of the totality. In the economy of the *Trionfi* there is a discrepancy between the plenitude of the dreamer's vision and the partial representation given by the poet's language. Totality is available as dream, just as is a dream the view of the self as a subject whose gaze attains a global understanding of the world and its values. In this dream, which unavoidably reminds one of Aeneas's dream in book 6 of the *Aeneid,* all the figures of history have become the object of the dreamer's gaze, and the whole of history is reduced to a spectacle destined to fade quickly, as dreams do, to a mere superficiality of names, which, like mobile figures, are quickly left behind. To make the world the object of one's vision is a way by which the self constitutes itself into a subject.[13] In this dream the significance of self and history are judged from the transcendent perspective of eternity. Petrarch's ethics is the dream of an absolute viewpoint wherein the self appears as a fragment of a larger world, and the world itself comes into being through the poet's dream.

CHAPTER V

The World of History

Because of his deep awareness that there is no temporal stability in the present, Petrarch cannot escape being involved in a sustained meditation on the past and the possible shape of the future. The spectacle of history's ruins confirms his sense that one's life is inexorably rooted in time and that time is the horizon within which any understanding of self is available. But time for Petrarch is also more than the framework of a solitary self-analysis. Time is rife with historical and cultural memories, and the inquiry about the significance and value of one's life is necessarily contextualized within their perimeter. The myth of Rome is both the foundation and crystallization of those memories and roots. As the opening chapter has shown, Petrarch seeks to retrieve the past's calcified and forgotten memories, and he does so with the goal of exposing the possibilities implicit in that tradition, of turning memory into the source both for the interpretation of the present and for the making of the future.

This chapter focuses on the central role history plays in the articulation of Petrarch's thought. In their efforts to determine his ideas of history, scholars have certainly not overlooked the specifically historical texts Petrarch writes, such as the two prefaces to *De viris illustribus,* the *Rerum memorandarum libri,* and the letters he exchanges with Cola di Rienzo. They have also rightly emphasized how in these various writings Petrarch forcefully probes classical historiographic questions, such as the methods of selection of historical evidence, the relationship between history and story, the moral purposes of history writing, the role of individual characters in the history of Rome, and, finally, the possibility of reviving in the present Rome's ancient glories.

These issues will refigure prominently in the course of the present discussion. For, no doubt, Petrarch understands historiography as an art that both uncovers, underneath the encrusted layers of records and legends, what has happened and reveals the underlying meaning of the totality of history. But I will also emphasize in my remarks a number of other matters, such as, for instance, Petrarch's reflections on the epistemology of history, or, to put it more directly, on the relation between history and philosophy; his sense of the role of the historian in relation to figurations of power (that of popes, princes, and tyrants); finally, his conviction that, since we are caught up in history, the historian's goal is the cultivation, in the broadly pedagogical sense of the word, of individuals who can shape the process of history.

There is a text in which Petrarch lucidly articulates the necessity of history as the unique context for and perspective on self-understanding, *On His Own Ignorance*. Mindful, as he certainly is, of the traditional medieval classification of *historia* as part of grammar,[1] he addresses this polemical tract, written late in his life, to a grammarian friend of his, whose name echoes that of the archgrammarian, Donato. I have discussed earlier in this book some features of this text; I shall repeat here some details from a different critical angle. As is known, the tract relates an autobiographical episode, the visit that four young friends, who had given their philosophical allegiance to Aristotelianism, pay the aged poet. Their call, however, is not a gesture of recognition of the moral and spiritual authority of the poet-sage. On the contrary, they accuse him of lacking any rigorous knowledge of philosophy, and they despise, so Petrarch writes, his eloquence as empty and worn out when viewed from the standpoint of their modern philosophical fashion. In short, they acknowledge that he has good character and is faithful in his friendships, yet their verdict is that he is altogether an illiterate.

Every single detail in Petrarch's introductory remarks will resonate in the unfolding of his counterarguments. Thus, the acknowledgment of the poet's good character and loyalty to friends prepares his extended reflections on the essence of virtue and its relationship to knowledge. The Socratic equation of virtue and knowledge is dismissed by Petrarch in the persuasion that virtue belongs to the will, whereas the object of the intellect is truth. Even the pretense of friendship of the four visitors is made to appear as an integral part of the larger pretense of philosophy.

Ideally, the claim of friendship, which for Aristotle is one of the virtues he examines in his *Ethics* and which resides in the very definition of philosophy (in every philosopher there is a friend, an interlocking of love and knowledge), places the question of knowledge away from any abstract theoretical configuration to a concrete context of human and political interactions. In fact, however, philosophy is not the sovereign discourse of intelligible significations and universal reason, and the error of philosophy, if anything, is to assume the benevolence of thought. By the end of the tract Petrarch explicitly forces on us the conviction that bitter disputes and polemics, not benevolence, are the very stuff of philosophical discourse. The tract surveys the history of philosophy with the overt suggestion that philosophical propositions are not immutable truths; their truth, rather, is historical and time-bound. Through the ideal of philosophical truth as the child of time, its history is cast, quite consistently, as an inventory of violence that ranges from Epicurus's hatred of Plato, Pythagoras, Aristotle, and Democritus, to the rivalry between two Spaniards, Quintilian and Seneca. The logically inescapable conclusion is that there are dark passions, such as envy and grudges, forfeiting philosophy's ideal claims, and they expose those claims as hollow.

On the face of it, the main thrust of *On His Own Ignorance* is to bring to a focus Petrarch's long confrontation with newly emerging philosophical fashions and to record his sense of the logical and moral inconsistencies in these new trends. Thus, these self-styled neo-Aristotelians come to challenge Petrarch's authority, but they do so from the point of view—and the irony of the philosophers' intellectual self-deception is flagrant—of Aristotle's *auctoritas* and from what they conceive to be the rigor of rational and scientific thought. In effect, inconsistency is for Petrarch the distinctive mark of the "new" philosophy, and he captures other damning instances of it in the young men's conduct in order to subtly intimate that what these dialecticians lack is exactly what they claim to uphold: a logical sense.

In a way, Petrarch is at pains to display in this text a forceful argumentative rigor as he refutes the objections leveled at him by the logicians. The young men's critique of Petrarch's authority, as the tract stresses, is an attack *ad hominem* and a violation of the old man's household. The visitors come to him, the letter says, "with astonishing winning manners" (p. 52); they call him "a good man, even the best of men," and they assert that he has "a good character" (p. 54). At the same time, they claim, as hinted above, that Petrarch has really no learning and they reject his eloquence as unworthy of a man of letters. Put simply, they judge him to be an *idiota,* in the etymological sense of the term, "altogether illiterate, . . . a plain uneducated fellow" (ibid.), and they envy, Petrarch writes, "my name and what fame I have already won within my lifetime" (p. 55). In these vituperations, however, the philosophers blindly lapse into an exercise of the very epideictic rhetoric they decry.

These textual details are meant to dramatize Petrarch's conviction that at bottom the new philosophical trend seeks to wrest knowledge from the false light of rhetoric and return it to the world of pure intellectual discourse where truth's sovereignty can be restored. Rhetoric for them is "an effective means of persuasion" (p. 61), phrases without wisdom, or, as they reportedly claim, "elegant and well chosen style" (p. 62), but without a strictly rational meaning. For Petrarch, however, as we shall see later and repeatedly throughout this study, style is a *force* by which the crystallized deeper sediments of language are animated, while rhetoric is both the theory of power, the art of persuasion of the will, and the discipline of history and of the commonplaces of memory.

Above and beyond these disagreements, it is clear from Petrarch's texts that the attack by the young philosophers aims at expelling what they conceive of as rhetoric's artifices from their version of the order of knowledge. By a subtle and lucid ruse, however, Petrarch suggests also that the real and radical target of their posture is nothing less than the separation of knowledge from history. This charge is not explicit. Yet the neo-Aristotelians' opposition to what they view as the vanity of eloquence logically leads to a view of philosophy as an intellectual discourse discontinuous from experience, and for Petrarch here lies their intellectual blind spot.

By these opening details of the narrative, which set up the stage for the ensuing polemic, Petrarch wants us to draw an inevitable inference. The discrepancy between, on the one hand, the philosophers' acknowledgment of the old poet's character, loyal friendships, and personal virtues and, on the other, their disparaging remarks about his learning is tantamount to their positing a sharp break between the realm of moral conduct and knowledge, between life and philosophy. The duplicitousness of the young men's behavior (they come to honor the poet and wish him good health and happiness, but they end up attacking him) is more than a hint of their personal immorality. In it Petrarch perceives their will to separate character from learning, ethics from knowledge. From this viewpoint, Petrarch goes on to argue that the Aristotelians' scheme of knowledge, as is peddled by the four neophytes, is flawed because it is blind to the sovereign moral aims of philosophy and because in the process it encroaches upon and dismisses the importance of knowledge as lived wisdom.

It is easy to show that the tract Petrarch writes is an elaborate, rhetorically controlled response to these explicit and implicit challenges in all their logical ramifications. The text, which by rhetorical necessity is written in the form of a personal letter (as if to insist on the necessity of genuine bonds of friendship in intellectual controversies), recalls the poet's encounter with the philosophers, and, as it does so, it dramatically stages a version of the perpetual quarrel of the arts. The polarity and opposition that historically structure the tradition of philosophical debates now reemerge as rhetoric battles logic, and language as eloquence and persuasion of the will is juxtaposed to an idea of knowledge divorced from the realities of experience.

The chief objection Petrarch levels at the neo-Aristotelian logic from the standpoint of his defense of the value of rhetoric is severe but is, as anticipated above, fairly conventional. The Aristotelian system of knowledge is saddled with ponderous abstractions that have nothing to do with the demands of lived, concrete experiences. This perceived bracketing of the importance of eloquence, ethics, and, in general, the complexities of personal history and time leads Petrarch to formulate a second objection which logically follows from the first. He objects to the apparent universalism of the neo-Aristotelian style of philosophy, its claim of total knowledge, and its pretension to know and organize into an intelligible totality the whole of reality.

With great clarity (and, oddly, the rigor of the argument stems from his will to expose the falseness of a merely intellectual clarity), Petrarch's first move in *On His Own Ignorance* is to trivialize the import of encyclopedic knowledge with its exorbitant premise that total knowledge is possible. In practice, however, the systematic pursuit of total knowledge abrogates any rigorous distinction between science and merely fanciful lore. The claim of a possible total knowledge is obliquely identified as the knowledge made available by medieval encyclopedists.

By a deliberate move, Petrarch shifts the sense of what philosophical knowledge is. He begins by giving a jaunty instance of what the young philosophers conceive of as scientific knowledge, and their knowledge is exposed as a weave of rational authoritarian assertions, untested logical absurdities, and hollow inventions handed down from antiquity. The "confused and undisciplined order" (p. 56) that Pe-

Medical encyclopedias don't tell us anything important
We know nothing about Man

trarch decries in the learning of one of the neo-Aristotelians is cast in a language that basically defines the encyclopedic structure of knowledge. One of these young men has much to tell, the text says,

> about birds and fishes: how many hair there are in the lion's mane; how many feathers in the hawk's tail; with how many arms the cuttlefish clasps a shipwrecked man; that elephants couple from behind and are pregnant for two years; that this docile and vigorous animal, the nearest to man by its intelligence, lives until the end of the second or third century of its life; that the phoenix is consumed by aromatic fire and revives after it has been burned; that the sea urchin stops a ship, however fast she is driving along, while it is unable to do anything once it is dragged out of the waves; how the hunter fools the tiger with a mirror; how the Arimasp attacks the griffin with his sword; how whales turn over on their backs and thus deceive the sailors; that the newborn of the bear has as yet no shape; that the mule rarely gives birth, the viper only once and then to its own disaster; that moles are blind and bees deaf; that alone among all living beings the crocodile moves its upper jaw. (p. 57)

The satirical tone of the passage is as unmistakable as it is fierce. No doubt, Petrarch wills to ridicule the nature of the neo-Aristotelians' knowledge. This mindless, indiscriminate, and yet diligent collection of untested beliefs and random lore textually echoes and, thereby, stages the pseudo-science of the encyclopedists such as Vincent of Beauvais, Alexander Neckam, and Bartholomaeus Anglicus, who, on the ultimate authority of Aristotle, repeat as facts fanciful assertions and absurd speculations by Aristotle, Pliny, and Isidore of Seville.[2]

This critique of the Aristotelian idea of universal and all-encompassing knowledge in *On His Own Ignorance* cannot be taken as a blanket dismissal of any encyclopedic project that aims to give a representation of the totality of knowledge. Petrarch's friendship with Boccaccio, who doggedly writes till the end of his life a mythographic encyclopedia, *De genealogia deorum gentilium* and the encyclopedic *De montibus,* which is influenced by Petrarch's own erudite archaeological-geographical compilation, the *Itinerarium syriacum,* and his bonds of friendship during the Avignon years with Pierre Bersuire and Giovanni Colonna,[3] who compiled two encyclopedic works, respectively, the *Reductorium morale* and the *Mare historiarum,* which is a universal world history, indicate that Petrarch well understands the feasibility and the validity of the universalizing mode of mythographic and historical writing.

Petrarch's critique of the encyclopedic project in *On His Own Ignorance* is to be taken in a technical sense. To these anachronistic, superstitious models of natural science and universal knowledge, which the four philosophers dogmatically view as the truth, Petrarch juxtaposes the sphere of one's own biographical individuality, the history of oneself as the concrete and truly inexhaustible domain of legitimate knowledge. From this standpoint, the narrative of Petrarch's own self-education, which occupies a central place in *On His Own Ignorance,* is a transparent strategy whereby he rejects the paltry challenge of his wisdom by the neo-Aristotelians. For him, knowledge cannot be mere bookishness and irrelevant erudition. Knowledge is simultaneously ethics and rhetoric in that they are disciplines of history and one's will, activities by which a man makes choices and dialogues with other human beings.

Quite in keeping with the thrust of Petrarch's vision, *On His Own Ignorance* contains a poignant autobiographical account of the poet's process of education, from his studies at Montpellier and Bologna (where he focused on law and rhetoric) to his travels to Toulouse, Paris, Padua, and Naples, where "the greatest of all the kings and philosophers of our age" resides. He also recalls the years spent at the papal court in Avignon, where with various unmentioned masters he continued studying the liberal arts (pp. 68–70). Through the recollection of his irreducibly personal *paideia,* thus, Petrarch shows how for him the world of thought is by necessity rooted in the geographical and historical particularities of one's own individual existence: *paideia* has to be understood, he maintains, as a shaping of a life in the light of a steady moral-intellectual self-examination. Thus understood, knowledge is necessarily historical in the measure in which it reflects and subsumes the depth of one's memories and one's experiences. Given this premise, it follows that philosophy, if it is to penetrate to the heart of a life and not simply dwell in the realm of logical abstractions, must border on or "descend" to areas of concern which are the purview of history and literature. The only worthwhile, imaginable knowledge, so runs Petrarch's argument in his discursive and poetic texts, is knowledge of oneself and study of one's character, or to say it a bit differently, true knowledge is coextensive with the concrete individualities of history.

Historians of the Renaissance, who in the wake of Burckhardt posit a clean break between the Middle Ages and the Renaissance, would in all likelihood see in Petrarch's personal, intellectual-moral claims of *On His Own Ignorance* another confirmation of the Burckhardtian sense of the Petrarchan discovery of the modern idea of individuality. And there is, no doubt, a measure of truth in holding that Petrarch here clearly drafts the outlines of the self as an empirical, unique individuality. There are, however, larger and more fundamental concerns at stake in Petrarch's procedure, and these concerns force us to redefine the current historical understanding of Petrarch's idea of individuality. I submit that by focusing on the autobiographical account of his education, Petrarch, in effect, echoes a rhetorical-historiographic tradition that makes biography the point of intersection between history and moral philosophy. For the chief aim of the biographical genre is to record the ethos or character of a man and to show the concrete shape the pursuit of wisdom takes in life.

The terms of the controversy over the exact relationship between biography and historiography are well known to students of Hellenism and Imperial Rome as well as New Testament and patristic scholars. I shall give here a brief synopsis. The relationship between them is cast originally as a drastic polarization between *fabula* and *historia* or *ethos* and *res gestae.* But the two rhetorical modes undergo radical shifts from the early Hellenistic separation of the two genres to a gradual fading of the boundaries distinguishing each from the other. The overlapping of history and biography occurs prominently in the history writing of the lives of the emperors in Rome.[4] The "lives of the Caesars" were in fact a deliberate eulogizing of emperors. The purists of historiography, who adhere to the principle that history is the domain of public events and not of personalities, had sought to stave off this encomiastic genre from the trajectory of history's concerns, but with the history of the Caesars it became impossible to distinguish the private from the public sphere. There were also specifically intellectual reasons for the overlay of one rhetorical genre onto the other.

On the basis of Plutarch, who states that he writes lives and not histories, Quintilian views history as an activity devoted to truth and the transmission of true events for the benefit of posterity and to win glory for its author ("ad memoriam posteritatis et ingenii famam componitur" [*Institutio oratoria* 10.1.31]). Since history, as he adds, has a certain affinity to poetry and may be regarded as a kind of prose poem, the historian employs a style that would break the monotony of the narrative. Behind Quintilian's principle lies (and he cites) the tradition of Sallust and, above all, Thucydides' and Cicero's sense of historiography as the narrative of true events, "for who is ignorant that it is the first law in writing history that the historian must not dare to tell any falsehood, and the next, that he must be bold enough to tell the whole truth? Also, there must be no suspicion of partiality in his writings, or of personal animosity?"[5] Cicero, to be sure, knows only too well that what confers immortality and grandeur to history is the skill of the orator; he writes, "By what other voice . . . than that of the orator, is history, the evidence of time, the light of truth, the life of memory, the directness of life, the herald of antiquity, committed to immortality?"[6]

Because the truth claims of history writing are inseparable from the incantatory power of rhetoric, any sharp distinction between biography and history fades. Biography had been kept out of the realm of history, as suggested above, on the grounds that it was a fabulous and not necessarily true narrative, one that focuses on the ethos of a person and whose purpose is the encomium of illustrious people. Biographers are labeled by Herodotus *logopoioi*, legend-makers, and their work is considered a branch of epideictic rhetoric.[7] But this neat demarcation between biography and history was to collapse. To paraphrase Montaigne, biography is found to be the window through which one can behold the larger horizon of history in the sense that the provisional meaning of the whole of history emerges through the retrieval of the historicity of individual lives.

What brings biography and history together from a technical viewpoint is the consciousness that rhetoric, which Petrarch's neo-Aristotelians dismiss as falsification of knowledge, is the discourse common to both. What is more, the two modes also share a concern with moral philosophy. Cicero in *De finibus* (1.10.36) understands the study of history as the discipline whereby one calls to mind "illustrious and courageous men and their deeds." Suetonius's *De vita Caesarum*, on the other hand, gives historical events as a way to highlight the character of the protagonists. In the biographies and saints' lives of late antiquity and the Middle Ages, the focus falls, as in history, on the celebration of the virtues of the heroic figures of the past whose achievements can be emulated in the present. In short, the world of history, which comprises both biography and the mighty events of Rome or of the Church, is seen as a rhetorical and ethical discipline.

Retrospectively, and in the light of these traditional debates, one can grasp the tight argument of *On His Own Ignorance,* in which the notion that knowledge cannot be conceived as absolute and that there is a historical, subjective dimension to knowledge triggers the text's exploration of the structure of the self. Appropriately, the unfolding of *On His Own Ignorance* shifts its ground and focuses sharply on Petrarch's autobiography: what seemed to be an *apologia* for one's life is, in fact, a hermeneutics of self. More precisely, the polemic against the young men turns into a narrative of Petrarch's own intellectual education and public achievements, and they are placed within the vindication of the values of rhetoric and ethics. From this standpoint, one can also grasp how for Petrarch history as biography is the central impulse of his imagination. No doubt, this is the context within which the *Canzoniere*'s confessional self-analysis belongs. The narrative organization of *De viris illustribus,* which relates history's play of forces through and as a sequence of biographies, as we shall see later, can only be understood in the light of the insight that history and biography constitute the foundation of genuine knowledge.

The statement about the pivotal role history plays in Petrarch's thought extends but cannot be limited to his study of the past, to the sort of more or less philosophical-antiquarian fascination with the disparate facts of Roman life—heroes, customs, topography, relics, numismatics, texts, and so on—that are a steady feature, as we partly saw in the first two chapters of this study, of Petrarch's discursive and poetic texts. At stake here is the relationship between history and antiquarianism, and I must proceed to explore its exact configuration by focusing on what might be termed the politics of the cult of antiquities. As a preamble to the discussion, let me stress that at bottom his all-too-real fascination with antiquarianism is a sign of what strikes me as Petrarch's historical nostalgia for Rome's irretrievable origins, his dream of recapturing a mythical time of historical purity and grandeur which ceaselessly proved to be elusive whenever he tried to revive it wholesale in the present. Both his *Liber sine nomine,* whose overt focus is a bitter polemic against the Avignonese papacy, and, especially, his correspondence with Cola di Rienzo summarize his reflections on the possibility of the imminent return of Rome's past and its dissociation from its degraded present.[8] The crisis initiated by Cola's visionariness and rhetoric—the desire to free Rome from the new barbarians and to have the popes back in the "city of the apostles"—plunges Petrarch into the midst of a political adventure which to him appears partly a turbulent dream, partly a sovereign and risky historical enterprise, but one which opens to him a vertiginous perspective. In Cola's dream Petrarch beholds the marvel of a possible renewed beginning of Rome's history, and this event leads him to the pursuit of a language that is to be by necessity absorbed by and that pulsates with the immediate demands of that history.

The exchange between the poet and the Roman tribune originates under the aegis of rhetoric and with a mutual recognition of their respective powers of eloquence.[9] The rhetoric of Rome's past grandeur, which is all-encompassing and circular in its repetitiveness, is the point of contact between Cola and Petrarch, and it reveals that Rome's liberty means to both the regaining of history's ground and, by the same token, the reconstitution of the eternal order of history. But neither is really deceived about the wide differences existing between them.

Petrarch's letters goad Cola to action by recalling the accounts of Livy, "prince of historians" (p. 20), or Sallust, among others, in the conviction that examples from the past can inspire the present: "What inspiration, truly, cannot be derived from the memory of the past and from the grandeur of a name once revered throughout the whole world? Who does not wish Rome the best of fortune in her efforts to attain her rightful empire? Both God and humanity champion such a just cause" (p. 25). But the part Petrarch can perform is the service of his pen in order to enhance, as he says, borrowing the language of Livy's preface to his *Ab urbe condita libri*, "the memory of the most noble people in the world" (p. 56). Cola's letter to Petrarch, by contrast, warmly thanks the poet for the affectionate care he lavishes on Rome (and him) but laments that Petrarch is not present in the city in person: "We and all the Romans feel warmly attached to you, and the more sincerely do we pledge ourselves to serve your glory and advantage. If only you were present at Rome in person! For, just as a most precious stone adorns a golden ring, so your illustrious presence would adorn and embellish the nourishing city" (p. 51).

Clearly enough, the passage profusely displays Cola's gratitude to the faraway poet, but the highlighting of the inexhaustible value of the poet's endorsement occludes—and reveals—Cola's clearheaded ploy. Petrarch thinks of his act of writing (wherein he urges Cola to read the histories and annals of Rome) as being in itself a historical action, but, in fact, as Cola laments, he is away from Rome—history's great stage—

in these most decisive hours for Rome's freedom. The lament is also a barely veiled reproach: unable to cross the threshold of action, Petrarch wraps himself in the web of his solitude, or, and the suggestion is oblique but not really sinister, he is enveloped in the pursuit of *his* own glory and *his* own advantage. It is possible, no doubt, to understand Cola's statement as a reference to Petrarch's ongoing familiarity with Cola's enemy in Avignon, Cardinal Giovanni Colonna. But in it there is a glimmer of a more powerful insight: in the concision of its language, the passage deciphers Petrarch's secret yearning that the roles between poet and tribune be reversed, that the tribune's own historical actions be in the service of the poet's imagination.

Cola was not off the mark. At any rate, there is a sharp difference between their respective visions of antiquity. Cola surrenders to the power of his own rhetoric and wishes to transform it into a present reality. One can say that the literalized quest for the revival of the grandeur of the Roman past best describes his theatrical and tragic archaicism, his deluded hope that it was possible to ignore or overhaul the mutations that the passage of centuries had inflicted on all things. In his literalism Cola envisioned the renewal of Roman history as that which could weave together, once again and forever, the strands of traditions in the Christian world into a powerful and still vital reality.

Petrarch is fascinated by the power of the tribune's vision and by the passions of his mind; he even stirs Cola for a while, as we have seen, to what could have been an epoch-making action, but he soon takes and keeps his skeptical distance from the (theoretical and practical) consequences of Cola's grievous, static literalism. From this standpoint, Petrarch's own antiquarian nostalgia never really becomes the limitation of his historical thinking. Quite to the contrary. His antiquarianism is the mark of his authentic historical consciousness, of his sharp realization that no fixed ideology—republican, despotic, or imperial—(and he knew them all) could bring back the glory that was Rome, that time had driven a wedge between past and present, and that nonetheless the present could only come out of the very possibilities embedded within the distant and dormant heritage of Rome. The ancient past of Rome, in short, is for him the realm of culture, of simulacra which are burdened with buried spiritual powers and which he turns into vital fictions of his memory and imagination.

"We are drawn," Petrarch says in the oration he delivered in Rome when he received his longed-for laurel crown (1341), "by the places, I do not know how, where there remain vestiges of those we love or admire."[10] He is directly quoting here Cicero's reflections on his attraction for the cultural memories of Athens recorded in his *De legibus* (2.2.4) but only to mark his disagreement with Cicero's sentimentality: "Michi autem, fateor, hec non ultima causa fuit Romam veniendi" (p. 1266) (But for me, I admit it, this was not the decisive reason for coming to Rome). He has not come to Rome solely to contemplate the sepulchers of the ancients or to dwell in the shadows of the remembrance of the city's "summorum virorum"; he trusts, rather, that a "non inglorium futurum" can flow out of the present coronation ceremony.

Within the celebratory horizon of the oration, delivered while Cola was in Rome, this future is heralded as the future of poetry itself because of the persuasiveness and force of poetry to counter the present and to be the source of all divine inventions.[11] At the origin of the history of Rome or Greece, then, there are poetry's imaginings and orations. Given Petrarch's sense of the irreducible uniqueness of all individualities, there is no desire for an impossible duplication of the past or its mechanical superimposition on the present. The text, actually, can be dubbed Petrarch's "discourse of Rome," in the double sense of the phrase—one of the senses being that he intends to give a representation of Rome's discourse (its morality, *studia,* wisdom, historical characters, values, and so on) for the future. Thus, the discontinuities of both past and future are reconstituted in memory and imagination, as poetry is acknowledged as the foundation of history's myths scattered through time. To put it somewhat differently, the assertion of the priority of poetry over all other discourses discloses the fact that historical genealogies have fabulous origins, that they unfold what the poetic myths crystallize. The claim, clearly, is meant to confer extraordinary authority on the historical role of the poet.

If the vision of the future of Rome in the oration is conceived to be coextensive with the empire of letters rather than with a literal re-creation of its past realities, there are many other elements in his various texts suggesting the exact contour of Petrarch's historical sense. These signs are visible everywhere from his holding steadfast to his conviction, laid bare in the self-analysis punctuating the *Canzoniere,* in the unfinished *Africa,* or in the *Trionfi,* that the foundational principle of the self, of the city, and of the whole of history lies in poetry and that poetry is the response to the gaps and finiteness of time. These signs are also visible from his *Invective contra medicum*, with its argument that rhetoric is the language of history, the cultural discourse that perpetuates for posterity the sedimented memories and myths of tradition. They are particularly evident from the specifically historical works Petrarch elaborates, *De viris illustribus* and *Rerum memorandarum libri*.

To grasp the lineaments of Petrarch's historical thought, thus, we must first examine in some detail the long preface to *De viris illustribus*, where he sets himself the preliminary task of accounting for the nature of and conceptual difficulties inherent to history writing, of reflecting on its style, and of laying out the criteria of his historical method. We know from reading, say, the *Invective* or *On His Own Ignorance* that Petrarch likes to explain how he writes his books. We quickly discover by his accounts of the various books' origins that polemics are for him never merely accidental, episodic occurrences. They are rhetorical, epistemologically necessary strategies by which he establishes his intellectual rigor and by which he ends up beholding the doubleness and contradictoriness of every experience. There is an intentional dramatization of arguments that are at odds with each other also in the preface to *De viris illustribus*.

The text was marked from its very conception by contrasting pulls. The reference in the *Secretum* to a projected work of history ("librum historiarum a rege Romulo in Titum . . . opus immensum") and, more poignantly, the different plans of redaction of *De viris illustribus* (one was envisioned as including figures from biblical history and mythology, from Adam to Abraham to Jason and Hercules; the final one narrows the focus down to biographies of characters from Roman history, from Romulus to Scipio to Cato the Elder and Trajan, with an abridged preface addressed to Francesco da Carrara) are striking symptoms of Petrarch's perplexities about the possible form the work was to take and, beyond that, of his bewilderment about the mode of representation of history.

In the preface, he views *De viris illustribus* as an exhilarating challenge to his critical judgment rather than to his poetic creativity. He is aware, as he says, that "just as it is glorious to invent new things in philosophical or poetic works, so it is forbidden to do so in history" (p. 139).[12] The sundry revisions of the original plan, however, make one suspect that history writing also turned out to be an unsettling and problematical experience for him, for what he had to decide were fundamental questions, such as the limits and legitimacy of his own historical account, the nature of "facts," the ambiguities and conflicts of his sources (p. 139), the principles of selection and exclusion from "the infinite quantity of events" (p. 140), whether or not to abide within a homogeneous (Roman) domain of historical experiences or place these within a biblical framework, and, finally, the feasibility of writing a total history.

On the face of it, the basic thrust of the longer preface is to describe the text's moral aims and techniques of compilation, to confront the stylistic options available to Petrarch as a historian, and to acknowledge the impossibility of circumscribing the vast diversity of history into one single narrative. There are no objective standards, the preface concludes, for determining the truth of past historical events. Confronted with "the disagreements of historians," Petrarch casts himself not as the "peacemaker" among their conflicting accounts, but as the "copier," a scribe guided by their "verisimilitude" and "authority" (p. 139). What is more, because of its remoteness in time and because the past is buried beneath the weight of unverifiable legends and pieties—and the statement resonates with Thucydides' own insight into the inaccessibility of historical events at the start of his *History of the Peloponnesian War*—it is impossible for him (as it was for Livy himself) to acquire a precise knowledge of bygone times. If this is the case, how then is a historical work to be justified or understood?

These sundry points and questions mark the conceptual articulation of the preface, yet its arguments are not constructed in a linear and systematic way. They are, rather, inextricably woven together around and sustain the preface's burden: Petrarch's self-reflexiveness on the task and predicament of the historian. His role, he says, is to engage in a scholar's research as he diligently collects facts and discriminates between fact and fiction. But it is quickly apparent that for Petrarch history is not a scientific discipline of firm and true facts. Livy himself, who "was so much closer to the events he was describing" (p. 139), was embarrassed, he writes, by the contradictions he found in his sources. The principles of "verisimilitude" and "authority" of the historical accounts to which Petrarch appeals for his own narrative suggest that he envisions history writing neither as *historia* nor as *fabula*, but as *argumentum*, as rhetoric's sphere, that is, of probable events, wherein facts and the imagination of facts are inextricably intermingled.

From this standpoint, it is understandable that he should seek to provide a fresh vision of the human traits of the characters involved in the drama of history (their manners, domestic life, sayings, bodily stature, genealogy, and manner of death) (p. 141). More than an inquiry into "objective" causes of events, history writing is the imaginative portrayal of personalities, the reconstruction of discrete frames which probe how a character, contextualized within the overall plan of Roman history, becomes a destiny. But the chief goal of the historian, that which justifies historiography, is the creation of a moral world.

The task of the historian, Petrarch says, following Livy's own preface to his *Ab urbe condita libri*, is "to point up to the readers those things to be followed and those to be avoided, with plenty of distinguished examples provided on either side" (p. 141).[13] Through the echo of Livy, the Ciceronian topos of history as *magistra vitae*, as the readers' scene of moral instruction, is made to depend on the historian's prior ethical judgment about what has to be followed or avoided in the rich storehouse of *exempla*. The recognition that the historian's role to give a critical separation not of history's facts but of history's contradictory moral values is not an isolated detail of the text. That the struggle for values constitutes the burden of Petrarch's vision of both history and culture is made manifest by the fact that the preface dramatizes other forms of opposition.

The impetus for Petrarch's history writing as an inquiry (in the technical sense of the word) into the past comes from his desire, as has been suggested in the paragraph above, to complement his other inquiries into ethics. But his specific point of departure is the juxtaposition of two alternate modes of conduct holding sway in his own time: the enemies of excellence (and this is the path treaded by the "insane mob") and the lovers of glory (who travel the path of virtue) are at odds with each other. This antagonism turns quickly into the consciousness of a moral discontinuity between past and present. The present can be best represented by Horatian satire, or, as he puts it, "Contemporary princes contribute material not for history but for satire" (p. 139).[14] Satire is to be understood here as the style appropriate to a quarrelsome and heroicomic world deserving the poet's moral harangue. The history of the past, on the other hand, is the reservoir of exemplary deeds by illustrious men the memory of whom "can lead to virtues" (p. 141). The imagination of the past, in short, sheds a blazing critical light on the decadence of the present age.

History is a guide to life /compass

"Illustrious men," as Petrarch defines them, are those whose achievements are not the result of "good luck" but "the product of glory and virtue" (p. 140). In Roman historiography "fortune" and "virtue" are antithetical and yet complementary terms designating, respectively, the imponderable, erratic elements of history and the human skill to bend to one's purpose the turns of the inscrutable goddess Fortuna. The tension between the two contradictory but mutually self-implicating poles is resolved in the acceptance of the transcendent myth of the eternity of Rome. By the erasure of luck from the domain of his present concerns, Petrarch intends to remove from his discourse fortuitousness and any other mythological pattern that would reduce history to an uncontrollable, fatalistic mechanism. He focuses, rather, on the personalities that embody the values of classical Rome, and he seeks to capture the principle of history in the contradictions of their individual heroic deeds and of their will.

The very title of the work, De viris illustribus, signals Petrarch's own will to inscribe his text within and at the same time to revise the classical and Christian tradition of treating history as biography. Scholars have consistently pointed out Petrarch's indebtedness to historiographers such as Livy, Valerius Maximus, Sallust, Suetonius, Orosius, and St. Augustine for both De viris illustribus and Rerum memorandarum libri.[15] But to the best of my knowledge they have not emphasized the existence of what can be called a rhetorical genre of "De viris illustribus," which Petrarch's title directly echoes.

The genre, which has been labeled "aretalogy" in that the miracles and virtues of exalted figures, such as pagan sages and Christian saints, are celebrated, would include a text by Suetonius, who, in addition to De vita Caesarum, compiled, according to St. Jerome, a now lost series of biographies of poets and orators known as De viris illustribus; it also would contain a work by Isidore of Seville as well as St. Jerome's own pivotal De viris inlustribus. The value of St. Jerome's work depends on many factors. It sketches some of Suetonius's biographies; secondly, in the preface to the text, St. Jerome lists Suetonius's Greek predecessors (Hermippus, Antigonus, and Aristoxenus). What is more, it became the model for Giovanni Colonna's own collection of famous lives.[16]

By focusing on personalities, much as Livy, Suetonius, or St. Jerome, Petrarch wills to detect the concrete, empirical embodiment of the classical and Christian virtues (justice, temperance, frugality, and so on) within Roman history rather than discuss their abstract, philosophical nature. The procedure allows him to keep a sure foothold in the realities of human existence and to stake his claims about the dignity of history over and against the coherence of philosophical paradigms. Thus, in *De viris illustribus* he depicts exceptional men's political achievements, their inward struggles and purposes, in order to show man's capacity for ill-doing and for virtue. From this standpoint, Petrarch moves within the fold of the tradition, sketched above, that casts history as biography, the hermeneutical tracing of the concrete design of an individual life. But Roman and Christian historians place their characters within the overarching schemes of, respectively, eternal Rome and providential history.[17] Petrarch certainly endorses the two myths of the continuity and providentiality of the Roman Empire, yet he radically redefines its ultimate sense. We should thus look in some detail at the fourth letter in *Liber sine nomine*, written anonymously to the Roman people late in 1352, while Cola was a prisoner in Avignon, to bring into the open the status of Rome's mythology in Petrarch's thought.[18]

Cola's unjust captivity, which is the immediate occasion of the letter, is an overt sign of Rome's own Avignonese captivity. Petrarch, as a Roman citizen (p. 53), feels implicated in this oppression, and at the risk of his own security and (therefore) under cover of anonymity, he speaks out of an irresistible passion for the "name" of Rome. His mind is caught between imagined (and certainly not unreal) terrors of political reprisals and an obsessive "romance" for Rome. This compound of fascination and dread (which, were I interested in adopting a psychological model, could be rendered as a mixture of grandiose fantasies and fear of annihilation) impels him to write prophetically, as it were *in place of* others, in the conviction that "there is no one who dares even whisper except in corners, in the shadows, in fear" (ibid.). The self-conscious heroic posture (whereby he intimates that his anonymity cannot really disguise the provenance of the letter and that its style will identify him as the author and make him vulnerable to possible punitive measures [ibid.]) is muted in the rest of the text as Petrarch shifts his focus to the Roman people.

In his climactic appeal to the people he incites them to "stand firm against injustice . . . protect the accused if innocent . . . dare something . . . in memory of the ashes and the glory of your forefathers, in the name of the empire . . . dare something, if not for his [Cola's] safety, then for your own honor" (pp. 55–57). The letter ends with his instigating the Roman people not to perish in the ashes of the past, to take action, and to overcome the defeatism in which they languish. It is evident even from this passage that the ills afflicting present-day Rome have for Petrarch many causes.

The first is psychological. The passion for distinction and honor, which for Petrarch is a natural impulse of all men living in a social compact, stands now eclipsed. The demoralization of the Romans is exemplified by the fear they now have of those who were once subjected to them, and the letter's final note stresses this aspect as it exhorts them not to be fearful, for "nothing is less Roman than fear" (p. 57). The second—and this is only suggested by the implications of the language of "fear" deployed in the letter—is hermeneutical. Fear, in fact, is to be taken as the experience of minds and wills overwhelmed and paralyzed by the power of the enemy. Because fear is tied to a perception of some awesome power, it is inevitable that one should view it from the perspective of the power emanating from the monumentality of Rome's ruins, which are both a sublime spectacle of her ancient glory and gloomy images of death. From this standpoint, it can be said that the *vetustas* of Rome, the very weight of its past that should arouse emulation, is what has frozen the contemporaries into inaction. It seems, thus, that the Romans are morally dead in spite or because of their familiarity with the landscape of their majestic history. One infers that their present moribund state is the more abject exactly because they yet rot in the midst of—indifferent to or unaffected by—Rome's ashes and petrified memories.

By this thematization of fear, Petrarch is showing the Romans, as he fiercely rebukes them for abandoning Cola to the injustices of the Avignonese court, their radical error of historical interpretation. Whereas Cola had yielded to the power of the ruins and in the imaginative excitement of his response he literally, and fearlessly, wants to resurrect them from their ashes as he refounds the Roman republic, the fear of these Romans can be said to be triggered by their own literal, idolatrous identification with the ruins themselves.

Cola's imagination is flared to action by the ruins, and he sees Rome as a phoenix remade from her own ashes; the Romans' imagination is stifled by those sepulchral traces left behind by time, and, thereby, they seal their own death. Eventually, with Cola's failure, Petrarch will come to see, and in this context he already suggests, that the two interpretations of the same past are each the specular reflection of the other, and both of them together cast their respective historical postures as modes of misreading history's metaphors. Against these, Petrarch makes distance, for which Cola reproaches him, the foundation of a historical interpretation that can both confront and transcend the pull of a cadaverous past.

There are other remedies Petrarch explicitly prescribes to overcome Rome's ills, and they exceed a narrowly political definition. The first and most obvious remedy lies in the pursuit of a spiritual and intellectual discipline of cohesion which would offset the present anarchy. In point of fact, the letter urges the Romans to speak with a single voice ("let the world know that it is the united voice of the Roman people" [p. 57]), for that united voice would inspire respect and "fear" in others. There are no practical suggestions as to how this unity, wherein dissenting elements can be made to cohere in an organic whole, can be achieved.

But there is an overtly organic lexicon in this fourth letter that allows us to root Petrarch's thought within a prominent tradition of medieval political theology. The possible order of the city is posited in terms of the unity of an organism, the *corpus politicum,* as the structure within which conflicting interests can be reconciled: "Each body," he writes as he argues for Rome as the sole head of the empire, "has been given one head. The universe, described by the poet as a great body, ought then to be content with a single earthly head, for every two-headed animal is a monster. How much more frightful and monstrous is the creature with a thousand different heads, all gnawing at and struggling against each other! Even allowing that there may be several heads, there still has to be one, surely, to restrain all the others and to preside over them in order that the peace of the entire body remain undisturbed" (pp. 47–48).

The adoption of this corporate ideology, which involves cosmos and empire, signals that corporatism is the way for Petrarch to control his own fear of confusion—the monster of differences—within the political world. Yet this corporate metaphor unveils his deeper conviction that the solution to Rome's ills lies in retrieving the dominant power-philosophy of classical Rome. The way out of Rome's submission to fear, the letter says, is nothing less than to have Rome once again inspire fear in its enemies. History, in short, is viewed as an economy of generalized competition for domination. The statement recalls Augustine's diagnosis in *The City of God,* where he interprets

THE WORLDS OF PETRARCH

the essence of Roman history in terms of Rome's *libido dominandi* and he denounces its claim of justice as a sham for power. But the power of Rome, Petrarch maintains against Augustine and somewhat in line with Dante, differs in kind from that of the other rivaling empires.

This unabashed endorsement of the might of classical Rome echoes, more precisely, Livy's historical vision, which deliberately presents itself as a propagandizing for and apotheosis of that might. Petrarch justifies Roman power as the *imperium legitimum* by arguing, much as Livy does, that the immanent order of justice established by Rome throughout the world goes unmatched: "When was there ever such peace, such tranquillity and such justice; when was virtue so honored, the good so rewarded and the evil punished; when was there ever such wise direction of affairs, than when the world had only one head and that head was Rome?" (p. 47). In opposition to the aberrant legal practices of Avignon, the legitimacy of Roman power, so runs the argument, resides in Rome's long-standing tradition of making laws, and not abstract justice as Aristotle would, the practical bond of a civil society.

The case for Rome's judicial traditions gives Petrarch the pretext to reaffirm the principle of the ongoing legality of the Roman Empire based in that city ("Furthermore, there are some outstanding jurists here who say that his claim clearly can be supported from civil law" [p. 53]). Finally, there is a theological perspective from which Petrarch vindicates the providentiality of the Roman Empire. Against St. Augustine, who had taken to task Vergil's belief in the immortality of the Roman Empire, in the persuasion that Rome is the latter-day incarnation of dead empires (pp. 49–51), Petrarch sides with Vergil's theology and, thereby, endorses the value of secularism.[19] The notion that Rome's history has been divinely ordained becomes the perspective from which the power of Fortuna (pp. 51–52), which is a specifically Roman goddess presiding over the perpetual fluctuations of all things, though not repudiated, appears subordinated to the design of Providence.

One cannot dismiss the letter's compendium of classical, Christian, and legal arguments as if they were empty platitudes syncretistically arrayed exclusively to both sustain and give utterance to Petrarch's rhetoric and vatic posture as he addresses the Roman people. They constitute, rather, the vital wares for his well-known assertion that history can only be the "praise of Rome." But it would be an error to regard the "praise of Rome" as a reduction of history to the stony, marmoreal immobility of her past, which is really Cola's position. The stability of the body-politic in the middle of the radical, unceasing changes brought about by fortune and time is the presupposition and foundation for his idea of culture as the transformation and reconstruction of the past. This idea is articulated through his sustained reflection on himself in the role of historian of Roman antiquity, which occupies, as I have already shown, a prominent place in the preface to *De viris illustribus,* and I briefly return to it.

De viris illustribus centers broadly on what Aristotle calls an *ethopoeia* (the representation of characters' achievements, mores, and natural dispositions) within the unalterable framework of Roman history. But the brunt of the preface is that history writing about Rome is not a universal, total history such as the salvation histories written by St. Augustine, Peter Comestor, or Otto of Freising, in which biblical and secular events are connected. Petrarch writes history as what must be called, by an oxymoron, a partial totality, a series of individual lives none of which encompasses the totality of Rome's pageant. From the standpoint of this time-bound and fragmentary history, the totality dramatized by the medieval encyclopedias of the neo-Aristotelians appears an illusory construct that evades time's constraints. In this Petrarchan world of history, no transcendent harmony of interpretive antinomies and viewpoints can be sought or attained. More precisely, as he arranges and compiles the contradictory morass of events that have lost their original self-evident transparency, Petrarch writes a commentary, in the etymological sense of the word (a recollection forward of the past), on the preexisting script of Roman history.[20]

As an experience of memory, a commentary is a displaced, secondary, and subjective discourse on the fragmentary traces of history's traditions. In point of fact, Petrarch goes out of his way in the preface to insist that he writes his own interpretive version of past events in opposition to and as a supplement of other versions. Appropriately, his narrative starts with the recognition of "the disagreements of historians" (p. 139), and it ends with the acknowledgment of the existence of other possible historical accounts ("Whoever desires to know these and similar things, let him consult other historians" [p. 141]).

Petrarch's own work of history, then, does not seek to reconcile or subsume opposing viewpoints within an overarching seamless unity but leaves them intact in their irreducible differences. It would be an error to understand this claim as merely a strategy to vindicate the absolute uniqueness and individuality of Petrarch's own discourse, which in reality explicitly disavows the myth of originality in history writing. What Petrarch, who never escapes the attraction of power, wishes to convey, rather, is the insight, partly described earlier in chapter 2, that culture is constitutively made of conflicts of interpretations, battles of books, polemics, and spiritual forces that are connected with each other and yet are at odds with each other. Just as the rights of the Roman people were to be determined by the power and control that Rome historically exerted over rival claims, so the myth of culture, whose empire Petrarch announces, displaces and reenacts the question of power onto the plain of values.

There is in the preface a direct analogy between Petrarch as a historiographer and Caesar Augustus that can help clarify Petrarch's sense of the establishment of the empire of culture and his role within it. The two laws of history, Petrarch says, quoting Cicero's *De oratore* (2.15.62), are, first, that an author "must not dare to tell anything but the truth, and the second that he must dare to tell the whole truth." Nonetheless, he acknowledges that, because of the infinite quantity of events, "it is virtually impossible to satisfy the curiosity to know everything." There must be a principle of selection for a possible narrative, and Petrarch makes Fama, who is the sister of Clio, or, to say it textually, "illustrious men," those who are "the product of glory and virtue," the law of the text's construction. To exemplify the legitimacy of the procedure, he relates an anecdote from Caesar Augustus's life, which he found in Suetonius's *Divus Augustus*. While Augustus was in Alexandria, he visited the mausoleum where the body of Alexander lay. When someone asked him if he also wanted to see the remains of Ptolemy, Augustus replied: "I want to see kings, not just corpses" (p. 140).

The story primarily dramatizes Petrarch's sense that the chief duty of the historian, to paraphrase Tacitus, is to see that virtue is placed on record and that history contains a variety of *exempla* from which one must choose "what to imitate."[21] Just as Augustus chooses to visit the tomb of Alexander—chooses, that is, to imitate him—but shuns Ptolemy, as if his ashes were the cadaver of history, so will Petrarch focus on "illustrious men" and shun all other obscure figures. But there is another, crucial resonance to the anecdote. Petrarch, in effect, confronts here the question which is at the center, as this chapter has been showing, of his historical and poetic thinking: the relationship between history and death. As the antiquarian who reflects on history's past, Petrarch fully grasps death's sovereignty and triumph over all historical achievements. This consciousness of death does not only define the belatedness of the historiographer in relation to the events to be narrated; it extends also to the existence of a historical agent such as Augustus, who recoils from one stifling image of death, Ptolemy's, as if he were a mere handful of ashes, and yet makes the memory of Alexander's death the point of origin of his heroic deeds.

In the preface to his *De genealogia deorum gentilium*, Boccaccio undertakes to explain to the king the structure he will impart to his mythographic compilation, and he wonders whether he can adequately extract the hidden meanings from the myths' *involucra*. "Who in our day can penetrate the heart of the Ancients?" he asks, "Who can bring to light and life again minds long since removed in death? Who can elicit their meaning? A divine task that—not human! The Ancients departed in the way of all flesh, leaving behind them their literature and their famous names for posterity to interpret according to their own judgment."[22] His answer to these questions defines for us his kinship with and distance from Petrarch's vision.

For Boccaccio, death makes the past wholly irretrievable, and this is the source of his vitalism as the desire to imaginatively turn away from the thought of death. But at the same time the collapse of the ancient myths marks the beginning of his *De genealogia*, which can only be a personal commentary on those myths. Petrarch, on the other hand, grants that history is under the dominion of death and that through history, which records the virtues of illustrious men, death enters life. But like Boccaccio the mythographer, Petrarch the historiographer shows (and from this viewpoint the anecdote he tells of Augustus is both synecdoche and metaphor of *De viris illustribus*) how in history life and death are never worlds apart, each hermetically sealed from and opposed to the other. On the contrary, life and death steadily communicate with each other, and each, in spite of the other, remains forever within the other. The Re-naissance, as it were, is the story of a life which circumscribes and is in turn circumscribed by finitude and death.

For Petrarch, as for Boccaccio, culture or historical action and reflection emerge from the heart of death and are a dialogue with it. But the *exemplum* he tells of Augustus (who is for Petrarch a repeated point of reference, as the *Epistle to Posterity* records) signals a poignant discrepancy and kinship between the emperor and himself in the oblique analogy he establishes between them. Leaving aside any possible irony in Petrarch's recalling Augustus, the analogy reveals his desire for a *translatio* of power, from the realms of politics to one of culture in the understanding that culture is politics. More to our concern, the historiographer chooses his sources and material as does the emperor, but there is a difference between them. Whereas Alexander's tombstone triggers Augustus's conquest of Egypt, Petrarch confronts the finitude of history, as Cola had done, but, unlike Cola or Augustus, he displaces the memories of the past and makes them building blocks of culture. In his humanistic vision, that he shares with Boccaccio, culture, which is the locus of divisions and conflicts, is the history of the future, and it is to be characterized by the values and meanings he struggles to control and impart to it.

It would be easy to show that in *Rerum memorandarum libri*, a compilation modeled on *Facta et dicta memorabilia* of Valerius Maximus, the values of history are viewed essentially in terms of the glitter with which culture is invested by Petrarch. Let us recall, to begin with, that the figures included in this compendium are not exclusively drawn, as happens in *De viris illustribus*, from the rubric of the Roman past. The boundaries of both space and time stretch into modernity (King Robert is present) and beyond the confines of Rome (there are memorable examples so-called *externa* as distinct from those specifically *romana*). Prominence is given to examples collected under the heading of "De studio et doctrina," where are to be found, among others, the lives of Livy, Pliny, Pythagoras, and a contemporary such as King Robert of Sicily, who in 1341 had cross-examined and proclaimed Petrarch worthy of the laurel crown. King Robert's passion for and mastery of humanistic studies—he was, in the widest sense, a student of philosophy, the sciences, and the Scriptures—cast him as a king-philosopher, who, as such, embodies for Petrarch the moral standard of action wedded to and inspired by knowledge.

The narrative of King Robert in *Rerum memorandarum libri* revolves around the notion that with his science and philosophy the king has attained absolute authority over all his subjects. Petrarch himself, by agreeing to be examined in Naples by the king, in fact acknowledges the king's mastery and dominance over the man of letters. But because for Petrarch the king's mastery has its pivot in his recognition of the power and prestige of the realm of letters (he would rather lose the crown, Petrarch has him say, than the "literae"), the general configuration of power between king and poet is reversible. In his perception of the distance separating Petrarch from him, Cola di Rienzo, it turns out, had lucidly uncovered the genuine scope and tyranny of Petrarch's historical-political discourse: the knowledge and production of literature are the constant measure by which power is determined and assigned.

This historical world of cultural discourse that Petrarch maps for his times and for the future constitutes both his modernity and his difference from the classical schemes of Roman politics. In keeping with his vision of the empire or republic of letters, of which he relentlessly reinvents the languages, molds the values, and establishes the foundation, Petrarch casts himself as the real hero, the spiritual head who aspires to be the educator of tyrants and princes.[23] From this perspective, the letter he writes in 1373 to Francesco da Carrara is especially valuable because in it he overtly insists that the prince must reserve the place of honor for the men of letters, as Augustus had done with Vergil, Varro, Ovid for a time, and Padua's own Livy, "the father of history" (p. 76).

The letter's force partly lies in the fact that Petrarch's political focus is here contracted. In hindsight, it seems that he has bracketed any possible lingering illusion that a *renovatio imperii* may be established, and he fixes his attention on the conduct of city government, on the ways in which general ideas, of which he is the bearer, have an impact on life. Nor does he think, as he says Plato did, that "the characteristics of a nation could be changed by changing the character of its music" (p. 73). Like Cicero, from whose *De legibus* (3.14.31) he is quoting, he believes that "a transformation takes place in a nation's character when the habits and mode of living of its aristocracy are changed" (p. 73). Ethics reemerges as Petrarch's form of thought for cultivating the elites and organizing the chaotic and fragmented experience of city life. But Petrarch, mindful no doubt of his past bonds with Gian Galeazzo Visconti, also knew, as the letter to Seneca shows (*Fam.* 24.5), both the tyrant's resistance to being educated and the teacher's delusion that a "savage beast" such as Nero can ever be tamed.[24]

By Seneca's failure to educate the emperor, Petrarch etches, as the next chapter will show, a view of history that decisively reappears in the *Canzoniere*. History is not pedagogical in a practical sense of the term; nor is it merely a story with a univocal moral lesson. The failure to shape the public world or to mold the mind of the prince, however, does not devalue history. Rather, history remains the crucial mode of understanding and self-understanding, and its truth lies in its disclosure of the temporal nature of existence. Petrarch is truly a historiographer when he constructs the poetic hermeneutics of his own life.

CHAPTER VI

Orpheus: Rhetoric and Music

In a memorable, Shelley-like page on Petrarch, Fredi Chiappelli wrote movingly of the poet's "obstinate will to climb beyond the shadows and perceive a free and perpetual image."[1] This characterization of Petrarch's restless quest comes now to mind as a silent gesture summoning us to reflect on how magisterially Chiappelli himself would traverse the shadowy, circuitous bypaths of Petrarch's style and on how relentlessly he would descend to the depths of that style and conjure up the "phantasms" of the poet's reveries.[2] But it also comes now to mind for the conceptual precision of the insight. Petrarch, one could say, following Chiappelli's lead, is, like Orpheus and from this narrow viewpoint like Dante, a poet of shadows. The shadows enthrall his vision, force him to gaze at them, and they ask to be imaginatively brought back to life by the poet's music and rhetoric. The myth of Orpheus plays a pivotal role in bringing together the issues of rhetoric and music, which for Dante constitute the essence of poetry and which, as I proceed to show, figure prominently in Petrarch's *Canzoniere*.[3]

There are in the *Canzoniere* a number of political poems, such as song 28, "O aspettata in Ciel beata et bella" (O soul awaited in Heaven, blessed and beautiful), song 53, "Spirto gentile" (Noble spirit), and song 128, "Italia mia" (My Italy). These poems have received considerable attention by scholars who have sought to shed light on what has often seemed to be Petrarch's contradictory and unclear political vision. If the political substance of these poems cannot be easily drawn within the general framework of a coherent ideology, they nonetheless all share a common essential concern. In a primary way, what each poem dramatizes is the poet's retrieval of classical eloquence, the discourse which belongs to the deliberative sphere of rhetoric. In the pages that follow I shall describe the sense of this retrieval, and I shall also pose a question which is usually brushed aside in the summations of the *Canzoniere*. What is the role of Petrarch's vatic, public utterances in a private love story which, as the praise of the beloved (the very name Laura, as has been remarked earlier, comes from *laus,* meaning praise), can be said to be under the aegis of epideictic rhetoric?[4]

That rhetoric, in the sense of eloquence, should appear prominently dramatized in the *Canzoniere* cannot come as a surprise. Texts such as *Invective contra medicum* and *On His Own Ignorance,* as has been shown earlier, provide sufficient evidence for Petrarch's view of eloquence as the ground of culture and the tool for its reorganization. Whereas for Dante, to state it simply, theology is the queen of the sciences, for Petrarch oratory is the discipline that encompasses ethics, poetry, and historiography. "The orator," Petrarch writes, "must master not only rhetoric but the whole of philosophy and the knowledge of everything else."[5] More precisely, rhetoric is the weapon by which the finespun abstractions of dialecticians, those who want to exclude rhetoric from the boundaries of rigorous knowledge, as well as the empty formulas of the Averroists and, in general, the myths of scientism are dismissed. The stings of speech, as Petrarch adds, have the power to arouse the sleepy and lift up those who are prostrate to the highest thoughts and to virtuous desire.

Such a concern with kindling passions is at the center of both the love poems and the political poems of the *Canzoniere.* Song 28, for instance, begins with an apostrophe to the soul of an unmentioned figure who embodies the Christian values of wisdom and service that Petrarch upholds.[6] More precisely, he is the man who, by force of his eloquence, can arouse the Italians to join the other Christians in their plans to free the Holy Land from the Moslems. The picture Petrarch draws in the poem is one of the molds of Western history cracking under the weight of Moslem oppression: to counter the breakdown of the West, he urges the Christians to do battle against the powers of darkness. The poem, in effect, is organized in terms of a clear-cut antithesis between the two Augustinian cities of Jerusalem and Babylon. In the second stanza, for instance, there is an allusion to the city of Jerusalem as the Christian city ("Ma quel benigno Re che 'l ciel governa, / al sacro loco ove fu posto in croce, / gli occhi per grazia gira") [ll. 22–24]) (But that good King who governs Heaven in His grace turns His eyes to the holy place where He was crucified). The stanza ends with a reference to the Moslem world as Babylon.

This antithesis of the two archetypal eschatological cities is given a secular, Roman definition by the description of the Christian West in Vergilian language. The third stanza evokes the various people of

France, Spain, and Portugal, the lands where "sona / dottrina del santissimo Elicona" (ll. 39–40) (sounds the knowledge of sacred Helicon), getting ready to undertake the Crusade. These people are referred to as "varie di lingue et d'arme et de le gonne" (l. 41) (differing in language and arms and costume). The line translates Vergil's "varied in their armor and their dress as in their languages" (*Aeneid* 8.723). In the *Aeneid* the line brings to a climax the *ecphrasis* of Aeneas's shield, on which Vulcan had wrought the story of Italy as well as the dazzling future triumphs of Rome.

As he reviews the savagery of Roman wars and the conquered nations appear marching in long processions, Vergil proleptically displays the fulfillment of the gods' promise, the divine gift of a world subdued to Roman hegemony. In Petrarch's poem the Vergilian allusion functions primarily as the imaginative recall of a past power that the degenerate historical present ought to emulate. It also functions as a technique to show Petrarch's sense of the inextricable unity of Rome and Christendom. But there is a great deal of irony visible in the Vergilian recall. For whereas Vergil speaks of a world of history and real actions, Petrarch, by an overt reversal, dramatizes how tarnished is the glory of the Vergilian world and how Italy is now a heap of ruins under the "giogo antico" (l. 62) (ancient yoke). In short, the world of history is for Petrarch the space of vanishing vestiges, of ghostly emblems of a past reality, and the past mythic actions of Rome survive only as the nostalgia of the poet's fantasy.

Vergil's language, in Petrarch's imaginative resuscitation of it, in fact asserts the cleavage between events and their literary accounts. From this standpoint, eloquence comes forth as an activity that embalms history and encloses it in the folds of its imaginative powers. At the same time, the poem is the parable of the dead memories and of impossible hopes for future epic actions. Nonetheless—and here lies the peculiar energy of the poem—Petrarch seeks to invest with a material substantiality what is retrieved as pure memory of the past heroic age. In effect, the poem explicitly contemplates the possibility that the poet's words produce events. The mythical figures for the transformation of eloquence into action are Orpheus and Amphion:

Dunque ora è 'l tempo da ritrare il collo
dal giogo antico, et da squarciare il velo
ch'è stato avolto intorno a gli occhi nostri,

et che 'l nobile ingegno che dal cielo
per grazia tien de l'immortale Apollo,
et l'eloquentia sua vertù qui mostri
   or con la lingua, or co' laudati 'ncostri.
Perchè d'Orfeo leggendo et d'Anfione
se non ti meravigli,
assai men fia ch'Italia co' suoi figli
si desti al suon del tuo chiaro sermone,
tanto che per Jhesù la lancia pigli. (ll. 61–72)

Therefore it is time to withdraw our neck from the ancient yoke and to rend the veil that has been wrapped over our eyes; let your noble mind, which you hold from Heaven by grace of the immortal Apollo, and your eloquence now show their power both through speech and through praiseworthy writings. For if reading of Orpheus and Amphion you are not amazed, the marvel will be even less when Italy with her sons wakes at the sound of your clear voice, so that she takes up her lance for Jesus: if this ancient mother looks at the truth, in none of her quarrels were there ever reasons so lovely and so gay.

That Petrarch's models for the powers of eloquence should be Orpheus and Amphion is somewhat predictable. Amphion, as one gathers from Horace's *Ars poetica* (ll. 394–96) and Statius's *Thebaid* (10.873–77), is the founder of Thebes' citadel. By the sound of his lyre, we are told, and by his supplicating spell, Amphion moves stones and leads them whither he would. The myth of Orpheus, on the other hand, is that of the poet who, by the sound of his harp or lyre, tames the beasts and charms the gods of the lower world in order to bring back to life Eurydice. Orpheus's own name is generally interpreted as *oraia phone* (that is, best voice), and his poetic activity is identified as the action of eloquence.[7] In a number of commentaries on Boethius's *De consolatione philosophiae* (3.12), such as that of William of Conches and Nicholas Trivet, we are consistently told that by "Orpheus we should understand the part of the intellect which is instructed in wisdom and eloquence [Orpheus ponitur pro quolibet sapiente et eloquente, et inde Orpheus dicitur quasi Oraphone, id est optima vox]; whence he is said to be the son of . . . Calliope, who is one of the nine muses . . . because he represents eloquence . . . and Apollo, the god of wisdom, because he instructed Orpheus in wisdom."[8] In these allegorical accounts the moral value assigned to Orpheus depends on his loss of Eurydice when, against the gods' prohibition, he glances backward. Eurydice is interpreted by Arnulf d'Orléans as vice, because "poisoned by the serpent, that is misled by the deceits of this life, . . . she judged the false and transitory things of this life to be durable and true."[9]

But Petrarch brackets in the poem Orpheus's loss of Eurydice, and the bracketing compels us into some legitimate speculations. In a way, the unnamed figure in song 28, "O aspettata in Ciel beata et bella," is literally unlike Orpheus. This soul is directed heavenward, whereas Orpheus's journey is a *katabasis,* a descent into the depths. In allegorical terms, however, they can be said to be alike, for the two figures signify the intellect's ascent to heaven after renouncing earthly cares. In renouncing earthly cares, Orpheus cannot animate the dead figure of Eurydice, and his song and eloquence are inexorably suspended in the void of a pure utterance. In the measure in which the unnamed hero is like Orpheus, moreover, the implication is that the eloquence of Petrarch's addressee also will fall short, like Orpheus's, of its target and fail in its stated aim to move the Italians to action. The consciousness that eloquence is unable to create history comes forth clearly in the *envoi* of song 28:

> Tu vedrai Italia et l'onorata riva,
> canzon, ch'a gli occhi miei cela et contende
> non mar, non poggio o fiume
> ma solo Amor, che del suo altero lume
> più m'invaghisce dove più m'incende,
> nè natura può star contra 'l costume.
> Or movi, non smarrir l'altre compagne,
> che non pur sotto bende
> alberga Amor, per cui si ride et piagne. (ll. 106–14)

Song, you will see Italy and the honored shore that is hidden from my eyes not by sea, mountain, or river, but only by Love, who with his noble light makes me desirous where he most enflames me: nor can nature resist habit. Now go, do not lose your other companions, for not only under a woman's veil does Love dwell, for whom we laugh and weep.

The passage states the poet's political-moral estrangement, his separation from the spiritual and martial pilgrimage to Jerusalem that the poem passionately calls for. There is no doubt that this assertion of the poet's solitude is a rhetorical move to dramatize the intensity of his love for Laura, who is the cause of his paralyzed will. But the move also denounces Petrarch's undeluded insight into the failure of political eloquence to sway and engender heroic deeds. In effect, the song articulates Petrarch's desire that eloquence be revived from its historical decay, that the declamatory art of discourse regain its prestige and power. At the same time, the poem discloses the futility of its own gesture.

A possible cause for this negative understanding of the power of rhetoric lies in Petrarch's ironic view of European political realities. As I have shown earlier, song 28 is structured along a simplified antithetical scheme of the two Augustinian cities: Babylon, which traditionally means the city of confusion of tongues, crystallizes the spiritual confusion of the Moslem world, and Jerusalem, which etymologically is *visio pacis,* is the Christian city. This polarity, however, resolves into a chiasmus, for the Christian Jerusalem, the city of peace, is, ironically, called to arms, and Rome, actually, is under the aegis of Mars:

> Tu ch' 'ai per arricchir d'un bel thesauro
> volte l'antiche et le moderne carte,
> volando al ciel colla terrena soma,
> sai, da l'imperio del figliuol de Marte
> al grande Augusto che di verde lauro
> tre volte triunfando ornò la chioma
>   ne l'altrui ingiurie del suo sangue Roma
> spesse fiate quanto fu cortese. (ll. 76–83)

> You who, to grow rich with a true treasure, have turned the ancient and the modern pages, flying up to Heaven even though in earthly body, you know—from the reign of the son of Mars to the great Augustus, who with green laurel thrice in triumph crowned his brow—who generous Rome often was with her blood when others were injured.

By the same token, the Christian countries appear as "varie di lingue et d'arme et de le gonne" (l. 41). The line implies that Rome succeeded in subduing the variety of people under its rule. It also literally describes Europe as another Babylon, a place of a variety of languages, customs, and arms. Finally, the successive stanza, which describes the German nation, the "tedesco furor" (l. 53) (Teutonic rage), as "nemica naturalmente di pace" (l. 50) (naturally the enemy of rest), blurs the moral opposition on which the poem is articulated, and, as it reverses Jerusalem into Babylon, it reveals the initial clear-cut demarcation of spiritual values to be illusory.

This ironic understanding of political eloquence does not occur only in this instance. The other two major political poems, "Spirto gentil" and "Italia mia," can also be shown to share the ambivalences of song 28. Song 53, "Spirto gentil," much like song 28 starts with an apostrophe to an unnamed figure. In the case of Laura, as has been shown earlier in this book, the power of the name is steadily acknowledged. Why is the name silenced in this poem? Scholars have long sought to identify the addressee variously as the Roman tribune Cola di Rienzo or as the soul, in the Scholastic sense of the word, of the character who is being apostrophized. The presence of this periphrastic construction in the apostrophe, here as in song 28, can be accounted for in a number of ways. It possibly implies that the referent is too well known to be explicitly mentioned; it also suggests the necessity for this stylistic *reticentia,* for the whole point of the poem is the vision of a time when the hero will earn "fama," a name for himself. "Fama," it may be added, is the other name of Clio, the Muse of history. For Petrarch, the inscription of self in the annals of history can only take place by accomplishing worthy deeds in the future:

> Però che quanto 'l mondo si ricorda
> ad uom mortale non fu aperta la via
> per farsi, come a te, di fama eterno,
> che puoi drizzar s'i' non falso discerno,
> in stato la piu nobil monarchia.
> Quanta gloria ti fia
> dir: "Gli altri l'aitar giovene et forte,
> questi in vecchiezza la scampò da morte." (song 53, ll. 91–98)

For, as long as the world can remember, to no mortal man was ever the way so open, as it is to you, to make himself eternal in fame; for you can raise to her feet, if I do not discern falsely, the most noble monarchy in the world. How much glory for you will be the saying: "The others helped her when she was young and strong: this man rescued her from death in her old age!"

The eternity that fame promises is, in fact, the transformation of a life into a legend. This promise is the reward for the power of the unmentioned hero (who has the attributes of *sapientia et fortitudo*—he is "valoroso accorto et saggio" [l. 3] [valorous, knowing, and wise]) who is the one likely to stir Italy from her spiritual drowsiness, to revive her from her sleep. A symmetrical balance, then, coordinates the song. The poet, who is here cast in the vatic posture of an Orpheus, deploys his eloquence in order to move the man of action to action. As a counterpoint, the man of action, referred to in terms of the strength of his arms to shake and lift the decrepit body politic of Italy, will be transformed into a poetic myth.

This symmetrical balance is not just a technical feature of song 53. It is, on the contrary, a sign of the organic bond Petrarch wishes to establish between *vita activa* and *vita contemplativa*, between the man of eloquence and the man of deeds. This organic link is given in terms of an explicit erotic bond that should join together the various entities of the political order. Thus, at the very outset, Italy is described through a personification: "Italia, che suoi guai non par che senta, / vecchia oziosa et lenta; / dormirà sempre et non fia chi la svegli? / Le man l'avess'io avolto entro 'capegli" (ll. 11–14) (What Italy expects or yearns for I do not know, for she does not seem to feel her woes, being old, idle and slow. Will she sleep forever, and will no one ever awaken her? Might I have my hand clutched in her hair!). The personification of Italy as a woman and Rome as its head enacts the theory of the *corpus politicum,* which is traditionally figured as a symbolic analogy between the biological body and the state, and which envisions the state as if it were an organic entity made up of interdependent, living parts. To accept the view of the state as an organic analogy to the human body logically entails the recognition that the state is not a mechanical conglomeration of interests but possesses a real capacity for an intellectual-moral activity. But it also implies that its reordering cannot be a matter of sheer contingency or of an a priori expectation of the periodic rejuvenation of the world, as in the Pythagorean *meta-cosmesis,* over the span of what is known as the great year, the cycle of 360,000 years when the world returns to its pristine purity.

The reordering, in Petrarch's vision, can be possible by an act of the will: actually, the man of action has to be, in a further extension of the organic metaphor sustaining the song, husband and father to Italy. The phrase "Tu marito, tu padre" (l. 82) (You be her husband, you her father) echoes Lucan's *Pharsalia,* the epic poem of the Roman civil war, in which Cato is called father and husband of Rome. That Petrarch should evoke here Lucan's text is apt. Lucan is understood by a long line of medieval literary theorists and compilers stretching from Isidore of Seville to Dante's *Convivio* not as a poet but as a historian.[10] By recalling Lucan and, obliquely, his poetics, Petrarch, in effect, conveys his desire to come through as the poet of history, and he is aware, no doubt, that Lucan's idea of history is one of generalized madness.[11] Lucan's epic discourse radically reverses Vergil's lingering and ironic faith in the Roman Empire. Lucan's perception about Roman history is the poetic background, as it were, for Petrarch's sense of the disintegration of Rome on which the reference to Cato in his role of father and husband focuses. Traditionally in medieval political theology the epithalamium between the figurehead and the state takes place in a garden. But Italy is now a wilderness in which ravenous beasts are prowling: "Orsi, lupi, leoni, aquile e serpi" (l. 71) (Bears, wolves, lions, eagles, and snakes). The enumeration deploys primarily the medieval moralized bestiaries; it also literalizes the wild, predatory attributes both enshrined in and concealed by the allegorical emblems of the great Italian families (the "bears" of the Orsini, the snakes of the Caetani, and so forth), which are the cause of present history's tragic disarray.

The presence of a literary echo from Lucan's epic in a lyrical-political poem forces a digression on Petrarch's own relation to the epic genre. The reduction of the complexity of Lucan's epic discourse to a textual, lyrical fragment in song 53 marks Petrarch's consciousness of both the historical-political fragmentation he lucidly describes in song 53 and the impossibility he painfully felt all his life of completing the projected epic or historical poem *Africa*. It is not without significance that he conceived the idea for such an epic after beholding the grandiose spectacle of the Roman ruins in 1338. Characteristically, in the *Epistle to Posterity*, the date he gives for the inspiration to such an undertaking is Good Friday. But in *Familiares* 2.14, it is the "reliquie" of Rome—greater than what he could ever imagine—that he records: *Africa* was conceived from the start in the shadow and in the recollection of these relics, and it was destined to remain itself a heap of fragments. The ideological hub of the poem—the celebration of Scipio's heroism in Rome's Second Punic War—which Petrarch had found in Livy's histories and in Cicero's *Somnium Scipionis*, was certainly a worthy theme for a unified epic. Accordingly, Petrarch's strategy is to recapitulate the *notitia vetustatis*, the findings of his laborious bibliographical research, as well as the voice of the epic and poetic tradition—Vergil, Ennius, Ovid, Horace, and others. But visible through these fragments is an imaginative impulse that counters and radically undermines the historical thematics. An example from book 2 of *Africa* will suffice. The narrative focuses on a dream: the shade of Publius Scipio appears to his son, Scipio the African, and he voices his elegiac vision of a future world wherein Rome's own dream of political hegemony over people of different languages is shattered. Time, the force that devours all things, encroaches upon the impulse to construct a totalizing, epic universe:

> Omnia nata quidem pereunt et adulta fatiscunt;
> nec manet in rebus quicquam mortalibus;
> . . . Facili labuntur saecula passu:
> tempora diffugiunt; . . . (2.344–48)

> All things which are born die, and grown in age wear out; nothing remains in what is mortal; . . . the centuries flow fast: the times get lost.[12]

This sense of time's power, whereby all designs are fragile and the desire to "producere nomen" (2.408) (make a name) and pursue glory—a central concern, if there ever was any, of Petrarch's humanism—is now madness, climaxes in Petrarch's dramatization of the death of, first, Sophonisba and, later, the young Magone (book 6): their deaths sanction the very death of the heroic imagination. To paraphrase Scipio's words in his dream, human beings and their deeds are faint shadows on the great stage of the world, and the world is a reliquary of those memories.

The hint of the necessary failure of the epic in song 53 can be formulated as follows: the poet's hope is that the man of action, like Orpheus, may tame the beasts and, like Orpheus and Amphion, may restore the stones of Rome: "L'antiche mura ch'ancor teme et ama / et trema 'l mondo quando si rimembra / del tempo andato e 'n dietro si rivolve, . . . tutto quel ch'una ruina involve" (ll. 29–35) (The ancient walls, which the world still fears and loves and trembles at when it remembers past time and looks back . . . and everything which this one ruin carries down). But this dream turns out to be insubstantial. For Cato, who is the historical model for the unnamed hero, succumbs to the predicament of the civil war and commits suicide. In a way, the recall of Lucan's text, as I have stated above, gives Petrarch a tragic paradigm of history: it exemplifies the persistent, aberrant recurrence of civil war within the Roman body politic. There is, furthermore, another textual element that dismantles Petrarch's political rhetoric and assigns it to the realm of an erotic wish. The last stanza is written in the mode of a *congé d'amour*:

Sopra 'l monte Tarpeio, canzon, vedrai
un cavalier ch'Italia tutta honora,
pensoso più d'altrui che di se stesso.
Digli: "Un che non ti vide ancor da presso,
se non come per fama uom s'innamora,
dice che Roma ognora,
con gli occhi di dolor bagnati e molli
ti chier mercè da tutti sette i colli." (ll. 99–106)

On the Tarpeian Mount, Song, you will see a knight whom all Italy honors, who cares more for others than for himself. Say to him: "One who has not yet seen you from close by, except as one falls in love through fame, says that Rome now with her eyes wet with tears keeps crying out to you for mercy from all her seven hills."

Unmistakably, the link between the poet and the "cavalier" is rendered through a convention of the Provençal love lyric. It alludes to the *amor de lonh*, the representation of desire as distance, which a troubadour such as Jaufré Rudel has prominently voiced. What the *amor de lonh* essentially tells in Jaufré's *vida* is the story of the poet-lover who, on hearing of the legendary beauty of a faraway woman, yields to the seductive fame of this beauty and undertakes what is known as a *peregrinatio amoris*. This is the journey of love, and, appropriately, at the end of the journey the lover dies, for the truth of love, as Petrarch fully knows, is to be at one with displacement and absence.

The shift from a political rhetoric to a love rhetoric, which is also signaled by the use of a Provençalism such as "chier" (l. 106), is not drastic. The love rhetoric, as I have shown, was present from the start in the metaphor of marriage, in the personification of Italy as a woman, and in the poet's wished-for erotic violence on the hair. It is also present in the *boustrophedon* Roma/Amor discreetly deployed in the syllables of the word "innamora" and in the two words "innamora . . . Roma." Retrospectively, this rhetoric casts the song as the poet's desire of and quest for a world of action which is finally disclosed as one of absence.

It is even possible to suggest, in effect, that Petrarch attempts to write political poems, but as their rhetoric fails, the failure gives him the alibi to retreat from a ghostly, unrealizable world of history to the obsessive absorption with his own private self, who is simultaneously empowered by love and powerless in love. A broad analog for this pattern occurs in St. Augustine's internalized quest, his confessional introspection, in the face of the collapse of the world of objective reality—the fall of Rome and, with it, the fall of the myth of the eternal earthly city. More to our concern, what joins the political and private poems in Petrarch is the rhetoric of absence as well as the question of sound, the music of linguistic utterances which unavoidably recoil from their objects, which alone is heard when the statement is voided of referential signification.

In song 28 the question of sound is explicitly linked to the myth of Orpheus: "Assai men fia ch'Italia co' suoi figli / si desti al suon del tuo chiaro sermone" (ll. 70–71) (The marvel will be even less when Italy with her sons awakes at the sound of your clear voice). The phrase "chiaro sermone" (clear voice), which is a faint recall of Dante's "chiare parole" (*Paradiso* 17.34), implies not the language of enigmas or the technique of wrapping truth in dark utterances but the plain eloquence coupled with passionate conviction. At the same time, "suon" is a metaphor that extends the reference to Orpheus two lines earlier and describes the seductively melodic quality of his song. We are all too familiar with the myth of the Thracian poet's sorrowful music and the incantatory power of his sounds, which make the woodland dance and the rivers stand still (*De consolatione philosophiae* 3.12). Petrarchan scholarship, however, has not explored the links between music and rhetoric that come together in the figure of Orpheus. Yet the link between the two arts and the myth of Orpheus were probed by Petrarch's beloved Quintilian in his *Institutio oratoria:*

> Orpheus and Linus . . . were regarded as uniting the roles of musician, poet and philosopher. Both were of divine origin, while the former, because of the marvel of his music, soothed the savage breasts of the wild, rocks and trees. So too Timagenes asserts that music is the oldest of the arts related to literature, a statement which is confirmed by the testimony of the greatest of poets in whose songs we have read that the praise of heroes and of gods were sung to the music of the lyre at the feast of kings. Does not Iopas, the Vergilian bard, sing "The wandering moon and the labours of the sun?" [*Aeneid* 1.742] and the like? Whereby the supreme poet manifests most clearly that music is united with the knowledge even of things divine. . . . There can in any case be no doubt that some of those men whose wisdom is a household word have been earnest students of music: Pythagoras, for instance, and his followers popularized the belief . . . that the universe is constructed on the same principles which were afterward imitated in the construction of the lyre. (1.10.9–12)

The yoking of rhetoric and music in Quintilian (which one can also find in Dante's *Convivio:* "molti si dilettavano studiare in Rettorica o in Musica" [3.11.9] [Many found delight in studying rhetoric or music] and in Boccaccio's *De genealogia deorum gentilium* [2.2.5]) is fully thematized in Petrarch's *Canzoniere.* The phonocentrism of the text is apparent from a number of overt elements. The literary forms Petrarch deploys—the song, the ballad, and the sonnet—reflect in themselves the musical origin of all poetry. While the etymology of "sonnet," from *sonitus,* calls attention to its acoustic origin, the song is understood in Dante's *De vulgari eloquentia* (2.8.6) as "nihil aliud esse videtur quam cantio completa dictantis verba modulatione armonizata" (nothing other than the complete action of one who writes, according to art, harmonized words for a musical setting).[13] More than that, the poems are systematically punctuated by references to musical instruments and terms (for example, *lira, cetra, tromba, choro, concento, caccia, voce*). The song is acknowledged as having the power to rectify the lover's perturbation of mind ("perchè cantando il duol si disacerba" [song 23, l. 4] [because, singing, pain becomes less bitter]); the vision of the poet's troubled heart as the battlefield of discordant strains depends on the mythography of Mars as the planet where music is assigned; the references to Orpheus, Amphion, and Apollo, the god versed in the secrets of music, poetry, and love, as well as the description of the natural world (such as swan, nightingale, swallow) and its sounds, are all elements which suggest that music is the aesthetic principle governing Petrarch's *Canzoniere.*

The centrality of this musical aesthetics in Petrarch has a primarily historical value, and I shall give here a brief synopsis of the problem. It is well known that whereas Provençal poetry is sung (the lute is the troubadour's instrument), the Sicilian poets' innovation was to separate from each other the sister arts of music and poetry. In *Purgatorio,* book 2, the conjunction between music and poetry is presented in the mode of nostalgia in the pilgrim's encounter with Casella, who sings Dante's own song, "Amor che ne la mente mi ragiona" (l. 112) (Love that discourses in my mind). It is Petrarch, however, who deliberately absorbs music into poetry and dramatizes the *rhythmica sonoritas* in his poems.

On the face of it, music is not to be understood merely as the *concinnitas,* the harmonious effect produced by the deployment of antitheses, parallelisms, assonances, alliterations, meter, and rhyme.

It is possible, actually, to inscribe Petrarch's aesthetic practice both within medieval musical theories and within the traditional meditations on music as an art of the quadrivium. Yet Petrarch's modernity, which scholars almost formulaically acknowledge but never define with any great precision, lies in his steady interest in the artistic experiments of his day. The traditional arts of the trivium and quadrivium are rigorously rethought by him, but he supplements them with the new arts such as painting and music. I have conducted elsewhere the analysis of his imaginative and intellectual concern for painting.[14] Let me stress for now that a sure emblem of his redefinition of the traditional encyclopedia of knowledge can be found in his keen promotion of the new musical theories that react against the polyphony of the north—the *ars antiqua* systematized by Johannes de Garlandia, Hieronymus of Moravia, and Johannes de Grocheo.

It would be impossible, let me say at the start, to guess the importance Petrarch attaches to music for poetry if one were to read Petrarch's dialogue on music. As is known, the dialogue is part of *De remediis utriusque fortunae* and is carried out by two allegorical figures, Joy and Reason. The dialectic between the two abstractions is fairly simple. Joy states her delight in song and the music of string instruments, and Reason counters that a better delight is found in tears and sighs. The two viewpoints are sustained throughout the unfolding of the text: thus, Joy points out the charms of music or how soothing music can be; Reason, on the other hand, responds by telling the story of Arion and the dolphins or by alluding to the Sirens' song as evidence of how music tricks wild animals. In brief, from Reason's perspective, mirth is shallow. Within this context, Reason recounts how Athanasius forbade the use of singing in church in order to ward off vanity; how Ambrose decrees that songs should be used reverently; and how Augustine in his *Confessions* admits to doubts about the spiritual value of music. Finally, Reason refuses to believe that Socrates in his old age devoted his efforts to the harp and concludes that the best music is that of the blessed, the song of the angels, and the Pythagorean music of the spheres.

If one were to follow from this dialogue, which owes so much to Isidore of Seville's reflections on music, one would hardly believe that Petrarch cared so much about music that in his *Testament* he refers to the lute he played or that the musician whom he called Socrates (the

Flemish Ludwig van Kempen) was his lifelong friend. He shares with his friend Pierre Bersuire an ardent enthusiasm for the *ars nova* of Philippe de Vitry, known as the heir to Orpheus and repeatedly hailed by Petrarch as a philosopher of that age.[15] In point of fact, however, Petrarch is also a friend of Louis Sanctus (Lodewijk Heyligen), whose *Sententia subiecti in musica sonora,* a treatise on *musica instrumentalis,* seeks to expand the technical innovations performed by Philippe de Vitry.

Petrarch's project of cultural renewal does not break, however, with the philosophical speculations of Boethius and Cassiodorus but resumes their view of music as the paradigm of the harmonious arrangement of the universe. It is well known that ever since Boethius three varieties of music are distinguished. There is *musica mundana,* which is characteristic of the planets and, as Hugh of St. Victor puts it, focuses "on the seasons, days (the alternation of day and night), months (the waxing and waning of the moon), years (the succession of spring, summer, autumn and winter)." The second is *musica humana,* the music of man, some of which is characteristic of "the body, some of the soul, and some of the bond between the two. . . . Music is characteristic of the soul partly in its virtues, like justice, piety and temperance; and partly in its powers, like reason, wrath and concupiscence." The third is *musica instrumentalis,* which consists partly of "striking, as upon tympani, partly in blowing as upon pipes; and partly in giving voice, as in recitals and songs."[16]

These various elements—philosophical, moral, and technical—are fully deployed in the *Canzoniere,* as if Petrarch meant to create a harmony within his own self and between his self and the order of the macrocosm.[17] But this wished-for harmony always seems to be outside of his reach. A brief examination of the first sonnet exemplifies this claim:

Voi ch'ascoltate in rime sparse il suono
di quei sospiri ond'io nudriva 'l core
in sul mio primo giovenile errore,
quand'era in parte altr'uom da quel ch'io sono:

del vario stile in ch'io piango et ragiono
fra le vane speranze e 'l van dolore,
ove sia chi per prova intenda amore
spero trovar pietà, non che perdono.

Ma ben veggio or sì come al popolo tutto
favola fui gran tempo, onde sovente
di me medesmo meco mi vergogno;

et del mio vaneggiar vergogna è 'l frutto,
e 'l pentersi, e 'l conoscer chiaramente
che quanto piace al mondo è breve sogno.

You who hear in scattered rhymes the sound of those sighs with which I
nourished my heart during my first youthful error, when I was in part
another man from what I am now; for the varied style in which I weep
and speak between vain hopes and vain sorrow, where there is anyone
who understands love through experience, I hope to find pity, not only
pardon. But now I see well how for a long time I was the talk of the
crowd, for which often I am ashamed of myself within; and of my raving,
shame is the fruit, and repentance, and the clear knowledge that what-
ever pleases in the world is a brief dream.

The sonnet, which is placed in the privileged position of opening the
collection, is a palinode in the sense that its ostensible aim is to provide
a principle of moral coherence from the standpoint of which the
paratactic, fragmentary sequence of the poems can be grasped as a
significant totality. From the perspective of the present ("Ma ben
veggio or sì come al popolo tutto"), the past appears as a spectacle of
vanity, a persistent oscillation between vain hope and vain grief. This
hollowness of the past—the epithet "van" is repeated twice and then
becomes the infinitive, "vaneggiar"—produces both shame and the
consciousness, on which the sonnet climaxes, that worldly pleasures
are illusory—"che quanto piace al monde è breve sogno."

The aphorism, which according to the canons of medieval rhet-
oric ought to mark the exordium of a text, condenses the knowledge of
the temporal precariousness of life's pleasures that are said to have the
abruptness and briefness of a dream. This consciousness of the in-
stability of time supports both the grammatical and thematic struc-
tures of the sonnet. The love passion the poems record, which is the
argument of this text, is assigned to the poet's youth and its errors
("giovenile errore"), and we are told that for a long time he was a
"favola" to the people. The word, which in the sense of rhetorical
genre means that which is fictive,[18] here is to be understood ety-
mologically from *fari* as that which is spoken. But if the pleasures of
the world are impermanent and therefore, according to the logic of the
text, deceptive, the poet is still within time. The sonnet displays an

explicit temporal tension: there is the desire to obtain the stability of a moral point of view, signaled by the infinitives scanning the last tercet—"vaneggiar," "pentersi," "conoscer"—as well as by the aphorism which has the unalterable fixity and generalized truth of a maxim.

At the same time, the poet is still caught in the contingencies and predicament of time. He says, using a verb of the future, "spero," that he hopes to find pity. More than that, the sonnet deliberately plays with the ambiguous indeterminacy of what actual changes time has wrought on the poetic self: in the line "quand'era in parte altr'uom da quel ch'io sono," the phrase "in parte" teasingly obscures the notion of whether or not the changes are moral or physical. More than that, the phrase stages Petrarch's sustained insight about the structure of the self: that it is a whole made up of parts. Finally, the rhyme scheme— "suono . . . sono" (ll. 1, 4)—suggests that, for all the poet's efforts to circumvent time and to rise to a selfless realm of temporal stability, the self's being is in time and that being *is* sound. Sound emerges as the acoustic perception of time, as the material audibility of time's arrow in its silent flight.

The "suono," let me add—a term which plays on the etymology of *sonetto* (from *sonitus*) and which is to be understood also in the technical sense of sound, not voice—is not repudiated: it is the metaphoric displacement of the tumultuous strains of the lover's heart. From this perspective the sound is the echo of the inward *concordia discors*. But the sound can overshadow and hamper the moral signification. St. Augustine, writing about the delights of the sense of hearing, acknowledges that when he hears sung "in a sweet and well-trained voice" Church melodies, he is occasionally deceived by the pleasure and is "more moved by the singing than by what is sung"; therefore, he prefers not to hear the music (*Confessions* 10.33). This moral ambiguity of music, its power to excite the mind, to conceal the meaning, and to make one share in the harmony of the world, is at the heart of Petrarch's first sonnet and of the whole of the *Canzoniere*. This ambiguity of music is adumbrated also by the metaphor of shame, which the poet says he feels at his past errors and which he repeats twice in the sonnet. To feel shame is, in a primary way, a strategy by which one abdicates ownership of oneself; by feeling shame one makes others the judge of oneself or judges oneself as others do, which is the same thing. In this sense, shame is the statement of a divided self; it is also theatrical, the narcissistic staging of oneself in the presence of imaginary listeners, the "voi" of the initial apostrophe, who disseminate untrue stories about the lover's past and to whom the poet's own story is addressed. But shame is also a figure of reversal in that it allows the retelling of past errors in the mode of remorse.

The ambivalence of shame is the ambivalence of sound. It would be difficult to read the opening poem of the *Canzoniere*, for all its ambivalent allegory of a new spiritual vision, without being enthralled by the power of its euphony, assonances, and alliteration ("di *me* me*desmo me*co *mi* vergogno," "del mio *v*aneggiar *v*ergogna è 'l *f*rutto," etc.). This stylistic trait is at odds with the tenor of the poem. Yet it announces that sound—perpetually resonant and perpetually vanishing—is the material trace of a rhetorical artifice by which Petrarch confronts and revives the silent harmonies of his tradition. In *De vulgari eloquentia* Dante defines poetry as a "rhetorical fiction set to music." Petrarch, the Apollonian poet, seeks to wrest the secrets of Orpheus's voice from the dim depths of forgetfulness and, thereby, heralds the vital and dismembered sound of the future.

In *The Republic* Plato makes music the instrument of the ideal *paideia* and the model of political association. For Petrarch, music is assigned not to the world of political history but to the interiority of the self and to the breath of poetry. As such, music and rhetoric come to constitute poetry as the new realm of a politics as culture. But can poetry alone be culture's foundation? The next and final chapter will ponder this question.

CHAPTER VII

Humanism and Monastic Spirituality

Possibly on account of his brother Gherardo's decision to enter the Carthusian monastery of Montrieux in 1343, Petrarch ceaselessly turned his thoughts to grasping the depth and substance of a monastic vocation. His steady interest in monastic spirituality is recorded by a host of texts, such as the correspondence he kept with Gherardo; the first eclogue of the *Bucolicum carmen,* which is a self-avowed allegory in which the poet, cast as Silvius, and the monk Gherardo, called Monicus, debate the spiritual distance separating one from the other; *De vita solitaria;* and, above all, *De otio religioso,* which is a systematic meditation on what to Petrarch seems destined to remain the forever elusive realm of the ascetic life.[1]

The opening suggestion that Petrarch discovered the spiritual value of a disciplined religious life through Gherardo's vocation is not to be taken in a deterministic sense. The uniqueness of Petrarch, indeed the uniqueness of any genuine poet, lies in his power to perceive the hidden historical significance of an existential choice. Gherardo's choice of the contemplative life certainly solicits Petrarch's affective memory; it also forces him to confront how, from their common origins and from their common memories, the two brothers could undertake such divergent paths of experience. More poignantly, his brother's vocation brings out in Petrarch the religious longing he had carried deep and constant within himself.

But the impact of Gherardo's call to holiness on Petrarch does not end simply with the personal acknowledgment of a desire, more or less frustrated, for a spiritual renewal. As a matter of fact, the mixture of intimacy and distance Petrarch feels toward Gherardo's journey of faith, toward his power to hear the word of God and to act on that word, summons the poet to rethink the very terms of a possible dialogue between the humanist and the monk. Such a dialogue, no doubt, comes forth primarily as a version of the ancient confrontation between the values of the *vita activa* and those of the *vita contemplativa,* which is conventionally figured through the familiar pairs of Leah and Rachel, Peter and John, Martha and Mary. Since the notion of "dialogue," which is a rhetorical structure Petrarch repeatedly deploys, has a number of important implications for Petrarch's sense of monastic spirituality and for his own sense of individuality and solitude, one should consider, however briefly, the premises and modalities of this genre.[2]

By its very form, the dialogue clearly challenges the assumption that the separate, solitary experiences of the monk and the humanist are hermetically closed off from each other. It establishes, on the contrary, the existence of a viewpoint that transcends the narrow limits of a subjective vision; at the same time it also posits the presence of an "otherness" with which one seeks to correspond. In this sense, the dialogic structure enacts a radical hermeneutical experience because it acknowledges an open exchange between two independent viewpoints and because it does not aim for a mere acquiescence to and convergence on one harmonious synthesis of opposites. Petrarch's own dialogues move lucidly within the horizon of such concerns. One, to be sure, could easily level the objection that his dialogues are in point of fact barely disguised soliloquies. The objection has a certain validity, but it matters little, for Petrarch's own soliloquies are never the unified, consistent voice of an undivided self. Petrarch's soliloquies are radically dialogic (just as much as the dialogues are monologic) in the sense that they epitomize the articulation of a fractured persona—in the etymological understanding of the word, the recognition of contradictory voices lodged in the reflective center of the self. At any rate, the fictive correspondence and dialogue between the humanist and the monk lead Petrarch to formulate a theory of culture that is rooted in leisure, *otium,* which is the core value of monastic contemplation and is the ideal of classical humanism.

The first letter Petrarch writes to Gherardo (*Fam.* 10.3) starts off by drawing attention to the poet's quest for a correspondence between the two of them, although the paramount aim of the dialogue is the poet's confessional self-analysis. Petrarch interrupts his long silence, as well as the novitiate's silence, he says with a mixture of humility and narcissism, so that he may explore his own heart, its desires and regrets, in the light of Gherardo's life of grace: "But now, to confess the truth, I have decided to write you not in your interest but in mine. . . . So while I do speak to you I am thinking of myself in the hope that perchance my worthless heart, sluggish and frozen by long inertia, would be warmed up by your holy ardor."[3]

What emerges from this denudation of a portion of the soul is Petrarch's conviction that one reaches the "self" deviously, that a detour through another's consciousness is a way to one's own desires. From a factual perspective, what emerges is the awareness, which Petrarch steadily restates elsewhere, that there is no durable, objective solidity to the world, that men are dupes of their passions and fashions, and that the anxieties which dominate the human lot are illusory. The marks of the mortality of all flesh, as it were, are palpable everywhere, but the primary metaphor for all that is perishable is fashion, as Petrarch writes:

> You will remember, our vain desire for expensive clothes, which still entraps me today, but daily grows weaker; what trouble we used to take repeatedly putting on and taking off fancy clothes morning and evening; what fear we felt that a single hair might fall out of place or that a light breeze might spoil our elaborate coiffures; or how we tried to avoid animals coming from any direction so that any dirt they kicked up might not soil our perfumed, spotless clothes or so that in the encounter they might not crumple our pressed creases. O true vanity of men, especially of youth.[4]

In this reverberation of memory, fashion, which is a metaphor of time in its fleeting essence and is linked especially to the past time of youth, comes forth as an ascetic, pure pursuit of style and formal perfection, albeit in the inverted realm of worldliness, as an elaborate ceremony of rites and practices and a renunciation of whatever may interfere with the achievement of that perfection. It can also be said that, as a rigorous system of ritual habits (one puts on and takes off clothes according to a rigid code of propriety, such as the hours of the day), fashion, though born from the need for change, seeks to mime, immobilize, or at least conceal the alterations and shifts synonymous with fashion. Petrarch, in short, casts fashion as the delusory perversion of liturgical acts, a perversion which Gherardo, but not the poet, has completely abandoned in favor of the liturgy of the devotional practices of monastic life. His turn to a life of contemplation, a term which etymologically suggests the suspension of time's flow and the turning of one's gaze to thoughts of eternity, is a direct repudiation of fashion's cult of modernity.[5]

The meditation on fashion brings to a head a number of other concerns present in this text. Because it stands for the vacuity of worldly values, for an artifice empty of any substantial content, and for sheer ostentation, fashion dramatizes the principle of life's fundamental theatricality, the belief that *esse est percipi*, that one's existence is reducible to style, to the way one appears, and is perceived on the great stage of the world. More poignantly, fashion calls attention to man's subjugation to the tyranny of time. Thus envisaged, the metaphor introduces in the economy of the letter Petrarch's extended reflection on his bondage to his own servants and, obliquely, on the true spiritual freedom Gherardo has achieved by his conversion to the contemplative life.

Gherardo's faith, which is the stable foundation of his theological and moral universe, certainly functions for Petrarch as a way to express his hope that his life is not merely an unalterable memory (although Petrarch often strives to make his life exactly that), a permanent and irreversible restlessness of heart. This poet of time, who understands the powerlessness of man in time, finds in his brother's conversion the failure of the notion of irreversibility of time as well as the concrete sign that time's inherent randomness and insignificance can be redeemed. Nonetheless, the very depth of Gherardo's vision of faith leads Petrarch to construct a symmetrical opposition between their parallel lives. At one end there stands the poet-humanist, caught in the actualities and precariousness of time-bound existence; at the other pole there is the monastery, a contemplative and idyllic world removed from the pressures and inauthenticities of daily life. More precisely, Gherardo's idyllic world is, paradoxically, a "heavenly journey" (and this paradox, as we shall see later, belongs to the vocabulary of monastic spirituality); in this journey Gherardo is engulfed in silence and in "angelic discussions." The poet, who, by contrast, is outside the spiritual boundaries of cenobitic life, figures his own difference from the monks through the deliberate evocation of classical texts.

Toward the beginning of the letter, in a section in which the rhetorical norm of *captatio benevolentiae* is observed, Petrarch gives the rationale for the style of his composition:

> Nor did Jupiter endow with greater courage against all terror his Hercules, fathered in adultery, than you were granted by the eternal Father of all, born of a virgin, who recognizes and assists the upright wills of those who have faith in him. Such being the case, you can listen to the voices of your dear ones and, should any free time become available amidst your

holy occupations, you can briefly respond. Allow me, however, to use with you words from secular authorities cited abundantly by Ambrose and our Augustine and Jerome which even the apostle Paul did not scorn to use. Do not close the door of your cell to words worthy of my mouth and not unworthy of your ears.[6]

Accordingly, Petrarch proceeds to allude to—and discard—Pythagoras's ideas about the transmigration of souls; later in the body of the letter he will refer to Cato, Cicero, Horace, Plato, and Aristotle and, above all, to some of Seneca's maxims, such as the one on the narcissistic impulse in caring for clothes, "Who has ever worn fancy clothing without desiring to be seen?," or the more general one, "Persist in your resolve and complete what you have begun." He even cites the proverb on servants, "every servant is an enemy," and registers his disagreement with Seneca's disapproval of it.

The chief reason for the rhetorical strategy of moving from one classical citation to the next as if they constitute and contain the formulation of specific experiences is to show the enduring value and, plainly, the immortality of the past. The classical legacy is unlike the ephemeral apparitions of fashion, and the modernity of the past is dramatized through the process of investing the disjointed fragments with the power to impinge upon and perhaps shape the realities of the present. Like fashion, however, the citations are also vehicles for the exhibition of one's erudition and one's own hard-earned authority. The authority of Petrarch's voice is coextensive with his becoming the mouthpiece of the authority or tradition. We should not see, however, simply a theory of impersonality at work here, as if the acknowledgment of the weight of tradition entailed the effacement of self. Quite to the contrary, as Petrarch writes to his brother through a pattern of citations, he emerges as a persona, as the mask through which the echoes of the past are again audible. At the same time, the quotations constitute him as a subject with the power to remake the sense of the past, to delete any trace of authoritarianism of the past, and to register his disagreements with the *doxa* of Plato, Aristotle, Pythagoras, and Seneca. The citational procedure, finally, is the strategy allowing Petrarch to reflect on and take sides in the long debate on the relationship between the rigorism of monastic self-understanding and the values of the liberal arts.

At least ever since Jean Leclerc's *L'Amour des lettres et le désir de*

Dieu, it has been clear that monastic *scriptoria* were places where classical texts were transcribed, manuscripts were illuminated, music was composed, and such a thing as monastic humanism—by which one has to understand the study of Vergil, Ovid, and Horace as well as the writing of verse, sermons, letters, legends, and *florilegia*—occurred. Figures such as Cassiodorus, Gregory, Romuald, and Benedict promote the ideal of the learned monk, while Vivarium in Calabria and Cassino in Latium epitomize the historical-spiritual centers where classical values were preserved.[7]

Nonetheless, these well-established links between religious cult and secular culture are often contested. The distrust of both pagan literature, because of the preciousness of its style, its often licentious themes, and the dangerous lure of its beauty, and of classical philosophy, which is to be understood as a way of living according to the dictates of natural reason, is crystallized by Peter Damian's vehement assertion: "Mea grammatica Christus est."[8] Petrarch certainly sides with the austere moral content of monastic discipline, but he rejects the monks' opposition to the liberal arts as is exemplified by Damian's sense of a split between Christ and the art of grammar.

Petrarch's polemic with the monks' distrust of grammar, which is a term for literature, focuses on the value and inevitability of style. He closes his letter to Gherardo, in fact, with the admission that he has written to his brother in the *sermo humilis,* in the plain language of monastic meditation stripped of all superfluities, "not in my customary style but in a strange one that is almost monastic, in consideration of you rather than myself." Discernible in the commonplace and ordinary statement is what can be called the artifice of Petrarch's adaptability to his interlocutors' language. His marvelous aptitude to appropriate their resources of thought serves him well in the intended aim of persuading his correspondent, an aim that is achieved by enveloping within the volubility of his own language the correspondent's viewpoint. Obliquely we are given here a formulation of what constitutes the essence of style. Style is without a doubt a technique of producing a certain effect on the listener. This energy or *dunamis* of style, and generally of rhetoric, is the clearest sign of its power. Yet, in addition to this, style is a cut or mark, a viewpoint, a way of looking at things and establishing links between separate worlds. Petrarch, as we know, attaches a historical role to questions of form and style because it is through style that one can fashion the temper and mood of one's times. The opening sonnet of the *Canzoniere,* which was discussed in some detail in the previous chapter, refers to the text's "vario stile" (l. 5) (varied style)—the poems' alternating or interlocked style of hope and sorrow. In effect, it can be said that Petrarch's authentic revolution is a revolution of style in the sense that he radically transforms the lexicon of European lyric poetry (which, paradoxically and with due respect to the theorists of Romantic myths of originality, is really at its best in England and Spain when it openly acknowledges its Petrarchan matrix), and, thereby, he alters the perception of the values of the lexicon. In his handling, for instance, the word for passion, *passione,* designates both Christian and his own amorous suffering. More to our immediate concerns, in this letter to Gherardo, style has the power to make the distant worlds of the monk and the humanist contiguous with each other, to bring into communication, without totalizing them or unifying them, the different spiritual dimensions of the two brothers.

If there is a contiguity between the world of the monk and the world of the humanist, that contiguity is the fabrication of the poet's imagination. It is *his* choice of style that forges—and by implication can disrupt—any possible bonds and relatedness between the two worlds. The second letter Petrarch writes to Gherardo (*Fam.* 10.4) conspicuously probes the distance between the realm of historical immanence, where the poet situates himself, and the life of contemplation, which Gherardo has chosen. By a sharp reversal, the letter simultaneously charts the historical links between poetry and theology.

The letter, as is well known, is sent to Gherardo along with the first eclogue of the *Bucolicum carmen* as an allegorical exposition of the poem's content.[9] The allegory of the pastoral poem involves, so the letter glosses the poem, Silvius, who stands for Petrarch himself, and Monicus, who stands for Gherardo and is called Monicus after one of the Cyclops, "as if he were one-eyed." The name is appropriate for Gherardo, Petrarch says, because, "of the two eyes we mortals usually use, one to gaze upon heavenly things and the other upon earthly ones, you renounced the one that beholds earthly things, being content with the better eye." The distance between the two brothers, which the letter at this point stresses, is figured in the poem both in terms of their vision and through the representation of the space they inhabit: Silvius is a troubled quester, a self-styled hapless vagrant roaming over "dumosos colles silvasque" (thorny hills and thickets). Gherardo, by contrast, lives in the cave of religious contemplation, away from the turbulence of city life.

As in all pastoral poems, here, too, the distance between the two shepherds is described as a poetic *agon*. Petrarch has yielded to the charms of two Muses, the songs of Vergil and Homer, yet "vox mea non ideo grata est michi, carmina quanquam / Laudibus interdum tollant ad sidera Nymphe" (For all that I am still by no means content with my singing, even though sometimes the nymphs will praise to the sky my verses). Gherardo, on the other hand, seeks to persuade Petrarch "durum hoc transcendere limen" (to step over this stony threshold), to enter his hut, the monastic solitude of Montrieux, where the sounds of the world are stilled and "notes of unrivalled sweetness are sung." Gherardo's shepherd, in fact, is David, the supreme poet of the lands of two rivers, Jor and Dan, and his songs are the psalms which the monks intone in their nocturnal chants. With perfect numerical symmetry (18 lines for each speaker, as if to suggest the equality of the two poetic modes), the eclogue goes on to enumerate the themes of Petrarch's Muses (11.72–90)—love, war, the Furies, Hades, and the gods and the heroes—as well as the simpler themes of Gherardo's single Muse (ll. 91–109)—the one God, his power, and his gifts of life and death. After Gherardo's speech, Petrarch promises that he will listen to his brother's Muse at some future time. For now this Odysseus of the heart heeds the Siren call of fame: he must sing of a hero born of the race of the gods and worthy of Orpheus.

While the delights of contemplative life are presented as the terminus of the poet's existential quest, the poem also suggests the extraordinary richness of the active experience of life. Actually, poetic vision, which is coextensive with active life and is cast as problematic and double for it uses simultaneously the two eyes mortals have, comes forth as superior to contemplative life. The contemplatives are traditionally saturnine souls whose gaze penetrates the highest reaches of God's essence.[10] Etymologically the word comes from *templum*, the space marked out, in the words of Varro's *De lingua latina*, by the seer with his divining rod as a location for his observation.[11] Because Saturn is the planet of contemplation and of time, it can be said that the contemplatives have taken "time out" of history in a single-minded vision of the heavenly bliss. By temporizing, by turning to this epic poem, *Africa*, before entering Gherardo's hut, Petrarch chooses to

implicate himself in history's contingencies, where heroic achieve-
ments as well as the vanity of those achievements are celebrated.

What makes active life, and with it poetic practice, superior to the
ascesis of the contemplatives is that the life of contemplation, notwith-
standing the lure of its visionariness, is a simplified, not risky enough
perspective on the complex demands of existence. Because ascetic life
sees the future as an infinite prolongation of the present, it brings
about a foreclosure of time and allows time to flounder in fore-
shadowed eternity. The poet, on the other hand, by his roaming over
the uncharted expanse of the landscape, confronts the contradictory
exigencies of history. Such a hierarchy of value is suggested by a
textual detail of the poem as well as by Petrarch's interpretive letter.
Scipio, we are told, is the hero who by force thrusts into the cave of
Polyphemus, the Cyclop who is interpreted as the one-eyed Hannibal.
Just as Scipio routs Hannibal, so Silvius's heroic poem—and the
analogy is established by the eclogue's allegorical interpretation—can
overwhelm the heroics of the one-eyed monk.[12]

The sense of the claim about the superiority of the poet over the
monk comes to a sharp focus in the allusion to Orpheus in the last line
of the eclogue ("Orphea promeritum modulabor harundine parva" [1.
123] [I will sing on a small reed things worthy of Orpheus]). Orpheus,
whose name, as shown in the previous chapter, etymologically means
"best voice," is the poet who, by the power of his music and eloquence,
tames the brutishness of man.[13] As such Orpheus is the very embodi-
ment of the ideals of the humanists. But Orpheus is also the emblem
of the *poeta-theologus*.[14] Accordingly, this second letter to Gherardo
(*Fam.* 10.4), written from Padua, opens with Petrarch's elaborate
statement on the theory of the *poeta-theologus*, that is to say, on the
relationship between literature and theology, which was central to the
concerns of the Paduan humanists.[15]

It is possible to infer that Petrarch, writing to his brother from
Padua, deliberately acknowledges the reflections of the Paduan hu-
manists on the doctrine of the *poeta-theologus*. Such a theory, to be
sure, was available to him from St. Augustine's *City of God* (18.14),
where the poet-theologians—Orpheus, Musaeus, and Linus—who
had made hymns to the gods are discussed. For St. Augustine, these
theological poets crystallize the rupture between knowledge and prac-
tice for they worshiped the one true God along with other false gods.
In *Invective contra medicum*, Petrarch subscribes to St. Augustine's

notion that the *prisci poetae* lacked the perfect knowledge of the one true God, which, at any rate, depends on heavenly grace and not on human study.[16] In the Paduan letter to Gherardo, however, Petrarch's emphasis falls on the proximity, which the Paduan humanists had charted, between poetry and theology in the persuasion that the Bible itself is a poetic verbal structure:

> I might almost say that theology is the poetry of God. What else is it if not poetry when Christ is called a lion or a lamb or a worm? In Sacred Scripture you will find thousands of such examples too numerous to pursue here. Indeed, what else do the parables of the savior in the gospels echo if not a discourse different from ordinary meaning or, to express it briefly, figurative speech, which we call allegory in ordinary language? Yet poetry is woven from this kind of discourse, but with another subject. Who denies it? That other discourse deals with God and divine things, this one with God and men; whence even Aristotle says that the first theologians were poets. That such was the case is indicated by the word itself. Research has been done on the origin of the word *poet,* and although opinions are varied, the most probable holds that men, once ignorant but desirous of the truth and especially knowledge of God—a desire natural to men—began believing in a certain superior power that governs mortal affairs. They considered it proper that this power be venerated with a submission more than human and a worship more than venerable. Thus they chose to build magnificent buildings called temples and to have consecrated ministers whom they named priests, as well as splendid statues and golden vases, marble altars and beautiful vestments. Furthermore, lest their praise remain mute, they determined to appease the divinity with high sounding words and to bestow sacred flattery on the divinity in a style far removed from common and public speech. In addition they employed rhythmical measures in order to provide pleasure and banish tediousness. Indeed it had to be an uncommon form of speech and possess a certain artfulness, exquisiteness, and novelty. Since such language was called *poetes* in Greek, those who used it were called *poets.* You will say, "Who is the source of such ideas?" . . . First there is Marcus Varro, most learned among the Romans; then there is Suetonius . . . ; and I would not add the third except that he is, I believe, more familiar to you. Isidore, therefore, briefly citing Suetonius, makes mention of this in the eighth book of his *Etymologies.* But you will retort: "I can even believe an old doctor of the Church, but the sweetness of your song does not behoove my rigorous life." Do not believe this, dear brother. Even the fathers of the Old Testament made use of heroic and other kinds of poetry: Moses, Job, David, Solomon, Jeremiah; the

Psalms of David that you sing day and night possess poetic meter in Hebrew. . . . Do not therefore, my brother, be horrified by what you know pleased men who were most devoted and consecrated to Christ. Concentrate on the meaning; if it is true and wholesome, embrace it regardless of the style.[17]

The burden of this extraordinary passage is to show that poetry and theology are not quite the antinomies they seem to be. What brings them to the same focus is the presence of figurative language and what summarily can be called poetic style in either discipline. From this standpoint Petrarch recasts the theoretical assertions by Albertino Mussato, Boccaccio, and Salutati, who effectively rhetoricize theology. The *poeta-theologus,* and here lies his unique role, is the figure empowered to bring together the perspectives of poetry and theology. Yet Petrarch, unlike the Paduan humanists, does not wish to appear as if he simply collapses theology into rhetoric. To this end he sets up an opposition between style and meaning and seeks to make it valid by evoking St. Jerome's perception of the intractable, untranslatable poetic specificities of the Bible. Petrarch even makes allowances for the moral perturbations style can introduce into the spiritual order of Gherardo's existence, and he tells his brother to bypass style, to embrace the eclogue's moral meaning, which Petrarch believes to be consistent with Gherardo's inflexible ethical standards.

But Petrarch knows too well that style and meaning are inseparable, that the style is the meaning and cannot be simply annihilated without annihilating the very statement of the allegory. In this exchange with Gherardo, in effect, Petrarch explores the dialectics at work in the question of style, its essence as a mode of vision, of looking at experience as well as its property as an instrument of simulation and enchantment, a way of saying things as well as a mask, a habit of thought as well as the tawdry variant of fashion. This dual component of style is not simply irreconcilable for him.

The adoption of the pastoral genre for the first eclogue of the *Bucolicum carmen* is ample proof of his effort to bring together the tensions he sees in the problem of style, for the pastoral is the point of intersection of the two distinct spiritual traditions the poem dramatizes. Petrarch's bucolic poem is, first of all, a stylized imitation of the Vergilian model.[18] The theme of poetic *agon,* the encomium of rural life, the dialogic form, Silvius's anxiety, which recalls the exiled Melibeus's longing for Tityrus's delight, and so on, underscore the imaginative value of the Vergilian canon in Petrarch's elaboration. This classical tradition coincides in the first eclogue with the awareness of the rich codification of monastic life as a pastoral existence.

The cloister's representation as a pastoral enclosure is a well-established motif in patristic sources. In the rhetoric of cenobitic life, the cloister is most commonly envisioned as a *paradisus claustri,* as the typological adumbration of the Earthly Paradise as well as a veritable paradise of delights where the fragrant scents of the virtues are breathed forth like sweet sop or glowing spice-flowers. There, as Peter Damian writes, "the roses of charity blaze in crimson flame and the lilies of purity shine in beauty."[19]

Such a celebration of the spiritual pleasures of monastic life jars, at least on the surface, with the ascetic principles whereby the monk, like Israel of old, must install himself in the desolation of the desert on the way to the promised land. In truth, the notion that the monk's life, in the formula of St. Benedict, ought at all times to be lenten in character is only the other side of the belief that the contemplative quest is joyful because it sees the divine meaning of all things. This coextensiveness of desert and garden, which is the central paradox of the monastic imagination, allows Petrarch to suggest in his eclogue that his spiritual detours, his being suspended in the existential region of ambiguities and contingencies, of being frozen on the *limen,* the threshold of conversion, constitute an experience which is contrary, but also proximate, to Gherardo's quest for the absolute.[20]

The chief characteristic of the pastoral form is the celebration of *otium,* leisure, or, as Vergil's eclogue states, "O Meliboee, deus nobis haec otia fecit" (O Melibeus, a god has given us this ease).[21] Gherardo enjoys the leisure of contemplation, whereas the poet chooses the excitement of active life, the high road of the epic vision. But a dialogue between their two perspectives is possible because, although writing is part of the *vita activa,* it brings the humanist to the threshold of contemplation as well as to the point where the realm of pure action is imagined. This double awareness of the humanist is figured in both letter and eclogue as his double vision; it is also reflected as the ambivalent value of style. A clearer understanding of what the essence of writing is for Petrarch emerges from a letter he writes to another Benedictine, Pierre, abbot of St. Bénigne (*Fam.* 13.7).

The burden of the letter, in point of fact, is to examine the poet's own vocation to write, and this vocation comes forth as a mania afflicting him. The lucid self-analysis centers on the origin of the affliction. To put it simply, writing for Petrarch is rooted in the universe of the passions, in an undefinable uneasiness and anxiety which Petrarch calls a "sickness." "Except when writing," he admits to the abbot, "I am always tormented and sluggish, whence (strangely enough) I feel belabored while at rest and rested while at labor." This ceaseless anguish of the mind is provisionally assuaged by writing, although in and of itself writing is not a cure. It is, rather, a disease and a "pestilence" infecting—as the humorous, semiautobiographical vignette of the student abandoning the study of law to follow in the poet's footsteps shows—"carpenters, fullers and farmers," who "have forsaken their plows and the other tools of their trade to discuss the Muses and Apollo."[22] Because it induces a forgetting of the contingencies of life, writing occupies a mixed, liminal place: it is an experience in which contemplation and action converge. In this liminal region the poet has the power to confront and engage in his discourse all other discourses, to tread "devious" paths of knowledge while he can also acknowledge the truth-value in Gherardo's contemplative impulse. The importance of this acknowledgment surfaces from a quick reading of *De vita solitaria* and *De otio religioso.*

De vita solitaria, dedicated to the bishop of Cavaillon, Philip of Cabassole, is primarily an encomium of leisure (*otium*) and its attendant virtues of quiet, silence, frugality, and freedom from the anxieties and cares of the tumultuous life of the city. These virtues are also the benefits of a life of solitude, which is to be properly understood as the opposite of *negotium.* As a strategy for building a solid, persuasive argument in favor of the desirability of the "letum otium" and freedom that solitude affords, Petrarch reviews and weaves into his moral treatise two traditions. Book 1 moves largely by citing the maxims on the values of tranquillity by Seneca, Cicero, Horace, and even Epicurus. Book 2, on the other hand, goes into an extended praise of cenobitic life and is, in fact, an inventory of the classical texts of monastic spirituality. The history of the world, accordingly, is summarized from the standpoint of its epoch-making figures who are said to have adhered to the practice of solitude: Adam, Abraham, Isaac, Jacob, Moses, Elijah, and Eliseus are all extensively described as proponents of the life of solitude. After the biblical characters, Petrarch considers the sequence of Christian contemplatives: Ambrose,

Martin, Augustine, Basil, Paula, Gregory the Great, St. Benedict, St. Francis, Bernard of Clairvaux, Romuald, and Pope Celestine are the witnesses of the spiritual values of solitude.

The collation of secular and Christian examples, drawn from different times and places, certainly dramatizes the harmonious, syncretic order of a mind given to leisure. There are questions, as is well known, as to whether Petrarch's mind favors Horatian and Epicurean ideas of leisure over and against the Christian tradition of contemplation in *De vita solituria*.[23] To believe that Petrarch is asking of us to recognize the subordination of the Christian contemplatives' leisure to the classical vision of leisure is an impoverishment of the text *because* it is an impoverishment of Petrarch's understanding of leisure, which by its very nature cannot be divided. Leisure, as a matter of fact, is not mere idleness or evasion into inactivity; it is, on the contrary, the foundation of culture and the condition for thought:

> Equidem solitudo sine literis exilium est, carcer, eculeus; adhibe literas, patria est, libertas, delectatio. Nam de otio quidem illud Ciceronis notum: "Quid dulcius otio literato?" Contraque, non minus illud Senece vulgatum: "Otium sine literis mors est, et homini vivi sepoltura."

> Solitude without culture is certainly an exile, a jail, a torture. Add culture and it becomes fatherland, freedom, delight. Apropos of leisure well known is that statement of Cicero: "What is sweeter than a leisure devoted to culture?" On the other hand, no less famous are the words of Seneca: "Leisure without culture is death, it is the burial of a living man."[24]

The point of leisure, which is at one with learning, is that it allows one to *see* life as a totality, that it allows everyone to fulfill one's potential, to step beyond this or that partial occupation. Leisure, in short, is freedom, a moral virtue that imparts each human existence with its own spiritual shape.[25]

This insight into leisure as the unifying trait of religious contemplation and philosophical *theoria* (which is the Greek word for contemplation) marks a rare but not unusual experience of equilibrium in Petrarch's thought. There is a passage in a letter Petrarch sent late in his life (1373, from Arquà) to the Augustinian friar Luigi Marsili which acknowledges the necessity for a theologian not to neglect the secular arts as well as the study of theology, while keeping the import of either in proper theological perspective. The passage, clearly inspired by St. Augustine's *De doctrina Christiana*, reads:

> But there is one thing I shall not pass over, so that you will not lend ear and heart to those who, under pretext of theological studies, try hard to dissuade you from acquaintance with secular letters. Without them, Lactantius and Augustine, not to mention others, would not have dislodged so easily the superstitious notions of the heathens, nor would Augustine have built the *City of God* with such skill and such walls. It behooves a theologian to know many things other than theology, indeed, if it were possible, to know nearly everything, to be prepared against the assaults by the world of the flesh. For sure, as there is one God to Whom all things are subject, there is but one knowledge from God, Whom all other gods obey. And that same Augustine discusses these matters in the second book of *On Christian Doctrine*. So read his conclusions, which you can do without prejudice to your main goal, and learn as much as your mind and memory permit; and always remember that you are a theologian, not a poet, nor a philosopher—unless, of course, a true philosopher, who is a lover of the true wisdom. And that true wisdom of God, the Father, is Christ.[26]

This all-encompassing vision of a harmonized, hierarchically arranged knowledge whereby secular, humanistic traditions are considered as preliminary to the true Christian wisdom still conveys the notion of a totality made of distinct parts, of boundaries that Petrarch cannot transgress even if he is fascinated by the possibility of transgression. The unity which is theorized, as it were, in *De vita solitaria* and is rooted in leisure is never a definitive solution for Petrarch. Boccaccio's *Decameron*, which is sustained by a metaphorics of play, revels in the imaginative spectacle of a rich, hybrid reality.[27] Petrarch, on the contrary, seeks to establish clear-cut partitions as if to retrieve and guarantee the pure shape of the various experiences and entities of reality.

De otio religioso, another text on contemplation, introduces, in fact, a disruption into the idyllic vision of leisure. *De otio religioso*, written after an extended visit to the monastery at Montrieux and addressed to Gherardo, can be read as a rethinking of the question of *otium* as spiritual creativity raised in *De vita solitaria* (which is alluded to in *De otio religioso*). Its point of departure is the citation of a line from Psalm 46.10, "vacate et videte," generally translated as "be still and know that I am God." The word, "vacate," which appears in the Vulgate, however, translates the Septuagint's "scholasate," which is rooted in *schole*, the Greek word for leisure. Consistently with the Greek text, "vacate et videte" has thus been translated as "have leisure and know that I am God."[28] Within this context, "vacate" carries out the inner sense of the psalm, which is about Jerusalem as God's dwelling place that will stand secure in the midst of the changes and tumults of the times. Like Jerusalem, the monastery is the refuge and strength against the shattered world, the shelter from cares, and the place where the covenant is kept.

On the face of it, the two books of *De otio religioso* draw lavishly from both Christian and pagan sources in order to emphasize their common moral principles about the misery of the human condition, embodied by the *contemptus mundi* motif, the fragility of life (large sections of book 2 consist of a lament in the form of the "ubi sunt?" questions), the evils of avaricious and dissolute living, and sibylline and biblical prophecies of peace to be realized with Christ's advent. The treatise, nonetheless, articulates a conclusion which is a far cry from the syncretic, harmonious vision of secular and religious values available in *De vita solitaria.* The pagan gods are all false, and the Scriptures, notwithstanding the humility of their style, are to be preferred to the empty eloquence of the arts in which children are nonetheless trained for the sake of lucre.

This final exhortation to the monks to seek nothing outside the Bible (David's psalms are viewed as the most fecund sort of writing) marks Petrarch's repudiation of his previous efforts to reconcile worldly wisdom and religious transcendence. He no longer seeks to shatter the partition wall between them. On the contrary, he even accepts the fact that faith and culture constitute the poles of an insoluble antinomy. In the first letter, as we recall, Gherardo appeared to be captive of a radical dualism in his belief that Petrarch's secular culture and his own religious experience were mutually hostile. In *De otio religioso* secular ideas founder and Petrarch endorses Gherardo's absolute formula for one's spiritual salvation.

To be sure, this is not an extraordinary about-face for Petrarch. "The Ascent of Mount Ventoux," which is a recollection of the two brothers' mountain climbing, dramatizes the distance between the spiritual ascent of the monk and the predicament of the humanist.[29]

More precisely, it juxtaposes Gherardo's easy ascent to Petrarch's halting movements and impasse with the overt end of discovering the imaginative richness of that moral crisis. *De otio religioso* elides the middle ground between culture and religious faith, and the Augustinian interiority, to which Petrarch still appeals, only leads to the recognition of the superiority of the spiritual life over the life of action.

The subordination of secular experiences to the truth of religious belief occurs also in the final poem of the *Canzoniere* (song 366), which is, rhetorically, a prayer to the Virgin. Preceded by a number of sonnets in which the poet variously regrets his past (sonnets 364 and 365), recalls the death of Laura (sonnet 363), and confronts his old age (sonnet 361), song 366 turns into a self-critique: the poet's love for Laura and his general attachments to the earth and to the practices of love lyrics are now the object of a palinode written from the standpoint of faith in the mercy of God.

The chief rhetorical strategy sustaining the movement of this prayer is one of opposition between the Virgin and Laura, or, to put it differently, between the self's own relation to heaven and its relation to the earth. From the transcendent perspective of the Virgin, the poet pledges to cleanse his wit and style, his tongue and heart ("ingegno et stile, / la lingua e 'l cor" [ll. 128–29]). By this anticipation of conversion to a purer mode of writing and living (of which the prayer is meant to be an emblem), the poem tells the deep longing of the poet's heart for a new spiritual condition. As a parable of longing and as the narrative of a quest for purification (and the contrite mood of spirit the poet evokes is its precondition), the prayer comes forth primarily as a confessional text, akin to St. Augustine's *Confessions.* St. Augustine's autobiography, which originates as a prayer and a journey to God, recounts the experience of a restless heart which will eventually be somewhat placated by signs of God's voice reaching him in his abjection. With the epiphany of grace the novel of the self records, St. Augustine turns prayer into a praise of God and into an interrogation or hermeneutics of the nature of God's language (the *Confessions* ends with an exegesis of the Book of Genesis). The reflection on God's language, no doubt, is also a way for Augustine to gauge the authenticity of his own voice. Petrarch's prayer to the Virgin, which is punctuated by epideictic rhetoric and is uttered through explicit metaphorics of a journey, dramatizes religious language both as a formulaic pattern of signification and as a language of desire. The object of this desire in the poem is the peace God may grant to the weary poet through the mediation of Mary.

Mary's classical role as *mediatrix* has a number of ramifications in Petrarch's poem. It should be said that the Virgin is singled out as the recipient of the poet's prayer and as the object of his love because she is the figure who stands in an intimate love relationship with God. This chain of love (the poet speaks compelled by love, the Virgin was directly touched by God, and so on) makes of prayer the privileged love language mediating between God and man. At the same time, by the prayer to the Virgin the poet casts himself as a quester for the human face of God—hence the insistence on the maternity of the Virgin and the Incarnation of Christ: "Vergine pura," reads one passage, "d'ogni parte intera, / del tuo parto gentil figliuola et madre" (ll. 27–28) (Pure Virgin, whole in every part, noble daughter and mother of your offspring). The paradox of the Virgin as daughter and mother of her offspring, which clearly recalls Dante's own prayer to the Virgin in *Paradiso,* canto 33, in turn stages Petrarch's insight into the essence of religious language as necessarily formulaic.

> Vergine bella, che di sol vestita,
> coronata di stelle, al sommo Sole
> piacesti sì che 'n te sua luce ascose:
> amor mi spinge a dir di te parole,
> ma non so' 'ncominciar senza tu' aita
> et di colui ch'amando in te si pose.
>   Invoco lei che ben sempre rispose
> chi la chiamò con fede.
> Vergine, s'a mercede
> miseria estrema de l'umane cose
> giamai ti volse, al mio prego t'inchina,
> soccorri a la mia guerra
> ben ch'i' sia terra et tu del Ciel regina. (song 366, ll. 1–13)

Beautiful Virgin who, clothed with the sun and crowned with stars, so pleased the highest Sun that in you He hid His light: love drives me to speak words of you, but I do not know how to begin without your help and His who loving placed Himself in you. I invoke her who has always replied to whoever called on her with faith, Virgin, if extreme misery of human things ever turned you to mercy, bend to my prayer; give succor to my war, though I am earth and you are queen of Heaven.

The text of this first stanza (much like the remaining parts of the *canzone*) is deliberately constructed with scraps and allusions drawn from the rich tradition of biblical and patristic sources. The first two lines, for instance, are modeled on the description of the portent in Apocalypse 12.1: a woman clothed with the sun, with the moon under her feet, and on her head a crown of twelve stars; the very attribute of beauty for the Virgin in the initial apostrophe recalls the "fairest among women" from Song of Songs 1.8; echoes from St. Bernard, Peter Damian, and Dante are conspicuous.[30] The technique is chiefly deployed in order to inscribe the poem within the tradition of devotional Marian literature, of the veneration (what in Greek is called *hyperdoulia*) due to Mary. Consistently with this, she appears here as the object of praise. But the staging of citations from the past is now a strategy to dramatize the self's utter surrender to the voices and fixed formulas of tradition which he, by repeating, reanimates.

For Petrarch, thus, to pray means to employ incantatory, ritual language (the poem's movement hinges on a sequence of anaphoras to the Virgin with changed qualifier) as if he were engaged in a timeless ceremony of propitiation of the Virgin; more fundamentally, it means to abide in a language that preexists oneself and that effaces the self; finally, prayer is a re-petition, in the etymological and deeper sense of the word as *re-petere*. We have seen earlier in this book that for Petrarch the self is not the locus of its own origination and that this conviction deflates all naive claims of mastery and self-mastery advanced by the poet-lover. In song 366 this insight defines the very structure of religious language as well as of the religious vision the self has of itself. In short, the poet's appeal to the Virgin and to God's mercy (which is really the argument of the poem) finds its metaphorical and conceptual extensions in Petrarch's figuration of the self and his conception of language as an allegory of desire.

To have song 366, the prayer to the Virgin, as the final composition of the song-book, which partly harks back to the first sonnet, is a way of conferring on it the privileged status of a final revelation, the revelation of one's own heart ceaselessly displaced and ceaselessly tending to the truth of faith. Prayer for Petrarch is this *tension*, this at-tention to a state that lies beyond his will, this in-tention to reach it. And although in the economy of the *Canzoniere* this prayer can be explained as one privileged moment among many other contrasting and equally privileged experiences, the religious perspective that the prayer to the Virgin posits is invested with the singular aura of felt convictions. Nonetheless, the sort of *panepistemon,* to use a term Poliziano will reinvent and utilize roughly a century after Petrarch's death, Petrarch's whole oeuvre drafts does not waver in preserving and promoting a variety of conflicting disciplines, viewpoints, and values.

Further, the claim, which Petrarch eloquently and repeatedly advances, that religious vision is superior to the impostures of secular culture cannot simply be seen as the triumph of the clarity of faith over the shadows of knowledge. If it is a triumph, as a matter of fact, there is a troubling underside to it: the belief that religion is a higher or better form of experience unavoidably ends up confining religion to the edges of history and deadening its powers in history. Paradoxically, then, the genuinely religious texts of Petrarch are not those that set theology apart from the critical debates as *De otio religioso* does. It can be said that Petrarch broadens the vast fields of theological reflection at the very moment when he confronts the figments of his vision and the demons of his own self. This is Petrarch's radical project. His long fascination with monastic spirituality has afforded him with the perspective of silence from which to hear the whispers and see the shadows of the soul.

Petrarch's Song 126

This analysis of one of Petrarch's most celebrated *canzoni* can certainly be construed as a parable, if little else, of the way I approach a literary text. How can the method I follow be described? The answer, putting aside the inclination to ignore the question, is that mine is a philological method.

The more orthodox practitioners of philology—those for whom erudite research into the storehouse of tradition is its own reward or those who professionally investigate the external features, the materiality, of a text (variants, emendations, sources, manuscript tradition, biographical data, and so forth)—will in all likelihood object to this definition and feel that my use of the term lacks any scientific rigor. And I would have to agree that my understanding of philology has little to do with what has come to be known, somewhat dismissively, as antiquarianism. It has even less to do with the philological positivism that still lurks, in a variety of sociological and ideological disguises, within historicist approaches to literary texts.

As I practice it, philology is involved, if I may distort Martianus Capella's title, in a troubled love affair with Mercury; that is, philology is primarily the discipline that accounts for the elements making up the historical specificity of any text. As Vico (who also knew how unaccountable the power of the imagination is) puts it, nothing lies outside the archives of philology: textual echoes, sources, etymologies, specialized vocabulary (terms that have specific identifiable frames of reference), topoi, genres, rhetorical and thematic structures—all are in the domain of its concerns. These concerns are scrutinized not as the preestablished apparatus of literary history or as generalized extratextual formulas but as they work within a text, as the text's metaphors. From this viewpoint, the philologist necessarily turns into a scrupulous reader of textual details, the sort of reader New Criticism has nurtured since the 1950s. This is tantamount to saying that what originally may appear as objective facts are in reality the other side of an interpretive choice, that disguised as philology there is always

Mercury, who makes his way hidden and, as he goes, unveils and assesses the textual value of each and every metaphor.

The reluctance to talk about method (which seems to have mixed motives: indifference to the theoretical implications and assumptions of one's practical criticism in the naive belief that practical criticism alone counts; resistance, in the name of some illusory intellectual autonomy, to being pigeon-holed in a fixed area; and even suspicion that a general method, codified a priori, always fails to render the unpredictability and wealth of individual texts) turns out to be the symptom of a genuine critical predicament. It points to the awareness of a split between "objective" philological facts and interpretive values, between the poet and tradition, and, more generally, between the core of a lyric text and the critical understanding of it.

Because of this gap, theoreticians of literature, such as Croce, have yielded to the temptation of dismissing philology altogether as a mere preamble to the purity of aesthetic appreciation or as a science that may well illuminate the mechanics of a literary text but is in no way essential to its interpretation. Although philology is devoid of any power to release the understanding of a text, it still has, I think, an ineliminable role to play in literary analysis: it establishes boundaries for what might otherwise prove the arbitrary, unwarranted vagaries of the critical imagination confronted with the elusive resonances, subtle hints, and clues—the dark secret, beneath a readable literal surface, of any poetic text.

As it happens, few poets have felt, as Petrarch has, the depth of the split between historical knowledge and the language of poetry. To begin with, the question that I ask of Petrarch (and that I would ask, with the proper adjustments, of, say, Dante or Leopardi) is why he writes poetry. What does poetry have to say, what message can it bear that other discourses do not? The question is legitimate because all these poets have written texts of moral philosophy, were translators and, in varying degrees, theorists of poetry. For Petrarch, poetry is the privileged language of specular self-reflection, and it is concerned with the crisis of moral knowledge. More than that, poetry to him marks the retrieval of the language of the imagination as the way to probe his unsettled sense of himself and the world.

There is, as a matter of fact, a Petrarchan vision of poetry, which can be gauged by what it excludes: other selves; crude Aristotelian philosophy with its simplified, rational formulas about the truth; the physics of love, peddled by scientific-medical authorities who are largely identified with the Aristotelians because they assume that the world of desire is contingent on and subject to objective conditions of reality. What it includes is the simple but vast sphere of the imagination, in which everything is implicated and complicated and in which mechanical laws of time, categories of sense, projects appear to be unstable forms. This understanding of the imagination is what Petrarch steadily evokes. Take, for instance, a discursive text such as "The Ascent of Mount Ventoux," a letter he addresses to an Augustinian monk, Dionigi da Borgo San Sepolcro. Like a true philologist, Petrarch begins the account of his mountain climbing by comparing sundry descriptions of mountains in Hellenic myth; he then translates the experience of his ascent into an allegory of the flight of the mind. The allegorical scheme he conjures up does not quite work, but once he reaches the top of the mountain and gazes toward the Alps, the power of the imagination emerges in the shape of memory and longing and new thoughts that seize him.

One would look in vain at a text such as "The Ascent of Mount Ventoux" for Petrarch's sustained thinking on the working of the imagination. The place to look is his poetry—for instance, song 126:

Chiare fresche et dolci acque
ove le belle membra
pose colei che sola a me par donna,
    gentil ramo ove piacque
(con sospir mi rimembra)
a lei di fare al bel fianco colonna,
    erba et fior che la gonna
leggiadra ricoverse
co l'angelico seno,
aere sacro sereno
ove Amor co'begli occhi il cor m'aperse:
date udienzia insieme
a le dolenti mie parole estreme.

    S' egli è pur mio destino,
é l cielo in ciò s'adopra,
ch' Amor quest'occhi lagrimando chiuda,
    qualche grazia il meschino
corpo fra voi ricopra,
e torni l'alma al proprio albergo ignuda;

la morte fia men cruda
se questa spene porto
a quel dubbioso passo,
ché lo spirito lasso
non poria mai in più riposato porto
né in più tranquilla fossa
fuggir la carne travagliata et l'ossa.

Tempo verrà ancor forse
ch' a l'usato soggiorno
torni la fera bella et mansueta
et là 'v ella mi scorse
nel benedetto giorno
volga la vista disiosa et lieta,
cercandomi, et—o pieta—
già terra infra le pietre
vedendo, Amor l'inspiri
in guisa che sospiri
si dolcemente che mercé m'impetre
et faccia forza al cielo,
asciugandosi gli occhi col bel velo.

Da' be' rami scendea
(dolce ne la memoria)
una pioggia di fior sovra 'l suo grembo,
et ella si sedea
umile in tanta gloria,
coverta giá de l'amoroso nembo;
qual fior cadea sul lembo,
qual su le treccie bionde
ch' oro forbito et perle
eran quel dì a vederle,
qual si posava in terra et qual su l'onde,
qual con un vago errore
girando parea dir: "Qui regna Amore."

Quante volte diss' io
allor, pien di spavento:
"Costei per fermo nacque in paradiso!"
Così carco d'oblio
il divin portamento
e 'l volto e le parole e 'l dolce riso
m'aveano, et sì diviso
da l'imagine vera,

ch' i' dicea sospirando:
"Qui come venn' io o quando?"
credendo esser in ciel, non là dov' era.
Da indi in qua mi piace
quest'erba sì ch' altrove non ò pace.

    Se tu avessi ornamenti quant' ài voglia,
poresti arditamente
ucir del bosco et gir infra la gente.

Clear, fresh, sweet waters, where she who alone seems lady to me rested her lovely body, gentle branch where it pleased her (with sighing I remember) to make a column for her lovely side, grass and flowers that her rich garment covered along with her angelic breast, sacred bright air where Love opened my heart with her lovely eyes: listen all together to my sorrowful dying words. If it is indeed my destiny and Heaven exerts itself that Love close these eyes while they are still weeping, let some grace bury my poor body among you and let my soul return naked to this its own dwelling; death will be less harsh if I bear this hope to the fearful pass for my weary spirit could never in a more restful port or a more tranquil grave flee my laboring flesh and my bones. There will come a time perhaps when to her accustomed sojourn the lovely, gentle wild one will return and, seeking me, turn her desirous and happy eyes toward where she saw me on that blessed day, and oh the pity! seeing me already dust amid the stones, Love will inspire her to sigh so sweetly that she will win mercy for me and force Heaven, drying her eyes with her lovely veil. From the lovely branches was descending (sweet in memory) a rain of flowers over her bosom, and she was sitting humble in such a glory, already covered with the loving cloud; this flower was falling on her skirt, this one on her blond braids, which were burnished gold and pearls to see that day; this one was coming to rest on the ground, this one on the water, this one, with a lovely wandering, turning about seemed to say: "Here reigns Love." How many times did I say to myself then, full of awe: "She was surely born in Paradise!" Her divine bearing and her face and her words and her sweet smile had so laden me with forgetfulness and so divided me from the true image, that I was sighing: "How did I come here and when?" thinking I was in Heaven, not there where I was. From then on this grass has pleased me so that elsewhere I have no peace. If you had so many beauties as you have desire, you could boldly leave the wood and go among people.[1]

    There is a certain amount of arbitrariness in isolating for a critical analysis one poem from the *Rerum vulgarium fragmenta* as if it were a self-sufficient unit, absolutely autonomous from the poetic sequence. The arbitrariness is the more evident in the present case of song 126, which is explicitly in antithetical and yet complementary position to song 125, its "sister song." In song 125 the poet quests for Laura in an uncharted, desolate landscape that yields no signs of her presence. Song 126 begins with the poet returning to the same landscape where the preceding poem ends. The landscape is the enchanted bower of Vaucluse and is the space of the original encounter between the lover and Laura. The spot, by a transparent extension of the etymology of the real place, is a *hortus conclusus,* and in song 126 it is imaginatively transfigured into a paradise (l. 55). This reversal of mood from the *planctus* of song 125 to the hymn of song 126 is not unusual in the *Rime sparse.* Another case in point is the pair of sonnets, 61 and 62. Sonnet 61 intones a blessing to the privileged time of the encounter—"Benedetto sia 'l giorno e 'l mese et l'anno / e la stagione e 'l tempo et l'ora e 'l punto" (ll. 1–2)—in which the polysyndeton gives an illusion of continuity to the antithetical movement of expansion and contraction. The subsequent sonnet, "Padre del Ciel, dopo i perduti giorni," is a *miserere,* the poet's lament for the wasted time of his passion.

The symmetrical coupling of contradictory experiences is, in one sense, the emblem of Petrarch's split, the steady play of attraction and repulsion for Laura that has come to be identified as the distinctive trait of his morality and of his voice. In rhetorical terms this oscillation of moods has other implications. The convention of the lyric, for instance, rests on the assumption of immediate and spontaneous emotions, while time is viewed as not a constitutive category of the lyrical expression. The movement between contrasting poles of moods implies, however, that each poem's autonomy is unreal, that the origin of each lyrical experience lies always outside of itself, and that each reverses and implicates others in a steady movement of repetition. From this perspective song 126 is a fragment that reenacts within its formal boundaries the same splits and tensions that exist between it and the adjacent poems in the sequence. But unlike song 125, which overtly tells the impasse of a poet in his quest for a poetic style, song 126 seeks to retrieve an original visionary experience.

The poem starts with an extended apostrophe to the waters, bough, grass, flowers, and air of the natural setting where Laura first appeared to the lover's eyes. The language of this opening stanza recalls a spring song, yet it is not a celebration of the general *reverdie* of

nature according to the conventions codified by the Provençal trou-
badours. For the troubadours, the description of the landscape tends
to be an ironic counter to the abiding winter in the lover's heart or a
way of dramatizing the inner renewal of desire. Petrarch's landscape,
however, is a particularized, concrete topography: we are near the
source of the Sorgue River, where the original vision of Laura oc-
curred. The main burden of the apostrophe, actually, is to localize
exactly the spot of the vision, and the insistent adverb, "ove" (ll. 2, 4,
11), seeks to define, within the contracted perimeter of the natural
enclosure, the marks left behind by Laura's body. The verb "pose"
(l. 3), which evokes the body, conveys the impression of a frozen, fixed
image, almost a lifeless statue, which is in sharp contrast to the easy,
spontaneous flow of the river, to the graceful fall of the flowers on
Laura's garment, and in general to the animation of nature that the
apostrophe suggests. This contrast in imagery is a hint of a deeper
contrast hidden in the stanza.

The opening line with its three adjectives gliding on to the noun
at the end (a case of *epitheton ornans,* for which Petrarch is justly
famous) calls attention to the symbolic interaction of light, touch, and
sound, which are blended in the figure of the water. The impression of
iridescent light produced by "chiare" is absorbed by the resonance of
"dolci," which is a musical attribute. In *De vulgari eloquentia* Dante
refers to *dulcedo* as a musical metaphor, the quality of style by which
harmony is engendered (2.8.3). More than that, there is an etymology
of "music" given by Hugh of St. Victor which is particularly striking
for this poem of "clear, fresh, and sweet waters." In the *Didascalicon,*
which is Hugh's meditation on the Victorine understanding of the
encyclopedia, Hugh writes about the term "music": " 'Music' takes its
name from the word 'water,' or *aqua* because no euphony, that is,
pleasant sound, is possible without moisture."[2] Within this context we
might remark the appropriateness of the choice of the *canzone,* which
technically is a harmonization of words for musical setting. The
rhetorical mode adds to the overall impulse to mime the melodious,
limpid fluidity of the waters, its seductive euphony, which in the line is
heightened, we might add, by the discreet alliteration of "ch-qu." But
the poet's is a song of sorrow, and the elegy he promises is markedly
out of tune with the musical pattern of the natural order.

This dissonance has an extended thematic counterpart. The lov-
er's retrieval of the place where Laura was seen turns into the aware-

ness of a temporal dislocation. The phrase "con sospir mi rimembra" (l. 5)—given parenthetically (and the parenthesis is a distinctive trait of Petrarch's poetry) as if to suggest the irrelevance, the secondary quality, of the remark—actually discloses that the experience is represented through the haze of memory. Memory is the metaphoric filter through which the past is reclaimed as present and that also accounts for the dematerialization of the landscape: the epithets "gentle branch," "angelic breast," "sacred air" openly spiritualize the substances they qualify. More to our concern, the image of the sigh, which implies simultaneously longing and loss, unveils the resurrections of memory not as the restitution of the past to the present but as a temporal disjunction.

Petrarch, in effect, is giving a special twist to St. Augustine's classical reflections of the category of time. It is too well known how in the *Confessions*—a text that Petrarch, as he tells us in "The Ascent of Mount Ventoux," always carried with him—time is experienced as a sequence of self-annihilating moments. This is what is known as fallen time, time in a random and hollow succession of itself, a pure fragmentation whereby no relation can be said to exist between a moment and what precedes or follows it. St. Augustine crystallizes this condition in the formula "praesens nullum spatium habet" (*Confessions* 11.15) (the present occupies no space). The three dimensions of time—past, present, and future—do exist as a sort of timeless time, as memory and expectation in the present, when fallen time is transformed by the *kairos,* the event that redeems and lends significance to the emptiness of *chronos.* Petrarch takes the vision of Laura, which happens on the day of Christ's passion, to be such an occurrence, but in this poem time and space are at odds with each other. The poem's dramatic pivot, in a sense, is to reflect on the discrepancy between the stability of the place and the radical instability of time.

The luminosity conjured up by memory is shadowed in the second stanza. The valedictory strain in the first stanza, triggered by the awareness of the gaps of time, takes over completely as the poet comes to grips with death as the imminent boundary of his own life. The intimation of mortality is marked by a verbal shift from the past of memory (l. 5) to the future tense (l. 20), as well as by the overt reversal in the role of Love. Love, a personification that appears in and gives continuity to the first four stanzas, is evoked first as opening the lover's heart (l. 11) and second as closing his eyes (l. 16). The antithesis between Love's steadiness and the self's subjection to mortality is further played out in this second stanza as a Platonic duality of perishable body (l. 18) and immortal soul (l. 19) or, later, as spirit (l. 23) and flesh (l. 26). The tension between the two terms is commonplace enough throughout Petrarch's poetry (with the apparent valorization of the "alma" over the "corpo"), but we must acknowledge the precision of the Neoplatonic vocabulary in these lines. Petrarch, I would suggest, is alluding to and bringing together a number of Platonic motifs that all focus on the myth of the soul's return to the place of its original dwelling. The phrase "torni l'alma" in the line "e torni l'alma al proprio albergo ignuda" (l. 19) translates what is actually the Platonic notion of the body as the integument, the cloth that wraps the captive, naked soul and impedes its flight back to its place of origin.[3] Even the reference to "porto" (l. 24) largely belongs to this tradition in that the Platonic metaphor of life as a sea itinerary conventionally ends up in the promise of the bark securely landing in the port of philosophical wisdom. Yet Petrarch recalls this Neoplatonic paradigm of the soul's redemption only to twist it around: the poet's concern is not the soul's fate alone but also the hope that the body will be buried in the place of his bliss.

The conversion of the love garden into a burial ground (a move adumbrated earlier in the *canzone* through the metaphoric equivalence of love and death) yields the figuration of the poet's posthumous existence. There is no tranquillity in the grave. As if struggling against the threat of a possible oblivion—he envisions the dross of his body scattered among the stones—Petrarch evokes the never-named figure of Laura, who, as she is looking for him, discovers his tombstone. The oblique hint of the poet's monument, disguised in the language of humility—he says he is "terra" (l. 34)—is not meant to convey the ironic insight into death's triumph over human life and its illusory artifices. The bleakness of such a perception is generally available from later iconographic motifs, such as the inscription "Et in Arcadia ego," or even from Petrarch's own *Trionfi*, which thematizes, among other things, how time is subsumed into death. In this *canzone*, however, the tomb is imagined as healing the rift that love has opened up. The shift of perspective in this stanza (whereas in the first stanza the poet is a sort of Actaeon spying on the bathing goddess, now we are told that the tomb is erected there where he first noticed her) signals that his tomb will receive her recognition. It will inspire Laura—who ironically comes to this place for her delight or "soggiorno" (l. 28)—to pity, while her sighs bring together, as if she belonged to the repertory of women of the "sweet new style," the double perspective of heaven and earth. This harmonization of opposites achieved through Laura's prayer is no deluded flight, as the pathos of her tears or her upward glance might suggest, away from the darker realities of the tomb. The ostensible statement of this third stanza—the tame vision of the future, wherein Laura will come to the place of his burial—hides a more radical threat to the poet. The phrase "tempo verrà" (l. 27) translates a line from Vergil's *Georgics* (1.493), "scilicet et tempus veniet," the context of which is of some moment to Petrarch's text.

Vergil's poem of the earth begins as a call to the labor of the plow, to the knowledge of nature's laws—of the soil, weather changes, and the cycles of the seasons—so that the land may be properly nurtured and be, in its turn, fruitful. The first book, however, climaxes both in the spectacle of the Italian farmlands, which, ravaged by civil war, lie forlorn, and in the prayer to Augustus that he restore peace to the world. The lament over the ruins of the times is preceded by Vergil's visionary celebration of the future golden age when the farmer, once again working the ground with his plow, will bring to light the tools of strife the earth had long concealed: javelins, empty helmets, and the huge bones in dug-up graves ("Gradiaque effossis mirabitur ossa sepulcris" [*Georgics* 1.497]).

There is no doubt that the brunt of the Vergilian passage is to affirm the creative value of the husbandman's toil: it renews the land and brings life where the spears had disseminated death. In this sense the disinterment, which will take place in some utopian future, cannot be said to carry any sinister suggestion that the farmer's work of peace actually causes the undesirable rediscovery of the tools of war and death. Nonetheless, there is an ironic (if more cryptic) undercurrent, which Petrarch shares, in this exalted Vergilian vision. The irony in this picture of a pacified future is made manifest by the verb "mirabitur," which describes the farmer's wondering eye at what will seem to him nothing more than archaeological marvels unearthed by his plow. In effect, the scene anticipates a time when the past will no longer be recognized and acknowledged and the earth will be a reliquary of spent and forgotten passions. It is precisely this threat of oblivion, paradoxically betrayed in a context in which Petrarch is most obstinately intent on remembering and being remembered by the woman who most harshly ignored him, that Petrarch wants to bury.

This hint of radical annihilation is abruptly erased as the poet retrieves in the fourth stanza the original vision of Laura. Futurity gives way to the pleasures of memory, and we are once again in the sparkling bucolic setting that echoes the first stanza. The pastoral scenery certainly obliterates the composite picture of the shadow of mortality, fallow fields, and raging violence that the *Georgics* has superimposed on the piety of Laura's grief. But the setting is further transfigured into the Garden of Eden, where Laura sits enthroned. The oxymoron for her stance, "umile in tanta gloria" (l. 44), revises the earlier one, "la fera bella et mansueta" (l. 29), which primarily attempts to capture her dual essence, her mixture of elusiveness and allurement, that in turn is the erotics of the text. But the attributes of humility and glory, which echo Dante's doxology for the Virgin Mary (one obviously thinks of "umile e alta" of *Paradiso* 33.2), collapse all hierarchies and intimate that the poet's visionary experience has abolished all boundaries and distinctions. The vision reverberates with another, less hidden, textual allusion to Dante. The rain of flowers falling on Laura's skirt is clearly patterned on the cloud of flowers within which Beatrice appears to the pilgrim in the Garden of Eden (*Purgatorio* 30.28–33). It is no doubt possible to view this poetic encounter as a variant of an *agon* (and like most poetic contests this one takes place in a pastoral setting, as if *agons* and the pastoral are bound together). But the representation of the ecstatic vision, which is patterned on Dante's *second* encounter with Beatrice, seems to be more Petrarch's acknowledgment of his predecessor than a polemical gesture, in which he frequently indulges elsewhere. It is, nonetheless, through this circuitous path that Petrarch reaches the point where the place and the present tense coincide, "Qui regna Amore" (l. 52).

The poet's trancelike experience is rendered through the incantatory repetition of "qual" (ll. 46, 47, 50, 51). The anaphora, to be sure, is primarily a technique employed to individualize the random rain of flowers. Thus one flower falls on Laura's skirt, another on her braids, and so on, in a process of individualization that dramatizes Petrarch's desire to impose a clear, purposeful, and distinguishable pattern on the "nembo" (l. 45)—a word that, in effect, describes either an undifferentiated vapor or a uniformly gray luminosity. More than that, "nembo" translates the Latin *nimbus* by which poets and painters conceal and at the same time reveal the Divinity. The anaphora, then, plays a double role in the stanza: it creates, first of all, the impression of a harmonious totality that blends together, for instance, the colors of Laura with the elegant curves, as if it were an airy dance, of the flowers; but it also undoes the plenitude and wholeness of the scene by enumerating the parts that compose it. Seen in this sense, the anaphora can be said to disclose the principle of repetition that sustains the articulation of the *Rime sparse.* The collection is a series of individual poems arranged to form a coherent unity and totality, but the unity always appears to be made of contiguous, adjacent parts that steadily repeat themselves, even while they aspire to mark new imaginative departures.

More to our concern, the poet's ecstatic vision comes forth as a flight from the bondage to time: it is said, more precisely, to charge the poet with forgetfulness, "carco d'oblio" (l. 56). The forgetfulness, in the first place, signals the reversal of the pattern of memory and future that structures the dramatic movement of the *canzone,* but more is at stake than simply another turn in the metaphoric system. For forgetfulness, which is the condition that accompanies the rapture (a kind of *torpor lethargi* that traditionally precedes or follows the *excessus* of the mind), announces the loss of the power to know the difference between the imaginary and the real. But the poet, far from receiving a higher, transcendent vision in the rapture, actually goes through the separation from the world of natural forms and the real Laura, the "imagine vera" (l. 60), as he refers to it. In a poem such as this, in which there is an extraordinary awareness of her physicality—her body is cherished as "le belle membra" (l. 2)—as well as a concern with the destiny of the poet's own body, the loss of Laura as a concrete image is not altogether a positive value. More important, what emerges from the poet's wonder at his paradisiac ecstasy is a radical disorientation, the sense of being somewhere else, of having lost contact with the spot that haunts his imagination: the question Petrarch raises, "Qui come venn' io o quando?" (l. 62), which calls attention to the transfiguration of the landscape, at the same time conveys the lingering consciousness of the wedge that divides the real from the visionary. The fact is that the rapture comes forth through the representation of memory, and Petrarch is undeluded about memory's power to bring back the original event. Hence the statement of acceptance of and pleasure in "quest'erba" (l. 65): the precise locale of the quest is acknowledged as the middle ground of the imagination, as the theater of memory where nostalgia for the past vision and longing for the new one are simultaneously played out.

In the hands of Petrarch, the language of the lyric is not the language of primary vision but is simulacrum, a secondary—prosaic, as it were—search for that original vision or its renewal. Retrospectively we can read the whole *canzone* as a series of searches into emblems of origin that, however close at hand they may be, become unavoidably elusive. The poet's memory, at the beginning, unfolds at the source of the river, but the source remains concealed, and we are allowed to see only the river's flow, a veritable image of self-dislocation. By the initial apostrophe, Petrarch animates nature, but the natural landscape becomes the place of his death; nature may even seem to speak, as one flower "con un vago errore / girando parea dir: 'Qui regna Amore'" (ll. 51–52). The voice is illusory, as the "parea" clearly announces and the slightly pleonastic "vago errore," which joins aimlessness and error, confirms. "Vago errore," one might add, is the poem's emblem in that the poem is *gyrovagus*, following a spiral path, rotating its metaphors and confronting its illusory moves. More to our concern, Laura herself, the main source of the poet's voice, appears always veiled, either literally behind her "bel velo" (l. 39) or evoked through metonymies (her garment, voice, face, and side) or covered with the loving cloud. The phantom of Dante is conjured up, but it is a Dante who is echoing another text of his, the *Vita nuova*. In short, all the possible sources of the poet's voice are interrogated, but none can yield the secret of the voice's origin.

We can perhaps grasp, finally, the authorial modesty of the *envoi:* "Se tu avessi ornamenti quant' ài voglia, / poresti arditamente / ucir del bosco et gir infra la gente" (ll. 66–68). The *envoi* places the poem in a landscape of nature, which is neither the landscape of vision nor that of memory: it acknowledges the failure of the lyric to live up to the poet's ideas, but it also seals the poem's unavoidable loneliness. From this point of view song 126, which begins by being antithetical to its sister song, ends in the same recognition of a voice that can never coincide with a vision, or, to put it differently, of an understanding that can never be at one with its lyrical origin.

The figure of Echo can best describe Petrarch's insight into his own poetry. Echo is the figuration of a desire that can never coincide with its object; it is the nymph whose body has faded away and who only exists in the articulation of sounds that originate outside of itself. To speak of Echo for Petrarch's sense of his own poetic predicament is not arbitrary. The myth of Echo may indeed be the story of some literary criticism and practice, but in song 126 there is an oblique recall of Ovid's account. The image of Laura in the first stanza is a faint echo of Narcissus by the treacherous pool (*Metamorphoses* 3.410–58), the scene when, spellbound by his own image, the youth sits on the bank, motionless, with a fixed gaze like a statue's, admiring his "smooth cheeks, ivory neck, lovely face where a rosy flush stained the snowy whiteness of his complexion." With Laura cast as Narcissus—as Petrarch does explicitly in sonnet 45, for instance—the poet becomes Echo, each the insubstantial and forever elusive shadow of the other, and each the double of itself.[4]

Ambivalences of Power

Few poets of antiquity or early modernity belong to the future as much as Petrarch does. Many of his works address problems of his own present and oppose the present's moral trends; others—the letters, the interrupted epic about Rome, the cult of antiquities—deal with the past and express a more or less ironic nostalgia for it. But although he certainly admired the past and used it as a gauge for what he perceives as a morally decrepit present, Petrarch's real, absorbing passion was the future. He envisioned the future, indeed he became the trumpeter of the new arts and sciences, sought to engender historical change and impart a clear direction and shape to it. This commitment to the future emerges most clearly from his *Epistle to Posterity*, which he began writing in 1351, and which serves as an autobiographical self-portrait from beyond the grave, as a posthumous voice reaching the future from a distant past.

Marked by an appearance of randomness as it goes from one subject to another (which, however does not detract from its overall cohesion), the letter is written in the plain, self-effacing and "familiar" style befitting authorial modesty. Petrarch has no wish to appear as a cumbersome, imperious voice of the past making demands on the future or claiming undue recognition. The opening sentence of the *Epistle* defines his discursive modality: "You may perhaps have heard something about me—although it is doubtful that my poor little name may travel far in space and time" (p. 5). Transparently, the exordium seeks to shun all possible postures of self-assertion or self-importance. On the contrary, the tone is one of unassuming familiarity and easy accessibility, and it aims at communicating an intimate atmosphere, at establishing a spiritual kinship or proximity between writer and reader as if this were a letter written for an unknown but possible friend across the vast distances of time.

Familiarity, as a rhetorical form of discourse and as a category of historical knowledge, is, of course, a concept Petrarch may be said to have invented or at least perfected. In the *Familiares,* which are letters he wrote to fictive or real correspondents of the past or the present, the term "familiar" has polysemous extensions: it describes the range of intimate subjects his letters will encompass; it casts Petrarch as a friendly man who is engaged in seemingly sincere self-confessions and who, thereby, draws his readers within the circle of his confidences; it also defines the principle of historical hermeneutics that writers of the past can become in the future objects of knowledge and affection, worthy of being remembered, and that to know them is to be familiar with them.

The tone of familiarity of the *Epistle to Posterity*, then, wills to counter the erasure time inflicts on one's name by making oneself known to the unknown future. The monument to the self Petrarch is to erect in order to keep alive the memory of the future entails a mode of history-writing which can be called an archaeology of the self. Whereas autobiographies—say, St. Augustine's *Confessions*—delineate the broad scope of a life and its vital truths to be delivered to their readers, the *Epistle to Posterity*, by contrast, drafts the tenuous and ghostly outlines of a life and sketches its barely visible substance. In fact, with its lacunae, its textual additions, and its seemingly random articulations of themes, the *Epistle to Posterity* gives the eerie impression of a silhouette of a text or of a phantasmatic, archaeological finding, of a torn document a fragment of which was snatched away from time's claws. Self-consciously posthumous, it primarily proposes to acquaint us with the essential quality and lineaments of Petrarch's life—the life of his mind, the features of his moral self, his education and his works—as if the phantasm of that life, doomed as it was to physical annihilation, were still in some ways unique and significant for the future. From this viewpoint the rhetoric of the letter is necessarily characterized by a predictable oscillation between two modes of exposition which are at odds with each other.

First, the overt impulse for writing this epistle is said to lie in Petrarch's will to dispel likely errors stemming from opinions and whims about his name and to establish the truth about his life. *Fama,* which can properly be called the language of history and which designates the future life of the self, is a sovereign concern for Petrarch as it is for all humanists. There is, however, no overt claim that Petrarch's life was extraordinary or famous enough to have him become the focus of public controversies and legends. If there is to be any self-monumentalization or self-vindication, the rhetorical procedures the writer deploys must deliberately mute any stridently triumphant tones. Predictably, the *Epistle* is marked by an opposite, seductive rhetorical strategy to counter and temper the impression of arrogance released by the very gesture of writing about oneself to an unknown posterity. The focus falls on the nature and limits of all individuality as a precarious moment in the unceasing succession of generations, in the persuasion that precariousness remains the perpetual point of recognition of all men, the experience that guarantees the possibility of resemblance between past, present, and future.

The unstated assumption governing the unfolding of the letter is the reader's likely curiosity for the past, which symmetrically balances Petrarch's own curiosity about the future. The symmetry wills to control the readers' responses by drawing them within an imaginative space of commonality, of shared experiences and mutual recognition. Petrarch—and this is the unequivocal implication of this strategy—is really no better than or all that different from his readers. Just as Petrarch did when he wrote about figures of the past, say, his *Lives of Illustrious Men*, so does posterity now look back at the past in its search for the shadowy and thin traces of human history, for knowing itself and recognizing itself within the detritus of time. Petrarch goes on to affirm overtly the common bond of ordinary humanity between himself and future readers: "I was one of your own flock," he says, "a little mortal man, neither of high nor base origin, of an old family—as Augustus Caesar says of himself . . ." (p. 5). The moral consciousness that he is one of the "wretched mortals, puffed with vain wind" (p. 5), who is now mindful of his past errors is the central lesson he draws from his life and passes on to posterity. At least on the surface, even the reference to the emperor Augustus, who is traditionally invested with attributes of divinity, is Petrarch's deliberate ploy to undo or "secularize" any notion of hierarchy between emperor and common people, and by extension, between himself and posterity.

The elaborate rhetorical design in the *Epistle*'s introductory paragraph, whereby he humbly seeks to ingratiate posterity's critical judgment, cannot hide the daring quality of Petrarch's gesture: the *Epistle to Posterity*, as a matter of fact, is a text in which Petrarch keeps alive for the future the memories of the past and, thereby, rejects the principle of the future's independence from the past; in which he asserts his modernity and extends his values on a present that is always in the future (and a future that is always present). *Modernus*, as is known, means "now" and the word primarily reveals the awareness that the present is different from the past. The distinctive feature of the *Epistle to Posterity* lies exactly in Petrarch's radical historical self-consciousness: he belongs to a different time from that of posterity, just as he did with antiquity; by the same token, the sense of a temporal discontinuity between the past and the present is flanked by a concomitant assertion of Petrarch's apartness from his own present. These temporal concerns, which preface and manifestly punctuate the dramatic movement of the *Epistle*, are central to Petrarch's figuration of modernity and its implication for his theory and practice of power.

The question of power is not immediately confronted in the letter. The narrative burden of the *Epistle to Posterity*, which in formal terms is a fragmentary, necessarily inconclusive (since his life is not yet over) and nonsystematic autobiographical account, focuses on the self, his peculiarities and distinctive traits. As stated above, Petrarch will not claim, as a way of starting, that he has launched a totally new cultural enterprise, that he has fashioned intellectual novelties, or that he has explored new territories of knowledge and opened up new paths of investigation. If there will be hints that he has inaugurated a "Petrarchan age," they will be available later (and surreptitiously) in the folds of the text.

His actual point of departure, on the contrary, is a brief but poignant description of his much changed physical appearance—as if the letter were chiefly a document of his empirical identity, an impossible way of retrieving the precarious, concrete form of his existence. The silent pathos implicit in this elegiac gesture of recalling the now lost physical suppleness serves Petrarch to displace the question of the empirical contents of his life toward the valorization of his intellectual achievements. By the same token, the image of a decayed and annihilated body casts Petrarch as a pure voice, or, to put it in mythical-poetic terms, as an insubstantial Echo. In his youth, he says, he was blessed with an active, agile, but not particularly strong body; he was not handsome, and yet he could make a good impression; and his "dark, ardent eyes" (p. 5) were very sharp.

This emphasis on the body, at present suddenly ravaged by old age and sicknesses, finally draws attention to the irreducible individuality of Petrarch's values: for all its limitations, the now absent body is the visible expression of his will, the foundation of his private and public existence, and more generally, of his unique viewpoint on history. And because the body is the very incarnation, as it were, of time's disconti-

nuities, it reveals individuality as a discontinuous succession of mo-
ments, each "now" both continuous with and yet separate from all the
others. This brief evocation of the precariousness of the body, which
for Petrarch is the metaphor of history, gives way to an extended
portrait of a durable, moral self. He was, he says, a scorner of money
(though in truth he died a rich man, as his detailed testamentary
dispositions show); he followed simple diets and shunned sumptuous
banquets. This presentation of self as a sort of Stoic sage introduces
Petrarch's recollection of the "overwhelming love affair" (p. 6) for the
unmentioned Laura from which, because of her "bitter but providen-
tial" death (p. 6) he managed to free himself.

Quite in keeping with the desire to project the moral rather than
the aesthetic existence of the self, nothing explicit is said here about
the *Canzoniere*, in which the phantom of that "overwhelming" love,
and its splendor and futility, are minutely recorded. For all the appar-
ent demotion of the love poetry to the status of a parenthetical,
aberrant experience in the ethical path of his existence, some evidence
of the *Canzoniere*'s love discourse is still preserved here. The text
stresses that Petrarch is now free of that passion's giddiness and
fascination; he has even rejected its "recollection," which I take to be a
tenuous allusion to the poetic writing of the amorous adventure that,
ironically, most defines his life. But the references to the "over-
whelming" love for Laura, to her "bitter and providential" death, and
to the ongoing stimuli of the flesh convey Petrarch's sense, respec-
tively, of death as an aggression perpetrated on the beloved, and of love
and lust as aspects of an involuntary hideous power on the rational
control the self exerts on oneself. These textual details open up, in
effect, the question that lies hidden in Petrarch's mind and will now
emerge in full force, as if this were the real concern of posterity: the
question of power and its ambivalences as well as the insight that
history (and the future) is under the sovereignty of a power ideology.
From this standpoint, it must be stressed that Petrarch's past poetic-
erotic experience, which he views as sheer futility in the economy of
his present moral philosophy, comes forth as an aesthetics of odious
powerlessness, as a mode that radically contradicts the pattern of Pe-
trarch's understanding of power as is related by the *Epistle to Posterity*.

The confession of the love-passion and generally of lust as weak-
nesses that need be transcended leads Petrarch to define further the
landscape of his soul. Among the other deadly sins that wounded his

rationality he focuses on two: he does not admit to the sin of pride, but acknowledges that of wrath. Envy, he adds, he aroused in others. The vainglory of having "honorable friendships" (p. 6) is a cipher for revealing his gravitation toward powerful social circles, though he claims he maintains his political-moral autonomy from kings and princes: ". . . my love of freedom was so deeply implanted in me that I carefully shunned those whose high standing seemed to threaten my freedom. Some of the greatest kings of our time have loved and cultivated my friendship. Why I don't know; that is their affair. When I was their guest it was more as if they were mine" (pp. 6–7).

Retrospectively, the image of Augustus Caesar that Petrarch evoked at the outset of the Epistle appears as more than an innocent technique to erase the importance of social degree from the perspective of the wretchedness of the human condition. In effect, Petrarch re-defines the vertical power relations within the social system. He counters the feudal principle of the poet's submission to the sovereign power of the king with the principle of horizontal juxtapositions. The poet's authority, power, and freedom (for which the divine Augustus is the term of comparison) exist side by side with the king's munificence and power. Petrarch even insinuates his sense of the poet's superiority over the king. At this point the *Epistle to Posterity* brackets this whole issue, the tortuous complications of which, however, cannot but resurface later in the text.

For now the self-portrait moves to an account of the growth of Petrarch's mind, which he says was "rather well balanced than keen" (p. 7). Initially interested in moral philosophy and poetry, he neglected poetry and discovered "the hidden sweetness" of sacred literature; because of his rejection of his own times (which makes him wish he had been born in another period) he was drawn to the charms of studying antiquity and history. This view of self-isolation and independence from his own times, which is one of the motifs of Petrarch's text, is crucial because of the light it casts on Petrarch's indirect suggestion about the nature of poetry.

Literature appears to be isolated from all other discourses and, in point of fact, it is itself a form of isolation. Neglected for a time by this supreme artificer, literature no longer plays the role of constituting the imaginative fold of the encyclopedia, as it had been for Homer, for Vergil, or, closer to home, for Dante. The encyclopedic unity is lost, and poetry is now opposed to or at least unlike history, theology, and philosophy—the disciplines which come forth as authentic forms of wisdom. Provisionally neglected, literature remains buried within itself and becomes its own object of narcissistic self-reflection. Petrarch will never stray far from meditating on language (including, as is the case here, the rhetoric of his speech: his clear utterance and the plain style of his ordinary elocution, which is unlike, he says, that of Caesar Augustus) and on what is known as the act of writing. But the neglect of poetry and the statement of his existential isolation both temper his claim of being intimate with kings and princes and prolong the consciousness of the powerlessness of self revealed by the poetry of the *Canzoniere* and by the love discourse it represents. The ideas of freedom from the official mechanisms of political power, his will to a moral dissociation from his own times, and the temporary neglect of literature together constitute what could appear to be a knot of the contradictory states of his mind. Freedom, as both the condition and aim of moral life, characterizes the state of creativity which Petrarch articulates as the trait of his mind and of modernity's own self-understanding. This state of freedom coincides, however, with freedom from the practice of secular literature, which effectively celebrates the free play of the imagination. The fact is that Petrarch wills to find an objective counterpart to freedom of the self so that this freedom will not appear as merely an imaginary self-construction. He relates the history of his family and his public life through their common experience of exile, in the persuasion that this circumstance was the real and symbolic source of the unique shape his life was to take.

Of Florentine origin, Petrarch was born in exile in Arezzo in 1304, and his childhood is marked by an ongoing instability: the family keeps moving from Incisa to Pisa and finally to Avignon, where the Pope himself lived "in shameful exile" (p. 7). His early schooling took place at Avignon and Carpentras, and later he studied law at Montpellier and Bologna (where, with interruptions, he was from 1320 to 1326). Uninterested in practicing law, he returned home to Avignon: "I call 'home,'" he adds, "that Avignon exile" (p. 8). The paradox of exile as home, which Petrarch lucidly stresses, calls attention to the doubleness, the ironic discrepancies and ambivalences visible in all his texts and in the depths of his consciousness, to what the *Epistle to Posterity* presents as that synthetic contradiction of freedom of creative subjectivity and assertion of his majestic intellectual power.

Back in Avignon he worked for the Colonna family, first for

Giacomo and later for Cardinal Giovanni Colonna. Petrarch is at pains to assure posterity that in this service to the Colonna family he was "practically independent" (p. 9), as if employment entailed political bondage that defiles the value of the imaginative work to come. This independence is dramatized as the excitement of travels throughout Europe. His "youthful curiosity" (p. 9) leads him to visit, first, France and Germany and, later, Rome. These voyages, without any apparent practical purpose for himself, can be construed as metaphors of Petrarch's self-displacement and exile, as analogues of his unspecified anxieties, and as efforts to deliver himself from his anxieties. More than that, the travels are said to be triggered by "curiosity."

This term, which in the Christian lexicon is charged with negative resonances, designates at the same time a self-consuming desire, the mind's unceasing mobility in its quest for novelties, and the mind's ceaseless estrangement from any one object when it is no longer a novelty. Curiosity eschews finalities, and from this viewpoint it is a metaphor for both time's motion and desire's endless articulations. It can be said that the curiosity that impels Petrarch to travel is the opposite of the ethical vision he now has of his past: as a mode of transgression of all boundaries, curiosity transforms the world into an aesthetic phenomenon, into fabulous shallow appearances which one's curiosity devours and onto which the mind can be fixed only for a brief time.

As a quester Petrarch knows that he must stand alone in a radical estrangement from the turbulence of the times and that his search, to be properly conducted, is to be internalized. Unable to bear "the congenital irritation and disgust" (p. 9) he feels for all cities and most of all for Avignon, he seeks refuge with his books in a solitary, narrow valley called Vaucluse, which is near the source of the Sorgue river, some fifteen miles from Avignon. This charming, secluded spot will give his imagination its coloration of regret and will wrap it in its distinctive state of permanent suspension. He cannot cling to the public myths and values the city upholds because they are doomed to perish, but he cannot sever all the bonds of love and grief for the world he has already renounced precisely because he would eventually lose it. In this place, which is a place of the mind, Petrarch will abide for many a year. Here he will undertake the writing of a pastoral poem, the *Bucolicum carmen,* and the treatise about solitary life, *De vita solitaria.*

Nothing is said of the *Canzoniere,* which more than any other text of his is rooted in the soil and is refracted with the light of this landscape. But the emphasis on these texts of solitude communicates one sense of Petrarch's understanding of literature. Writing is for him a self-recollection, a location of oneself at the edge of history, at the dividing line between the *saeculum* (a word that, in opposition to *mundus,* the Middle Ages took in the double sense of time and space, as the encompassing horizon, as it were, of the "world") and one's own inner realities. There is, however, a public counterpoint to this understanding of writing as the practice of estranged solitude. On a Good Friday, which is also the day when his passion for Laura began, he was seized by the inspiration to write an epic poem, which he calls *Africa* after its hero, Scipio Africanus. He begins the poem "with a great burst of enthusiasm, but soon, distracted by various concerns, I put it aside" (p. 10).

There is in Petrarch what must be called a compulsion not to finish what he begins (the *Epistle to Posterity* is a case in point, just as the *Africa* is). He records with obvious excitement the beginnings of his works, as if he still were fascinated by novelties, but he keeps them as projects to be accomplished in the future or to be picked up on the spur of the moment. Years later, as the *Epistle* reports, while roaming the woods of Selvapiana in the Reggio region, suddenly "struck by the beauty of the site, I was moved to pick up my interrupted *Africa*" (p. 11). This taste for fragmentariness, which is revealed also by the aphoristic bent of his writing, betrays the quality of a mind that can be "distracted," whose intellectual grasp is always shifting as well as his sense of the openendedness of the problems he confronts. Paradoxically, his disposition to interrupt his works suggests his emancipation from the present, a freedom which can be defined as a self-projection into the future, as if he forever belonged to the future. Petrarch's modernity, then, is chiefly to be defined as the awareness of a self's temporal and spatial apartness; as the recognition of a creative, aesthetic freedom which is to be a central component in the self's own self-articulation; as a figuration of a self that is a radically unfinished and future-oriented project. But there is another side to his conception of modernity and of posterity. What turns out to count most in the definition of the self is power, and there is an overt thematic strain of the fascination with power in the *Epistle to Posterity.*

Africa, which was meant to be the epic of history, was left unfinished, and yet it changed the poet's fate. On a single day, as the

Epistle to Posterity goes on to relate, "letters arrived from the Roman Senate and from the Chancellor of the University of Paris. They summoned me, as if in competition, to receive the laurel crown of poetry in Rome and in Paris" (p. 10). In Petrarch's letter there are intimations of a secret logic binding the failure of writing *Africa* to the extraordinary public success of the poet, marked by institutional acts of recognition. *Africa* could not be finished because Petrarch, one infers, no longer entertained any illusions about the feasibility of representing the epic heroes of antiquity for the present. The failure of the epic, thus, is the obverse side of and gives rise to Petrarch's discovery and construction of himself *qua* poet as the hero of modernity.

History's heroic values are radically altered as the poet displaces and eclipses tradition's figures of power. He has now become so utterly a public persona that the future anonymity he feared at the outset of the *Epistle* is revealed as unfounded. The image of the "competition" between the University of Paris and the Roman Senate, which stand for modernity and antiquity in the historical paradigm of the *translatio studii,* certainly conveys Petrarch's sense of playfulness and surprise at the honor bestowed on him by competing power structures. The image has another side: it stages the domain of culture as a confrontation of conflicting forces and interests. The value of the poet, to put it simply, depends on the desires of the competing institutions. More than that, at this point the *Epistle to Posterity* radically shifts its ground and squarely focuses on the relationship between the poet and figures of political power.

Compared with Plato's autobiographical seventh letter, in which the philosopher relates his efforts to educate the tyrant, as if this were a necessary compromise for the philosopher, Petrarch's account of his ties with the princes and despots of fourteenth-century Italy is bound to appear evasive and even mediocre. The *Epistle to Posterity* lacks the grandeur of Plato's text: whereas Plato felt the need to retrace and justify the coherence of his dazzling philosophical vision at the moment when it is shattered by the tyrant's subornation, Petrarch is at pains to record his independence in the face of the (insidious and yet welcome) generosity of the princes. Nonetheless, Petrarch's rhetorical evasiveness is the sign of a contradictory complexity in his relation to political power.

It is well known that the poet will opt to receive the laurel crown on the steps of the Roman Capitol, for "the prestige of Rome was to be preferred to all else" (p. 10). The poet's imperial dream is close to being fulfilled. But he first goes to Naples to be examined over a period of three days by "the noblest of kings and philosophers, Robert, illustrious in his government and in literature" (p. 10). After Robert decided that Petrarch is worthy of the laurel, he goes to Rome to be crowned; from Rome he goes to Parma with the Correggi, and eventually to Padua as a guest in the household of the Carraras. The letter breaks off with the remark that Petrarch returns to France, "not so much from a desire to see again what I had seen a thousand times as, like a sick man, to be rid of distress by shifting position" (p. 12).

The morbid consciousness made explicit by the letter's closing sentence is the inverted reflection superimposed on Petrarch's rhetorical evasiveness. Power's seduction is irresistible for this cosmopolitan and uprooted man of letters, and its lure is made visible by Petrarch's admission of the power of the poet-intellectual to celebrate, preserve for posterity, and confer values on kings and princes (who in turn seek out the poet and lavish gifts on him). A dark and yet quite decipherable complicity is established as the natural privilege of the princes (whose empirical identities keep changing) and the earned privilege of the poet (who remains singular, as if irreplaceable) are symmetrically linked together in a power network.

Petrarch lucidly recognizes history as an implacable pattern of power relations and decisively inserts himself in that pattern by remaining distinct and preserving himself within his own identity. But his *Epistle to Posterity* encloses in its fold contradictory signs of his discourse on power. The poet's sovereignty over the statesmen, which is the brunt of the letter, is countered by evasiveness, and this evasiveness can be construed as a saving strategy: the distress he feels, the need that he, "like a sick man," shift position by traveling back to Vaucluse, are symptoms that Petrarch's mind is deeply divided against itself: exile, the disabling love-passion, the knowledge of finiteness of all experiences, the imaginative freedom he enjoys while roaming over the hills of Provence and Selvapiana, and his isolation in time and space—questions that punctuate the movement of his letter—are nothing less than the radical antithesis of his power-cult and, almost certainly, they are also the alibi of his quest for power and recognition. He represses and gives up, in short, the interior love world of the *Canzoniere,* imaginatively rich but powerless, for the public ceremonies of power.

The slender archaeology of the self that the *Epistle to Posterity* retrieves traces Petrarch's impasse between exile and power. Obliquely, as the *Epistle* is the imaginative recall of the phantasm of posterity, it constitutes the enigmatic divination of a modernity, which, like the fragmented text reflecting it, imagines familiar aesthetic routes of escape, but is inescapably caught within the ambivalences of power. The torn message reaching the future from the depths of the past offers to our view the image of the ironic, perpetual contradictions of history. It is as if Petrarch had read Plato's seventh letter and thinks it over.

Notes

1. Antiquity and the New Arts

1. The bibliography on the question of historical periodization is obviously vast. Some of the works I have found particularly valuable are Giorgio Falco, *La polemica sul Medio Evo,* vol. 1 (Turin: Falco, 1933); Lynn Thorndike, "Renaissance or Prenaissance," *Journal of the History of Ideas* 4 (1943): 65–74, an issue devoted to "Tradition and Innovation in Fifteenth-Century Italy" and also containing important contributions by Hans Baron, Ernst Cassirer, Paul O. Kristeller, and others that are pertinent to the questions at hand; and George Boas, "Historical Periods," *Journal of Aesthetics and Art Criticism* 11 (1953): 248–54, and "The Problem of Periodization," in *The Late Italian Renaissance,* ed. Eric Cochrane (New York: Harper and Row, 1970), pp. 23–73, which contains an English version of Benedetto Croce, "La crisi italiana del Cinquecento e il legame del Rinascimento col Risorgimento," *La critica: Rivista di letteratura, storia e filosofia* 37 (1939): 401–11.

2. These viewpoints are sketched in Erwin Panofsky, "'Renaissance': Self-Definition or Self-Deception?," in *Renaissance and Renascences in Western Art* (New York: Harper and Row, 1960), pp. 1–35. See also Eugenio Garin, "Interpretazioni del Rinascimento," in *Medioevo e Rinascimento* (Bari: Laterza, 1976), pp. 85–100.

3. The notion that there is no dividing line between the culture of the Middle Ages and that of the Renaissance is upheld in Thorndike, "Renaissance or Prenaissance," esp. p. 70. The uniqueness of the Italian Renaissance is debated in Charles H. Haskins, *The Renaissance of the Twelfth Century* (Cambridge: Harvard University Press, 1927). See also the remarks in Jacques Boulenger, "Le Vrai Siècle de la Renaissance," *Humanisme et Renaissance* 1 (1934): 9–12, which are in the same spirit as Haskins's assumptions. Of interest may also be the following statement by Etienne Gilson: "La différence entre la Renaissance et le moyen age n'est pas une différence par excès, mais par défaut. La Renaissance, telle qu'on nous la décrit, n'est pas le moyen age plus l'homme, mais le moyen age moins Dieu, et la tragédie, c'est qu'en perdant Dieu la Renaissance allait perdre l'homme lui-meme" (*Les Idées et les lettres* [Paris: J. Vrin, 1932], p. 192). For a different sense of continuity, see Paul Renucci, *L'Aventure de l'humanisme européen au Moyen-Age (IVᵉ–XIVᵉ siècle)* (Clermont-Ferrand: Bussac, 1953). For a modern view of historical continuities and discontinuities, see Albert Russell Ascoli, "Petrarch's Middle

Age: Memory, Imagination, History, and 'The Ascent of Mount Ventoux,'"
Stanford Italian Review 10, no. 1 (1991): 5–43.

4. Hans Blumenberg, "Aspects of the Epochal Threshold: The Cusan and the Nolan," in *The Legitimacy of the Modern Age,* trans. Robert M. Wallace (Cambridge: Massachusetts Institute of Technology Press, 1983), pp. 457–596. The main impulse behind Blumenberg's polemics is the desire to offset the opinions in Karl Lowith, *Meaning in History: The Theological Presuppositions of the Philosophy of History* (Chicago: University of Chicago Press, 1949). The opinions by Hans-Georg Gadamer are debated by Blumenberg on pp. 476ff.

5. Henry Osborn Taylor, *The Mediaeval Mind,* vol. 2 (London: Macmillan, 1938). For the issue devoted to the "Alterity of the Middle Ages," see *New Literary History* 10 (1979).

6. This sense of the past as not entirely past is best conveyed by a famous image that John of Salisbury in the twelfth century attributes to Bernard of Chartres (eleventh century) and that Alexander Neckham picks up in the thirteenth century: "We are dwarfs on the shoulder of giants: thanks to them, we see better and farther away than they did."

7. Gordon Leff, *Paris and Oxford Universities in the Thirteenth and Fourteenth Centuries: An Institutional and Intellectual History* (York: John Wiley and Son, 1968). See also *Chartularium Universitatis Parisiensis,* ed. Heinrich Denifle and Emile Chatelain, 4 vols. (Paris: Didier, 1889–97); Pierre Mandonnet, *Siger de Brabant et l'Averroisme latin au XIIIe siècle,* 2 vols. (Louvain, 1908–11); and Daniel A. Callus, "The Introduction of Aristotelean Learning to Oxford," *Proceedings of the British Academy* 29 (1943): 229–81. More generally, see Charles H. Haskins, *The Rise of the Universities* (Ithaca, N.Y.: Cornell University Press, 1957). For Marsilius, see his *The Defender of Peace,* trans. Alan Gewirth (New York: Columbia University Press, 1956). See also Gewirth, "John of Jandun and the 'Defensor Pacis,'" *Speculum* 23 (1948): 267–72, and Gaines Post, "*Plena Potestas* and Consent in Medieval Assemblies," *Traditio* 1 (1943): 355–408. On biblical exegesis, see Henri de Lubac, *Exégèse médiévale: Les quatre sens de l'Ecriture* (Paris: Aubier, 1959–64). For another version of this argument, see Giuseppe Mazzotta, *Dante's Vision and the Circle of Knowledge* (Princeton: Princeton University Press, 1993).

8. See the still classic article, Theodor E. Mommsen, "Petrarch's Conception of the 'Dark Ages,'" *Speculum* 17 (1942): 226–42, reprinted in *Medieval and Renaissance Studies,* ed. Eugene F. Rice, Jr. (Ithaca, N.Y.: Cornell University Press, 1959), pp. 106–29. See also Franco Simone, "La coscienza della Rinascita negli Umanisti," *La Rinascita* 2 (1939): 838–71, 3 (1940): 163–86, and Wallace K. Ferguson, "Humanist Views of the Renaissance," *American Historical Review* 45 (1939): 1–28. G. Stuart Gordon, *Medium Aevum and the Middle Ages,* Society for Pure English, no. 19 (Oxford: Oxford University

Press, 1925), studies the early occurrences of terms such as *media tempora, media aetas,* and *medium aevum.*

9. The history of the attitudes toward the Middle Ages has been studied in Lucie Varga, *Das Schlagwort vom "finsteren Mittelalter"* (Baden: R. M. Rohrer, 1932).

10. The quotation is from *De sui ipsius et multorum ignorantia,* in *Opere latine di Francesco Petrarca,* ed. Antonietta Bufano, 2 vols. (Turin: Unione Tipografico-Editrice Torinese, 1975), p. 1070. In *De Africa* Petrarch envisions a better future time when "Letheas . . . sopor" will cease and the pure radiance of the past will be regained: "Poterunt discussis forte tenebris / Ad purum priscumque iubar remeare nepotes" (9.453ff.).

11. The phrase *uso moderno* occurs in *Purgatorio* 26.113. The "new" or modernity is not necessarily a term for progress in the *Divine Comedy.* There is a ceaseless pattern of alternation between times of artistic achievement and ages of barbarism—and never simple progress—in Dante's imagination. See the lines in *Purgatorio* 11: "Oh vana gloria de l'umane posse. / Com'poco verde in su la cima dura, / se non è giunta da l'etati grosse. / Credette Cimabue ne la pittura / tener lo campo, e ora ha Giotto il grido, / sì che la fama di colui è scura. / Così ha tolto l'uno a l'altro Guido / la gloria de la lingua; e forse è nato / chi l'uno e l'altro caccerà del nido. / Non è il mondan romore altro ch'un fiato / di vento, ch'or vien quinci e or vien quindi, / e muta nome perchè muta lato" (ll. 91–102).

12. Giovanni Boccaccio, *Lettere edite ed inedite,* ed. Francesco Corazzini (Florence: Sansoni, 1877), pp. 189ff. The translation is mine.

13. This is *Fam.* 6.2. Here and throughout I use the text from *Le familiari di Francesco Petrarcha,* ed. Vittorio Rossi and Umberto Bosco, Edizione nazionale delle opere di Francesco Petrarcha, vols. 10–13 (Florence: Sansoni, 1933–42), unless noted otherwise. For the date of the letter, see Ernest H. Wilkins, *A Tentative Chronology of Petrarch's Prose Letters* (Chicago: University of Chicago Press, 1929). On the letter, see the excellent remarks in Thomas M. Greene, *The Light in Troy: Imitation and Discovery in Renaissance Poetry* (New Haven: Yale University Press, 1982), pp. 88–93. Greene brings to bear both the *Mirabilia urbis* and book 8 of the *Aeneid* on Petrarch's imaginative reconstruction of Rome. Also of interest are the remarks in Mommsen, "Petrarch's Conception of the 'Dark Ages,'" pp. 114–18. On the motif of Roman ruins, see Walther Rehm, *Der Untergang Roms in abendlandischen Denken* (Leipzig: Dieterich, 1930). On the question of antiquarianism, which I shall examine again from a different angle in chapter 5, see Angelo Mazzocco, "The Antiquarianism of Francesco Petrarca," *Journal of Medieval and Renaissance Studies* 7 (1977): 203–24.

14. The translation from *Fam.* 6.2 is taken from *Rerum Familiarum Libri I–VIII,* trans. Aldo Bernardo (Albany: State University of New York Press,

1975), 1:294. All translations of books 1–8 of *Le familiari* are from this work, unless noted otherwise.

15. The sense of place, which is central to Petrarch's imagination, can best be illustrated by this memory of Vaucluse: "There, I remember happily, I began my *Africa*. . . . There I wrote a large share of my letters in prose and verse, and I composed almost all of my *Bucolicum Carmen*. . . . No locality ever gave me more leisure or a keener stimulus" (*Fam.* 8.3). The translation is taken from *Letters from Petrarch,* trans. Morris Bishop (Bloomington: Indiana University Press, 1966), pp. 69ff.

16. The translation is taken from Mommsen, "Petrarch's Conception of the 'Dark Ages,'" p. 115.

17. For this question of Rome in the Middle Ages (which includes St. Augustine's *City of God* as well as Dante's *Monarchia* and *Divine Comedy*), see Charles Norris Cochrane, *Christianity and Classical Culture: A Study of Thought and Action from Augustus to Augustine* (Oxford: Oxford University Press, 1968); Charles T. Davis, *Dante and the Idea of Rome* (Oxford: Clarendon, 1957); and Giuseppe Mazzotta, *Dante, Poet of the Desert: History and Allegory in the Divine Comedy* (Princeton: Princeton University Press, 1979).

18. The fall of Rome had been predicted, according to biblical exegetes, by Nebuchadnezzar's dream of the statue as told in Daniel 2.31ff. See the gloss on this by Philip of Harvengt, "De somnio regis Nabuchodonosor," in *Patrologia Latina* [hereinafter *PL*], ed. J. P. Migne (Paris, 1844–64), 203, col. 586. On this, see J. W. Swain, "The Theory of the Four Monarchies: Opposition History under the Roman Empire," *Classical Philology* 35 (1940): 1–21. Vergil's prophecy is from *Aeneid* 1.278ff. It was the event of the fall of Rome, furthermore, that lay behind St. Augustine's decision to write *The City of God,* in which the eternity of the earthly city is a counterfeit of the real eternity in the Heavenly City. On this, see Mazzotta, *Dante, Poet of the Desert,* pp. 170–75. For the reaction of St. Jerome, see note 21 below.

19. Irenaeus, *Contre les hérésies* (Paris: Editions du Cerf, 1952), 2.5, 26; Tertullian, *De resurrectione carnis,* in *PL* 2, cols. 791–836.

20. Lactantius, "De postremis temporibus ac de urbe Roma," in *De divinis institutionibus,* bk. 7, ch. 25, in *PL* 6, col. 811. For an excellent treatment of St. Augustine's reflections on the city in ruin, see Theodor E. Mommsen, "St. Augustine and the Christian Idea of Progress: The Background of 'The City of God,'" *Journal of the History of Ideas* 12 (1951): 346–74, reprinted in *Medieval and Renaissance Studies,* ed. Rice, pp. 265–98. My indebtedness to this excellent article is great. The lines by the Pseudo-Bede are from *Flores ex diversis, quaestiones et parabola,* in *PL* 94, col. 543.

21. St. Jerome is quoting here Psalms 39.2. The passage, here given in the translation from Mommsen, "St. Augustine and the Christian Idea of Prog-

ress," p. 266, comes from his *Commentaries on Ezekiel* 25.15–16. The remark is
an introduction to the exegesis of the first book.

22. "Itaque die quodam, dum in eam mentionem incidessemus, flagitasti
ut dicerem explicite unde putarem liberales et unde mechanicas initium
habuisse, quod carptim ex me audieras. . . . Accipe igitur quod tunc dixi,
verbis forte aliis sed eadem profecto sententia. Verum quid agimus? Nam et
non parva res est et epystola hec abunde crevit, . . . differamus que restant in
proximum diem, . . . sed quid rursum cogito, quid ve polliceor tibi diem
proximum epystolamque alteram? Nec diei unius opus est nec epystolare
negotium; *librum exigit*, quem non prius aggrediar—si tamen curis maioribus
non retrahor atque disturbor—quam in solitudinem meam me fortuna revex-
erit" (*Fam.* 6.2; emphasis added). See also the speculations in L. Venturi, "La
critica d'arte e Francesco Petrarca," *L'Arte* 25 (1922): 238–44.

23. *Sine nomine: Lettere polemiche e politiche*, ed. Ugo Dotti (Bari: Laterza,
1974). See especially letter 10, to Francesco Nelli, in which Avignon is called
"Babylon," "golden labyrinth," etc.

24. Ibid., letter 2, to Cola di Rienzo, has the following: "O Avinio, cuius
vinea, si quid coniectoribus fidei est, botros amarissimas et cruentam proferet
vindemiam" (p. 20). The pun is operative in sonnet 137 from the *Canzoniere:*
"L'avara Babilonia ha colmo il sacco / D'ira di Dio e di vizi empi e rei / Tanto
che scoppia, ed ha fatti suoi dèi / Non Giove e Palla ma Venere e *Bacco*"
(emphasis added).

25. See *Babylon on the Rhone: A Translation of Letters by Dante, Petrarch,
and Catherine of Siena on the Avignon Papacy*, trans. Robert Coogan (Madrid:
J. P. Turanzas, 1983), for the various spiritual perspectives on Avignon.

26. The translation is taken from ibid., letter 4, p. 54.

27. "When was there ever such a peace, such tranquillity, such justice,
such esteem for virtue, such reward for goodness, such punishments for the
wicked, and such sound judgement in the affairs of state as when the world
had one head and that head was Rome? Was it not in that epoch when the
most powerful lover of peace and justice chose to be born of a virgin and to
visit the earth?" (ibid.). See also the corresponding notions in Dante's *Monar-
chia* 1.16.1–3, 1.11.10.4, 2.11–12.

28. "'Imperium sine fine dedi.'" Here Augustine reasonably comments:
"For how shall he give an empire without end who never gave nor was ever
able to give anything except that which a sinful and mortal man can give? . . .' I
will not treat this matter of who passed down the Roman Empire, for it is
certain that none but the omnipotent God gave it. . . . Augustine asks where
this kingdom might be: 'Is it on earth or in heaven? Certainly it is on earth. . . .
If those things that God himself has made shall pass away, how much more
swiftly will pass that which Romulus founded!' In these things Augustine

reproaches Vergil. . . . And so in this instance, Augustine, employing different words, accuses and excuses Vergil as I understand it" (letter 4, trans. Coogan, pp. 57–59). For Dante's oblique polemic with St. Augustine over the vale of Rome, see Mazzotta, *Dante, Poet of the Desert,* pp. 180–88.

29. *Contra eum qui maledixit Italie,* in *Opere latine di Francesco Petrarca,* ed. Bufano, p. 1164. The statement is the radical reversal of St. Augustine's conviction that Rome is one of the series of earthly cities. See *City of God* 15.5.

30. Quintilian, *Institutio oratoria,* ed. Jean Cousin (Paris: Société d'édition "Les Belles Lettres," 1975–80), book 8, chap. 6, para. 4.

31. Useful information on the city of Avignon at the time of the popes is available in Robert Brun, *Avignon au temps des papes* (Paris: Librairie A. Colin, 1928), and E. Castelnuovo, *Un pittore italiano alla corte di Avignone* (Turin: Einaudi, 1962). See also Beryl Smalley, *English Friars and Antiquity in the Early Fourteenth Century* (New York: Barnes and Noble, 1960), esp. pp. 240–307. Of great interest, although tangentially relevant to the present argument, is Eugenio Garin, "La cultura fiorentina nella seconda metà del trecento e i 'barbari britanni,'" *Rassegna storica della letteratura italiana* 62 (1960): 181–95.

32. Jean H. Hagstrum, *The Sister Arts* (Chicago: University of Chicago Press, 1958); R. Lee, *Ut Pictura Poesis* (New York: Norton, 1967); Mario Praz, *Mnemosyne* (Princeton: Princeton University Press, 1970); Erwin Panofsky, *Studies in Iconology* (New York: Icon Books, 1972). See Horace's *Ars poetica,* lines 361–65; Plato's *Republic* 10.605A; and Aristotle's *Poetics* 1448a.5.

33. Isidore of Seville, *Etymologiarum sive originum libri XX,* ed. W. M. Lindsay (Oxford: Clarendon, 1966), bk. 19, ch. 16, pars. 1–2: "Pictura autem est imago exprimens speciem rei alicui, quae dum visa fuerit ad recordationem mentem reducit. Pictura autem dicta quasi fictura; est enim imago ficta, non veritas. Hinc et fucata, id est ficto quodam colore inlita, nihil fidei et veritatis habentia. Unde et sunt quaedam picturae quae corpora veritatis studio coloris excedunt et fidem, dum augere contendunt, ad mendacium provehunt." The translation is mine.

34. On the subject, see Adolfo Venturi, "Le arti figurative al tempo di Dante," *L'Arte* 24 (1921): 230–40. See also the excellent articles by Creighton Gilbert: "Cecco d'Ascoli e la pittura di Giotto," *Commentari* 24 (January–June 1973): 19–25, and "The Fresco by Giotto in Milan," *Arte Lombarda,* n.s., 47–48 (1977): 31–72. Compare *Purgatorio* 11.91–99. The praise of Giotto, however, is placed within the context of punished pride—a strategy by which Dante undercuts the belief in the permanence of artistic achievements. Boccaccio's praise of Giotto is in *Decameron* 6.5: "E per ció, avendo egli quella arte ritornata in luce, che molti secoli sotto gli error d'alcuni, . . . era stata sepulta." Boccaccio's metaphor of light, to describe Giotto's exhuming the buried art,

reverses the image of eclipse ("sí che la fama di colui oscura") in *Purgatorio* 11.96. For Petrarch's involvement with painting, see also his *Testament,* ed. and trans. Theodor E. Mommsen (Ithaca, N.Y.: Cornell University Press, 1957). See also M. Meiss, *Painting in Florence and Siena after the Black Death* (Princeton: Princeton University Press, 1951) Compare Petrarch's *De remediis* 1.40; *Fam.* 5.17, 23.19; and *Seniles* 2.3.

35. Enrico Castelnuovo, *Un pittore italiano alla corte di Avignone,* pp. 15ff.; Valerio Mariani, *Simone Martini e il suo tempo* (Naples: L.G.E., 1968). For the pictoral descriptions of allegorical moralizations (figures, images, pictures, etc.), see Beryl Smalley, "Commentators and Preachers in France," in *English Friars,* pp. 240–64.

36. Here and throughout, the Italian text is from *Canzoniere,* ed. Gianfranco Contini, annotated by Daniele Ponchiroli (Turin: Einaudi, 1964), and the English translation is from *Petrarch's Lyric Poems: The "Rime sparse" and Other Lyrics,* ed. and trans. Robert M. Durling (Cambridge: Harvard University Press, 1976), unless noted otherwise. I rely heavily on the comments in *Le rime,* ed. Giosuè Carducci and Severino Ferrari (Florence: Sansoni, 1960).

37. *Metamorphoses* 10.243ff.; Jean de Meun, *Le Roman de la rose,* ed. Ernest Langlois (Paris: E. Champion, 1924), 5.20817ff.

38. Arnulf d'Orléans, "Arnolfo d'Orleans, un cultore di Ovidio nel secolo XII," ed. Fausto Ghisalberti, *Memorie del reale Istituto Lombardi di Scienze e Lettere de Milano* 24 (1932): 223.

39. See Hebrews 11.1 for the standard definition of faith. See also *Paradiso* 24.64–66. For a definition of beauty in terms of vision, see *Summa Theologiae* 1.5.1. See also note 33 above for Isidore's sense of the links between "fides" and "painting."

40. *Roman de la rose* 5.21154.

11. The Thought of Love

1. The phrase, which summarizes the standard view of Petrarch, is in Paul Oskar Kristeller, *Eight Philosophers of the Italian Renaissance* (Stanford: Stanford University Press, 1964), p. 5. See also Francesco Fiorentino, *La filosofia di Francesco Petrarca* (Naples: D. Morano, 1875); Giovanni Gentile, *Studi sul Rinascimento,* 2d ed. (Florence: Sansoni, 1936); Ernst Cassirer, *The Individual and the Cosmos in Renaissance Philosophy,* trans. Mario Domandi (New York: Harper and Row, 1963); and Eugenio Garin, *La cultura filosofica del Rinascimento italiano* (Florence: Sansoni, 1961), and "La cultura fiorentina nella seconda metà del trecento e i 'barbari britanni,'" *Rassegna storica della letteratura italiana* 64 (1960): 185–87.

2. *The Didascalicon of Hugh of St. Victor: A Medieval Guide to the Arts,* ed. and trans. Jerome Taylor (New York: Columbia University Press, 1968), 1.2, p. 48.

3. All quotations from the *Invective contra medicum* and *Contra eum qui maledixit Italie* are taken from *Opere latine di Francesco Petrarca,* ed. Antonietta Bufano, 2 vols. (Turin: Unione Tipografico-Editrice Torinese, 1975). The quotations from *On His Own Ignorance and That of Many Others* are taken from Hans Nachod, trans., in *The Renaissance Philosophy of Man,* ed. Ernst Cassirer, P. O. Kristeller, and J. II. Randall, Jr. (Chicago: University of Chicago Press, 1948), pp. 47–133.

4. Umberto Bosco, *Petrarca* (Turin: Unione Tipografico-Editrice Torinese, 1946).

5. The quotations from the *Epistle to Posterity* are taken from *Letter from Petrarch,* trans. Morris Bishop (Bloomington: Indiana University Press, 1966), pp. 5–12. A still valuable, if conventional, account of Petrarch's intellectual role is Kristeller, *Eight Philosophers,* pp. 1–18. See also Arnaud Tripet, *Pétrarque ou la connaissance de soi* (Geneve: Librairie Droz, 1967), esp. pp. 157–65, and Charles Trinkaus, *The Poet as Philosopher: Petrarch and the Formation of Renaissance Consciousness* (New Haven: Yale University Press, 1979). A succinct intellectual portrait of Petrarch is Aldo Scaglione, "Petrarca 1974: A Sketch for a Portrait," in *Francis Petrarch, Six Centuries Later: A Symposium,* ed. Aldo Scaglione, Studies in the Romance Languages and Literatures, no. 3 (Chapel Hill: Department of Romance Languages at the University of North Carolina, 1975), pp. 1–24.

6. The letter known as "A Self-Portrait" was written by Petrarch to Francesco Bruni, who was a teacher of rhetoric at the stadium of Florence beginning in 1360. The detail given in the letter accounts, to a great extent, for Petrarch's skeptical language. For the idea of probable truth and the rhetorical disputation, see Wesley Trimpi, "The Quality of Fiction: The Rhetorical Transmission of Literary Theory," *Traditio* 30 (1974): 1–118. See also Warren Ginsberg, *The Cast of Characters: The Representation of Personality in Ancient and Medieval Literature* (Toronto: University of Toronto Press, 1983), pp. 98–133.

7. The translation is taken from the fragment of the letter on a "A Self-Portrait," Nachod, trans., in *Renaissance Philosophy of Man,* pp. 34–35.

8. *Epistle to Posterity,* trans. Bishop, p. 7.

9. The *Psychomachia* (The fight for mansoul) is available in *Prudentius,* trans. H. J. Thomson, Loeb Classical Library (Cambridge: Harvard University Press, 1949), 1:274–343.

10. Cicero's critique of Socrates is found in *De oratore* 3.16.60–61. The admission by the Sophist Gorgias that rhetoric is "the kind of persuasion which produces belief, not knowledge" is found in *Gorgias* 454e.8. The

antagonism between rhetoric and philosophy in historical terms is treated in George A. Kennedy, *Classical Rhetoric and Its Christian and Secular Tradition from Ancient to Modern Times* (London: Croom Helm, 1980).

11. The tract has recently been examined as a defense of rhetoric in Trinkaus, *Poet as Philosopher*, pp. 90–113.

12. I have studied in some detail the debate and its history in *Dante's Vision and the Circle of Knowledge* (Princeton: Princeton University Press, 1993). See also Giuseppe Mazzotta, *The World at Play in Boccaccio's Decameron* (Princeton: Princeton University Press, 1986), for Boccaccio's own understanding of the debate between the arts.

13. The editor of the *Invective* correctly cites the classification of the arts in Hugh of St. Victor's *Didascalicon* (2.vi–xx). A passage from the *Invective* (p. 828) shows clearly Petrarch's dependence on the *Didascalicon:* "Quid te autem non ausurum rear, qui rhetoricam medicine subicias, sacrilegio inaudito, ancille dominam, mechanice liberalem?" On the historical links between medicine and rhetoric, see Jacqueline de Romilly, *Magic and Rhetoric in Ancient Greece* (Cambridge: Harvard University Press, 1975), esp. pp. 45–66. See also Mazzotta, *World at Play*, pp. 13–46, for the relationship Boccaccio establishes between rhetoric and medicine.

14. I would only change Durling's "filled with care" (which is meant to render Petrarch's "pensoso") into "thoughtful" or even into "pensive" in order to stress openly the importance of *thinking* in Petrarch's lyrical vocabulary.

15. As part of the rhetoric of the eyes in the sonnet, one could point out phrases such as "gli occhi porto" (l. 3), "schermo" (l. 5), symmetrically antithetical adjectives "manifesto" (l. 6) and "celata" (l. 11), etc. For a systematic study of Petrarch's rhetoric in his lyrical works, see William Kennedy, *Rhetorical Norms in Renaissance Literature* (New Haven: Yale University Press, 1978), esp. pp. 1–41.

16. A doctoral student of mine, Françoise Brito, developed in my Petrarch seminar (Yale, fall 1991) and elaborated with rich documentation, which I hope to see published in the near future, the notion of Petrarch's nationalization of culture as part of Italy's (and Petrarch's) self-identity over and against French claims.

17. A strong reading of this song, within the larger context of Petrarch's place in history, is Albert Russell Ascoli, "Petrarch's Middle Age: Memory, Imagination, History, and 'The Ascent of Mount Ventoux,'" *Stanford Italian Review* 10, no. 1 (1991): 5–43. See also Timothy Bahti, "Petrarch and the Scene of Writing: A Reading of *Rime* CXXIX," *Yale Italian Studies*, n.s., 1 (1982): 45–63.

18. A definition of memory in terms of gathering, which is the sense in which St. Augustine understands thinking, is available in Hugh of St. Victor's *Didascalicon:* "Concerning memory I do not think one should fail to say here

that just as aptitude investigates and discovers through analysis, so memory retains through gathering. The things which we have analyzed in the course of learning and which we must commit to memory we ought, therefore, to gather. Now 'gathering' is reducing to a brief and compendious outline things which have been written or discussed at some length" (3.11, trans. Taylor, p. 93).

19. The *signa amoris* described in the first stanza of song 129, "or ride or piange or teme or s'assecura, / e 'l volto, che lei segue ov'ella il mena, / si turba et rasserena" (ll. 8–10), echo "Move, cangiando color, riso in pianto, / e la figura con paura storna" (ll. 45–46) of Cavalcanti's poem. *Donna me prega* is available now in *The Poetry of Guido Cavalcanti,* ed. and trans. Lowry Nelson, Jr. (New York: Garland, 1986). For the gloss by Dino del Garbo, see *Guido Cavalcanti: Le rime,* ed. Guido Favati (Milan-Naples: Ricciardi, 1957), pp. 348–78. Dino's interpretation of the lines quoted above reads: "In *move cangiando colore, riso in pianto* (l. 46), Guido considers his consideration of the motions of love, i.e., of the various alterations which it is able to cause the body to undergo. Thus love causes the body to change now to this color and again to its opposite, at one time to laughter, and another to weeping; which Guido declares in *move cangiando colore, riso in pianto.* Likewise it turns the lover at one time to joy and hope and at another to fear and desperation, as Guido declares in *et la figura con paura storna,* that is to say, it at times makes the face of the lover like that of a joyful man" (Otto Bird, "The Canzone d'Amore of Cavalcanti According to the Commentary of Dino Del Garbo," *Medieval Studies* 3 [1941]: 131). See also Bernard of Gordon, *Lilium medicinae* (Venice, 1550). More generally, see Massimo Ciavolella, *La malattia d'amore dall'antichità al medioevo* (Rome: Bulzoni, 1976).

20. The motif is studied in Joseph C. Plumpe, "*Vivum Saxum, Vivi Lapides:* The Concept of the Living Stone in Classical and Christian Antiquity," *Traditio* 1 (1943): 1–14.

21. An updated bibliography on the *Secretum* is available in *Petrarch's "Secretum" with Introduction, Notes, and Critical Anthology,* ed. and trans. Davy A. Carozza and H. James Shey, ser. 17, Classical Languages and Literature, vol. 7 (New York: Peter Lang, 1989). I quote from this translation. Some particularly noteworthy works on this text are Hans Baron, "Petrarch's 'Secretum'—Was It Revised and Why?: The Draft of 1342–43 and Later Changes," *Bibliothèque d'Humanisme et Renaissance* 25 (1963): 489–530; Pierre Courcelle, "Pétrarque entre saint Augustin et les Augustiniens du XIV siècle," *Studi petrarcheschi* 7 (1961): 58–71; Giulio A. Levi, "Pensiero classico e pensiero cristiano nel *Secretum* e nelle *Familiari* del Petrarca," *Atene e Roma* 35 (1933): 63–82; Bortolo Martinelli, *Il Secretum conteso* (Naples: Loffredo, 1982); Adelia Noferi, "Alle soglie del *Secretum,*" in *L'esperienza poetica del Petrarca* (Florence: Le Monnier, 1962), pp. 55–66; Francisco Rico, *Vida y obra de Petrarca,*

vol. I, *Lectura del "Secretum"* (Padua: Antenore, 1974); and Victoria Kahn, "The Figure of the Reader in Petrarch's *Secretum*," *PMLA* 100 (1985): 154–66.

III.   The *Canzoniere* and the Language of the Self

1. All quotations of the Italian texts are from *Canzoniere*, ed. Gianfranco Contini, annotated by Daniele Ponchiroli (Turin: Einaudi, 1968). English translations are from Petrarch's *Lyric Poems: The "Rime sparse" and Other Lyrics*, ed. and trans. Robert M. Durling (Cambridge: Harvard University Press, 1976). I have also consulted the notes in *Le rime*, ed. Giosuè Carducci and Severino Ferrari, new introd. by Gianfranco Contini (Florence: Sansoni, 1960).

2. The question of selfhood in Petrarch has been studied in historical terms in Charles E. Trinkaus, *In Our Image and Likeness: Humanity and Divinity in Italian Humanist Thought,* 2 vols. (Chicago: University of Chicago Press, 1970), esp. 1:3–50. The question was first probed, from a literary perspective, in Thomas Greene, "The Flexibility of the Self in Renaissance Literature," in *The Disciplines of Criticism,* ed. Peter Demetz, Thomas Greene, and Lowry Nelson, Jr. (New Haven: Yale University Press, 1968), pp. 241–64.

3. Adelia Noferi, *L'esperienza poetica del Petrarca* (Florence: Le Monnier, 1962), an essay that admittedly develops some suggestions advanced in Giuseppe De Robertis, *Studi,* 2d ed. (Florence: Le Monnier, 1953), pp. 32–47.

4. Raffaele Amaturo in *Petrarca* (Bari: Laterza, 1971) acknowledges that the *Canzoniere* is not a spiritual itinerary from sin to redemption, but he also claims that for Petrarch "la letteratura diventa un mezzo di conoscenza, di dominio intellettuale, di rasserenamento etico" (p. 356).

5. Robert M. Durling, "Petrarch's 'Giovene donna sotto un verde lauro,'" *MLN* 86 (1971): 1–20. See also John Freccero, "The Fig Tree and the Laurel: Petrarch's Poetics," *Diacritics* 5 (Spring 1975): 34–40.

6. This is suggested in his introduction to Dante Alighieri, *Rime,* ed. Gianfranco Contini (Turin: Einaudi, 1965), p. vii.

7. Gianfranco Contini, "Preliminari sulla lingua del Petrarca," *Varianti e altra linguistica* (Turin: Einaudi, 1970), p. 175.

8. Natalino Sapegno, *Storia letteraria del trecento* (Milan-Naples: Ricciardi, 1963), p. 253. See also Robert M. Durling, *The Figure of the Poet in Renaissance Epic* (Cambridge: Harvard University Press, 1965), pp. 67–87.

9. Noferi, *L'esperienza poetica,* pp. 7ff.

10. Francesco De Sanctis, *Saggio critico sul Petrarca,* ed. N. Gallo (Turin: Einaudi, 1983). The centrality of desire and of the sense of mortality in the *Canzoniere* has been treated by Umberto Bosco in his important monograph, *Francesco Petrarca* (Bari: Laterza, 1968).

11. Noferi, *L'esperienza poetica*, pp. 9ff.

12. *Etymologiarum sive originum libri XX*, ed. W. M. Lindsay (Oxford: Clarendon, 1966). For the definition of *amor*, see 10.4–5. Isidore derives *amicus* from *hamus*, that is, "from chain of love (catena caritatis)." Andreas substitutes chains of cupidity (*cupidinis vinculis*) for Isidore's *catena caritatis*.

13. We might point out, in passing, that this topos is playfully deployed by Eugenio Montale: "ho cominciato anzi giorno / a buttar l'amo per te (lo chiamavo il lamo)" (*La bufera e altro* [Milan: Mondadori, 1961], p. 113).

14. Andreas Capellanus, *De amore libri tres*, ed. Salvatore Battaglia (Rome: Perrella, 1947). The definition occurs in 1.3.

15. Ibid., p. 13.

16. Amaturo, *Petrarca*, p. 281. See also Gianfranco Contini's edition of *Canzoniere* and his "Preliminari sulla lingua del Petrarca" (note 7 above) for some cogent suggestions on Petrarch's reading of the stilnovists.

17. *Aeneid* 1.319: "She had let her hair stream in the wind" (Vergil, *The Aeneid*, trans. W. F. Jackson Knight [New York: Penguin, 1956], p. 37). For the allusion in Petrarch, see Amaturo, *Petrarca*, p. 282.

18. *Metamorphoses* 1.529: "Her hair streamed in the light breeze" (Ovid, *Metamorphoses*, trans. Mary M. Innes [New York: Penguin, 1982], p. 43).

19. "Bound them in a knot, though her own hair hung loose" (*Metamorphoses*, trans. Innes, p. 78). The Latin original is to be found in *Metamorphoses* 3.169–70. For a most valuable reading of the myth of Diana and her connection to Laura and to Petrarch's poetics of fragmentation, see Nancy J. Vickers, "The Body Re-membered: Petrarchan Lyrics and the Strategies of Description," *Mimesis: From Mirror to Method, Augustine to Descartes*, ed. John D. Lyons and Stephen G. Nichols (Hanover, N.H.: University Press of New England for Dartmouth College, 1982), pp. 100–109.

20. *Metamorphoses* 3.192–93: "Now, if you can, you may tell how you saw me when I was undressed" (trans. Innes, p. 79).

21. This metaphor of the mirror faintly recalls Bernard de Ventadour's lines: "Be deurì aucire / qui anc fetz mirador / Can be m'o cossier, / no n'ai guerrer peyor. / Ja l jorn qu'ela s mire / ni pens de sa valor, / no serai jauzire / de leis ni de s'amor" (*Chansons d'amour*, ed. Moshé Lazar [Paris: Librairie Klincksieck, 1966], 2.41–48, p. 208).

22. For the dramatic function of the *losengier* in troubadoric poetry, see Moshé Lazar, *Amour courtois et "fin amors" dans la littérature du XIIᵉ siècle* (Paris: Librairie Klincksieck, 1964), pp. 161–63. For the *trouvers*, see Roger Dragonetti, *La technique poétique des trouvers dans la chanson courtoise: Contribution à l'étude de la rhétorique médévale* (Brugge, Belg.: De Tempel, 1960), pp. 272ff. For a more general treatment, see Maurice Valency, *In Praise of Love* (New York: Macmillan, 1969), pp. 171ff.

23. *Metamorphoses* 3.435. Innes translates: "In itself it is nothing" (p. 85).

For a study on the Narcissus theme in medieval literature, see Frederick Goldin, *The Mirror of Narcissus in the Courtly Love Lyric* (Ithaca, N.Y.: Cornell University Press, 1967).

24. *Metamorphoses* 3.463. The whole passage, in Innes's translation, reads: "I am myself the boy I see. I know I . . . it is I who kindle the flame" (p. 86).

25. *Metamorphoses* 3.141–42. Innes translates the whole passage as follows: "But calm reflection will show that destiny was to blame for Actaeon's misfortunes, not any guilt on his own part" (pp. 77–78).

26. This motif occurs frequently in the *Canzoniere*. See, for example, sonnet 2, where love is said to have come by stealth.

27. The figure of the veil, in its allegorical overtones, occurs, for instance, in 2 Corinthians 3.12–16, where Paul discusses the possibility of seeing the spirit beneath the surface of the Old Testament and adds: "Having therefore such hope, we are very bold, not like Moses, who put a veil over his face so that the Israelites might not see the end of the fading splendour. But their minds were hardened; for to this day, when they read the old covenant, that same veil remains unlifted, because only through Christ is it taken away." Dante, of course, systematically uses the metaphor of the veil ("velo," "velame") in the context of allegory. Compare, for example, *Inferno*, 9.61–63, and *Purgatorio* 8.19–21.

28. The theory of *rithimorum asperitas* and *lenitas* is to be found in *De vulgari eloquentia* 2.13.12, where Dante quotes his own "Al poco giorno" to which Petrarch alludes (see note 29).

29. The lines "Miri ciò che 'l cor chiude / Amor et que' begli occhi, / ove si siede a l'ombra" echo "ch 'Amor li viene a stare a l'ombra" from "Al poco giorno."

30. The translation from Dante's *Rime Petrose,* here as well as earlier in the text, is taken from *Dante's Lyric Poetry,* trans. Kenelm Foster and Patrick Boyde (Oxford: Clarendon, 1967), p. 171.

31. I am here paraphrasing a more extended analysis of the poem in my *Dante, Poet of the Desert: History and Allegory in the Divine Comedy* (Princeton: Princeton University Press, 1979), esp. pp. 277–90. For the importance of the Medusa myth for Petrarch, see Kenelm Foster, "Beatrice or Medusa: The Penitential Element in Petrarch's *Canzoniere*," in *Italian Studies Presented to E. R. Vincent* (Cambridge: Cambridge University Press, 1962), pp. 41–56.

32. St. Augustine, *Confessiones,* in *Corpus Scriptorum Ecclesiasticorum Latinorum,* vol. 32. The passage on the weight of love occurs in 13.9.

33. Ibid., 1.13ff.

34. The passage in its entirety reads: "Who remindeth me of the sins of my infancy? For in Thy sight none is pure from sin, not even the infant whose life is but a day upon the earth. Who remindeth me? . . . What then was my sin? . . . Myself have seen and known even a baby envious; it could not speak,

yet it turned pale and looked bitterly on its foster-brother. . . . Passing hence from infancy I came to boyhood, or rather it came to me . . . for I was no longer a speechless infant but a speaking boy" (*The Confessions of St. Augustine,* trans. Edward B. Pusey [New York: Collier, 1961], pp. 15–16). The Latin original is found in *Confessiones* 1.7–8.

35. 1 Corinthians 15.53.

36. A. T. Macrobius, *Commentarii in Somnium Scipionis,* ed. James H. Willis (Leipzig: Teubner, 1970), esp. 1.2.11, p. 6.

37. One could point to the fact that Amor is personified; to the personification of the natural landscape; to the fact that the *canzone* is articulated on a series of oppositions between an "inside" that is concealed and an "outside."

38. The implications of the technique of the anagram have been treated in Jean Starobinski, *Les Mots sous les mots: Les anagrammes de Ferdinand de Saussure* (Paris: Gallimard, 1971). See also François Rigolot, "Nature and Function of Paranomasia in the *Canzoniere,*" *Italian Quarterly* 18, no. 69 (1974): 29–36.

39. *Etymologiarum* 17.7.2. The translation is mine.

40. For the idea of the calendar as a structural principle of the *Canzoniere,* see Thomas P. Roche, "The Calendrical Structure of Petrarch's *Canzoniere,*" *Studies in Philology* 71 (1974): 152–72. The notion of *recommencements* as a way of defining Petrarch's variations is suggested in De Robertis, *Studi,* p. 42.

41. Sonnet 224 has the line "un lungo error in cieco laberinto" (l. 4). Sonnet 89, on the other hand, focuses on the "pregione" of Love and on the insoluble "errore" (l. 14) of his passion.

IV.   Ethics of Self

1. The importance of this practice has been highlighted in Ronald Witt, "Medieval *Ars dictaminis* and the Beginnings of Humanism: A New Construction of the Problem," *Renaissance Quarterly* 35 (1982): 8–14, and "Medieval Italian Culture and the Origins of Humanism as a Stylistic Ideal," *Renaissance Humanism: Foundations, Forms, and Legacy,* ed. Albert Rabil, 3 vols. (Philadelphia: University of Pennsylvania Press, 1988), 1:29–30, 51–55.

2. "It may happen that you could receive these trifles, read them and then call to mind nothing more than past events in our life and those of our friends. This would make me very happy since your request will not seem neglected and my fame will be safe. I will not fool myself into thinking any differently. How can we believe that a friend, unless he is another me, could read all these things without aversion or boredom since so many of them conflict and are

contradictory because of their uneven style and uncertain goal?" (*Fam.* 1.1, trans. Bernardo, p. 7).

3. "I am in good health, as is customary with bodies composed of contrary elements. Indeed I am making every effort—and I wish it were a success—to be of healthy mind; otherwise my good intentions are deserving of praise. You certainly know my ways: I refresh my mind, wearied by affairs, through a change of location. Thus, after two years in France I was returning to my homeland" (*Fam.* 16.11, from *Letters on Familiar Matters: Books IX–XVI,* trans. Aldo Bernardo [Baltimore: Johns Hopkins University Press, 1982], 3:318). All translations of books 9–16 of *Familiares* are from this work.

4. *De officiis* obviously was not exclusively the textbook on ethics. See Petrarch's *Fam.* 1.2 for a reference to Cicero's *De finibus.* See also E. Vernon Arnold, *Roman Stoicism, Being Lectures on the History of Stoic Philosophy with Special Reference to Its Development within the Roman Empire* (New York: Humanities Press, 1958), pp. 310ff.

5. Seneca, *Epistula* 89.22. Compare Arnold, *Roman Stoicism,* pp. 345–46. I am much indebted for these categories, as is clear, to Michel Foucault, *Histoire de la sexualité,* vol. 2, *La Chair et le corps* (Paris: Gallimard, 1979).

6. See Phillip De Lacy, "Stoic Views of Poetry," *American Journal of Philology* 69, no. 3 (1948): 241–71. See also Berthe Marti, "The Meaning of the Pharsalia," *American Journal of Philology* 66 (1945): 352–76, "Seneca's Tragedies: A New Interpretation," *TAPA* 76 (1945): 216–45, and "The Prototype of Seneca's Tragedies," *Classical Philology* 42 (1947): 1–16.

7. I am paraphrasing here the opening lines of the letter he writes to Tommaso da Messina (*Fam.* 1.9) on the question of eloquence.

8. The question has been treated recently in Antoine Compagnon, *La Seconde Main ou le travail de la citation* (Paris: Seuil, 1979). See also Gérard Genette, *Palimpsestes: La littérature au second degré* (Paris: Seuil, 1982); Gian Biagio Conte, *Memoria dei poeti e sistema letterario* (Turin: Einaudi, 1974); and Angelo Jacomuzzi, "La citazione come procedimento letterario: Appunti e considerazioni," in *L'arte dell'interpretare: Studi critici offerti a Giovanni Getto,* Università degli studi di Torino, Facoltà di Lettere e Filosofia, Istituto di Italianistica (Cuneo: L'arciere, 1984), pp. 3–15.

9. In another letter Petrarch writes to Giovanni Colonna (*Fam.* 6.4), in response to critics who have accused him of using in his writings too many examples from the authors of the past, Petrarch admits that "there is no better way to learn than by having the mind desire to emulate these greats as closely as possible" (trans. Bernardo, p. 314).

10. The bibliography on the *Trionfi* is scant. See Aldo Bernardo, *Petrarch, Laura, and the Triumphs* (Albany: State University of New York Press, 1974), which ought to be read in conjunction with the still vital study, Marguerite

Waller, *Petrarch's Poetics and Literary History* (Amherst: University of Massachusetts Press, 1980). Compare the recent *Petrarch's Triumphs: Allegory and Spectacle,* ed. Konrad Eisenblacher and Amilcare Iannucci, University of Toronto Italian Studies, no. 4 (Ottawa: Dovehouse Editions, 1990).

11. See Ezio Raimondi's review of Cesare F. Goffis, *Originalità dei Trionfi,* in *Studi petrarcheschi* 4 (1951): 262. For further views on the problematical quality of this poem, see Giovanni A. Cesareo, "L'ordinamento dei 'Trionfi,'" in *Studii e ricerche sulla letteratura italiana* (Palermo: Sandron, 1929), and Emilio Pasquini, "Preliminari all'edizione dei 'Trionfi,'" in *Il Petrarca ad Arquà: Atti del Convegno di Studi nel VI Centenario,* ed. Giuseppe Billanovich and Umberto Bosco (Padua: Antenore, 1975), pp. 199–240. For further bibliography, see Zygmunt Baranski, "A Provisional Definition of Petrarch's *Trionfi,*" in *Petrarch's Triumphs,* ed. Eisenblacher and Iannucci, pp. 63–83.

12. Massimo Verdicchio, "The Rhetoric of Enumeration in Petrarch's *Trionfi,*" in *Petrarch's Triumphs,* ed. Eisenblacher and Iannucci, pp. 135–46, has sharply identified the dominant rhetorical figure of the poem. See also John Smurthwaite, "Petrarch's *Trionfo dell'eternità:* Aesthetics of Conversion," *JRMMRA* 8 (1987): 15–32.

13. See Domenico Pietropaolo, "Spectacular Literacy and the Topology of Significance: The Processional Mode," in *Petrarch's Triumphs,* ed. Eisenblacher and Iannucci, pp. 359–68, for the semiotics of spectacles.

v. The World of History

1. "Grammatica est scientia recte loquendi, et origo et fundamentum liberalium litterarum. Grammatica autem a litteris nomen accepit: enim *Grammata* enim Graeci litteras vocant. Divisiones autem Grammaticae artis a quibusdam triginta dinumerantur, id est, . . . schemata, tropi, prosa, metra, fabulae, historiae" (Isidore of Seville, *Etymologiarum sive originum libri XX,* ed. W. M. Lindsay [Oxford: Clarendon, 1966], 1.5). See also St. Augustine, *De musica* 2.1.1: "Atque scias velim totam illam scientiam, quae grammatica graece, latina autem litteratura nominatur, historia custodiam profiteri . . . grammaticus, custos ille videlicet historiae" (*Patrologia latina* 32.1099). See also *The Didascalicon of Hugh of St. Victor: A Medieval Guide to the Arts,* ed. and trans. Jerome Taylor (New York: Columbia University Press, 1968), p. 88.

2. We know that one of the early books Petrarch read was Isidore of Seville's encyclopedic *Etymologiarum,* which he received as a gift from his father in 1325.

3. Petrarch sends several of his *Familiares* to the Dominican Giovanni Colonna. On Colonna's historiography, see Ross Braxton, "Giovanni Colonna, Historian at Avignon," *Speculum* 45 (1970): 533–63.

4. The bibliography on the subject is vast, and I will limit myself to listing a few items: Friedrich Leo, *Die griechisch-romische Biographie nach ihrer litterarischen Form* (Leipzig: Teubner, 1901); Georg Misch, *Geschichte der Autobiographie*, 2d ed. (Leipzig: Teubner, 1931); N. I. Barbou, *Les Procédés de la peinture des caractères et la vérité historique dans le biographies de Plutarque* (Paris, 1934); Gennaro Lomiento, "La Bibbia nella composizione della Vita Cypriani di Ponzio," *Vetera christianorum* 5 (1968): 23–60; Jacques Fontaine, "Alle fonti dell'agiografa europea," *Rivista di storia e letteratura religiosa* 2 (1966): 187–206; Paul Lehmann, "Autobiographies of the Middle Ages," *Transactions of the Royal Historical Society* 5, no. 3 (1953): 41–52; Santo Mazzarino, *Il Pensiero storico classico* (Bari: Laterza, 1966) 2.1, pp. 117–211; Arnaldo Momigliano, *The Development of Greek Biography* (Cambridge: Harvard University Press, 1971); Patricia Cox, *Biography in Late Antiquity: A Quest for the Holy Man* (Berkeley: University of California Press, 1983); and Pierre Courcelle, *Recherches sur le Confessions de saint Augustin*, 2d ed. (Paris: Boccard, 1968). See also Thomas C. P. Zimmerman, "Confession and Autobiography in the Early Renaissance," in *Renaissance Studies in Honor of Hans Baron*, ed. A. Molho and John A. Tedeschi (DeKalb: Northern Illinois University Press, 1971), pp. 119–40, and Roy Pascal, *Design and Truth in Autobiography* (Cambridge: Cambridge University Press, 1960). Of general interest to this issue is David Wallace, "Carving Up Time and the World: Medieval-Renaissance Turf Wars, Historiography and Personal History," in *Working Papers*, University of Wisconsin–Milwaukee Center for Twentieth-Century Studies, no. 11 (1990–91), pp. 1–24.

5. Thucydides theorizes the historian's craft as the inquiry into observable facts. "And with reference to the narrative of events," he writes, "far from permitting myself to derive it from the first source that came to hand, I did not even trust my own impressions, but it rests partly on what I saw myself, partly on what others saw for me, the accuracy of the report always tried by the most severe and detailed tests possible" (*History of the Peloponnesian War*, trans. Charles Foster Smith, 4 vols., Loeb Classical Library [London: Heinemann, 1919–23], 1:23). The citation from Cicero is from *De oratore* 2.15.62. The edition and translation I am using here is *Oratory and Orators*, trans. John S. Watson (Carbondale: Southern Illinois University Press, 1970), p. 99.

6. "Historia vero testis temporum, lux veritatis, vita memoriae, magistra vitae, nuntia vetustatis, qua voce alia, nisi oratoris, immortalitati commendatur?" (*De oratore* 2.9.36, trans. Watson, p. 92).

7. A passage from Dante's *Convivio* (1.3.2–15) on the encomiastic character of autobiography illustrates the enduring quality of this notion in the late Middle Ages. The passage reads: "Non si concede per li retorici alcuno di sè medesimo sanza necessaria cagione parlare, e da ciò è l'uomo rimosso perchè parlare d'alcuno non si può che il parladore non lodi o non biasimi quelli

di cui elli parla" (*Convivio,* ed. Cesare Vasoli and Domenico de Robertis [Milan-Naples: Ricciardi, 1979]). The passage reads in English: "The teachers of Rhetoric do not allow anyone to speak of himself except on ground of necessity. And this is forbidden to a man because, when anyone is spoken of, the speaker must needs either praise or blame him of whom he speaks" (*Dante's Convivio,* trans. William Walrond Jackson [Oxford: Clarendon, 1909]).

8. *The Revolution of Cola di Rienzo,* ed. Mario Emilio Cosenza, 2d ed., with a new introduction by Ronald C. Musto (New York: Italica, 1986). The passages are quoted from this text. Of considerable interest for the history of the cult of Roman antiquities is Hendrik J. Erasmus, *The Origins of Rome in Historiography from Petrarch to Perizonius* (Leiden: Van Gorcum, 1962).

9. "As I recall that most inspired and earnest conversation we had two days ago as we stood before the portals of that famous and ancient sanctuary," Petrarch writes in his first letter to Cola di Rienzo, "I glow with such zeal that I consider your words those of an oracle issuing from the innermost recesses of that temple. I seem to have listened to a god, not to a man. You bemoaned the present conditions—no, the very fall and ruin of the republic—in words of such divine inspiration, and you probed our wounds with the shafts of your eloquence to such depths that whenever I recall the sound and meaning of your words, tears leap to my eyes, and grief again grips my soul" (*Revolution of Cola di Rienzo,* ed. Cosenza, p. 6). It is of interest to recall an answer by Cola di Rienzo to Petrarch: "Your numerous and most charming letters, so eloquently written and so thickly crowded with inspiring arguments, have filled the eyes of the reader and the ears of the hearer with pleasure. When their contents had been more deeply and maturely considered, the intellect feasted on them with greater pleasure. In your very gratifying letter of exhortation, you have summoned the praiseworthy examples of the heroes of old to spur us on to emulate their virtuous deeds, whereby our spirits are and have been thoroughly revived" (ibid., p. 50).

10. "Movemur enim, nescio quo pacto, locis ipsis, in quibus eorum, quos diligimus aut admiramur, assunt vestigia" (*Collatio laureationis* in *Opere latine di Francesco Petrarca,* ed. Antonietta Bufano, 2 vols. [Turin: Unione Tipografico-Editrice Torinese, 1975], p. 1266).

11. *Collatio laureationis,* p. 1270. Petrarch continues, referring to Macrobius's *In somnium Scipionis* (2.10.11), by relating poetry to history, ethics, and physics. The difference between, on the one hand, poets and, on the other, historians and philosophers is the same as between cloudy and serene skies, "cu, utrobique eadem sit claritas in subiecto, sed, pro captu spectantium, diversa."

12. I quote from the translation by Benjamin G. Kohl in "Petrarch's Prefaces to *De viris illustribus,*" *History and Theory* 13 (1974): 132–44.

13. Compare Livy's preface to *Ab urbe condita libri:* "Hoc illud est praecipue in cognitione rerum salubre ac frugiferum, omnis te exempli documenta in inlustri posita monumento intueri; inde tibi tuaeque rei publicae quod imitere capias, inde foedum inceptu, foedum exitu, quod vites." The citation is taken from *Livy*, ed. B. O. Foster, Loeb Classical Library (Cambridge: Harvard University Press, 1976), 1.10, p. 7.

14. Horace's *Ars poetica* (lines 149–50) is echoed by Petrarch later in the preface: "Since it is virtually impossible to satisfy the curiosity to know everything, I have instead taken the position that I shall treat only those things which acquire splendor in the treatment."

15. The issue has been frequently studied. Some of the major works on this subject are Pierre De Nolhac, "Pétrarque et les historiens romains," in *Pétrarque et l'humanisme*, rev. ed. (Paris: Librairie H. Champion, 1965), 2:1–65; Giuseppe Billanovich, "Petrarca e gli storici romani," in *Francesco Petrarca: Citizen of the World*, ed. Aldo S. Bernardo, Proceedings of the World Petrarch Congress, Washington, D.C., April 6–13, 1974 (Padua: Antenore, 1980), pp. 101–14; Guido Martellotti, "Storiografia del Petrarca," in *Scritti petrarcheschi*, ed. Michele Feo and Silvia Rizzo (Padua: Antenore, 1983), pp. 474–86.

16. For the idea of "aretalogy," see Morton Smith, "Prolegomena to a Discussion of Aretalogies, Divine Men, the Gospels, and Jesus," *Journal of Biblical Literature* 90 (June 1971): 174–99. Compare Cox, *Biography in Late Antiquity*, pp. 3–12. St. Jerome's *De viris inlustribus* is available in *Nicene and Post-Nicene Fathers*, ed. Philip Schaff and Henry Wace, 2d ser., vol. 3 (New York: Christian Literature Company, 1892). On St. Jerome and Suetonis, see Andrew Wallace-Hadrill, *Suetonius: The Scholar and His Caesars* (New Haven: Yale University Press, 1984). Colonna's *De viris illustribus* is explicitly modeled on St. Jerome's 330 biographical entries. Jerome writes about Christians; Colonna writes about both pagans and Christians. See Remigio Sabbadini, "Giovanni Colonna biografo e bibliografo del secolo XIV," *Atti delle R. Accademia delle scienze di Torino* 46 (1911): 282–85. See also G. L. Forte, "John Colonna, O.P.," *Archivum Fratrum Praedicatorum* 20 (1950): 369–414.

17. The tradition of eternal Rome has been suggestively studied in Charles Norris Cochrane, *Christianity and Classical Culture: A Study of Thought and Action from Augustus to Augustine* (Oxford: Oxford University Press, 1968), esp. pp. 74–176. See also Kenneth J. Pratt, "Rome as Eternal," *Journal of the History of Ideas* 26 (1965): 25–44.

18. The quotations from this letter are taken from *Petrarch's Book without a Name: A Translation of the "Sine nomine,"* trans. Norman P. Zacour (Toronto: Pontifical Institute of Mediaeval Studies, 1973). A recent and cogent exploration of the significance of Avignon for the poets of the Italian trecento is Emilio Pasquini, "Il mito polemico di Avignone nei poeti italiani

del Trecento," in *Aspetti culturali della società italiana nel periodo del papato avignonese* (Todi: Accademia Tudertina, 1981), pp. 259–309. See also the introductory remarks, with which I am in substantial agreement, by Ugo Dotti in *Sine nomine: Lettere polemiche e politiche,* ed. Ugo Dotti (Bari: Laterza, 1974), as well as Carlo Muscetta, *Crisi e sviluppi della cultura dal comune alle signorie,* in *Letteratura italiana, storia e testi* (Bari: Laterza, 1971), 2.1, pp. 4–23.

19. The general contour of Petrarch's argument supplements Dante's own polemic with political Augustinianism both in *Monarchia* and in the *Divine Comedy.* For a full discussion of Dante's interpretive strategies between Vergil and Augustine, see Giuseppe Mazzotta, *Dante, Poet of the Desert: History and Allegory in the Divine Comedy* (Princeton: Princeton University Press, 1979), esp. pp. 147–91.

20. "Commentaries (*com-mentaria*) are so named as from *cum mente* (with the mind) or from *comminiscor* (call to mind); for they are interpretations, as, for example, commentaries on the Law or on the Gospels" (*Didascalicon,* trans. Taylor, 4.16, p. 119). The quotation is adapted, as Taylor also points out (p. 218), from Isidore of Seville's *Etymologiarum* 6.8.2–3.

21. The quotation is taken from *Livy,* trans. Foster, 1.10, p. 7. For Tacitus, see *Annals* 3.65.1. On Roman historiography, see Donald R. Dudley, *The World of Tacitus* (London: Secker and Warburg, 1968), esp. pp. 13–75, and Wallace-Hadrill, *Suetonius.*

22. I am quoting from *Boccaccio on Poetry,* trans. Charles G. Osgood (Indianapolis: Bobbs-Merrill, 1956), p. 11.

23. That Petrarch's letters to various princes, such as Francesco da Carrara, belong to the tradition of the "mirrors for princes" has long been acknowledged by scholarship. For an outline of the tradition, see L. K. Born, "The Perfect Prince: A Study in Thirteenth- and Fourteenth-Century Ideals," *Speculum* 3 (1928): 470–504; Wilhelm Berges, *Die Furstenspiegel des hohen und spaten Mittelalters* (Leipzig: Hiersemann, 1938); and Arpad Steiner, "Petrarch's *Optimus Princeps,*" *Romanic Review* 25 (1934): 94–111. Benjamin G. Kohl gives a detailed review of the tradition in his introductory remarks to his complete translation of Petrarch's letter to Francesco da Carrara, *Rerum senilium liber XIV. Ad magnificum Franciscum de Carraria Padue dominum. Epistola I. Qualis esse debeat qui rem publicam regit.* The text is available in *The Earthly Republic: Italian Humanists on Government and Society,* ed. and trans. Benjamin G. Kohl and Ronald G. Witt, with Elizabeth B. Welles (Philadelphia: University of Pennsylvania Press, 1978), pp. 35–78.

24. For an overview of the question of tyranny (a historical question that is at the center of attention in the *Policraticus* of John of Salisbury and in *De regimine principum* and that climaxes with *De tyranno* by Coluccio Salutati

and in the reflections of Bartolo of Sassoferrato), see Ephraim Emerton, *Humanism and Tyranny,* Studies in the Italian Trecento (Cambridge: Harvard University Press, 1925).

VI. Orpheus: Rhetoric and Music

1. Fredi Chiappelli, *Studi sul linguaggio del Petrarca: La Canzone delle Visioni* (Florence: Olschki, 1971), p. 228.

2. See Fredi Chiappelli, *Il Legame musaico,* ed. Pier Massimo Forni (Rome: Edizioni di Storia e Letteratura, 1984), p. 15.

3. Dante's definition of poetry as "fictio rhetorica musicaque poita" (a rhetorical fiction set to music) occurs in his *De vulgari eloquentia* 2.4. For an analysis of what the definition entails and for further bibliography, see Giuseppe Mazzotta, *Dante's Vision and the Circle of Knowledge* (Princeton: Princeton University Press, 1993).

4. No doubt, this motif of praise—or epideictic rhetoric—marks the deliberate point of contact between Dante's discovery of the "stilo de la lode" (style of praise), which in the *Vita nuova* is presented as the lover-poet's extraordinary invention signaling a new poetry worthy of Beatrice, and Petrarch's dramatization of Laura as "owning" her own praise in the very folds of her name's syllables. In either case the religious resonance of the *laudi* adds poignancy to the representation.

5. *On His Own Ignorance,* trans. Hans Nachod, in *The Renaissance Philosophy of Man,* ed. Ernst Cassirer, P. O. Kristeller, and J. H. Randall, Jr. (Chicago: University of Chicago Press, 1948), p. 126.

6. Song 28, which I shall largely discuss here, reads as follows:

O aspettata in Ciel beata et bella
anima che di nostra umanitade
vestita vai (non, come l'altre, carca):
perchè ti sian men dure omai le strade
(a Dio diletta, obediente ancella)
onde al suo regno di qua giù si varca,
    ecco novellamente a la tua barca,
ch'al cieco mondo à già volte le spalle
per gir al miglio porto,
d'un vento occidental dolce conforto;
lo qual per mezzo questa oscura valle
ove piangiamo il nostro et l'altrui torto
la condurrà de' lacci antichi sciolta
per drittissimo calle
al verace oriente ov'ella è volta.

Forse i devoti et gli amorosi preghi
et le lagrime sante de' mortali
son giunte innanzi a la pietà superna;
et forse non fur mai tante nè tali
che per merito lor punto si pieghi
fuor de suo corso la giustizia eterna.
    Ma quel benigno Re che 'l ciel governa,
al sacro loco ove fu posto in croce,
gli occhi per grazia gira;
onde nel petto al novo Carlo spira
la vendetta ch'a noi tardata noce
sì che molt'anni Europa ne sospira;
così soccorre a la sua amata sposa
tal che sol de la voce
fa tremar Babilonia et star pensosa.

Chiunque alberga tra Garona e 'l monte
e 'ntra 'l Rodano e 'l Reno et l'onde salse
le 'nsegne cristianissime accompagna;
et a cui mai di vero pregio calse
dal Pireneo a l'ultimo orizzonte
con Aragon lassarà vota Ispagna.
    Inghilterra con l'isole che bagna
l'Occeano intra 'l Carro et le Colonne,
in fin là dove sona
dottrina del santissimo Elicona,
varie di lingue et d'arme et de le gonne
a l'alta impresa caritate sprona.
Deh qual amor sì licito o sì degno,
qua' figli mai, qua' donne
furon materia a sì giusto disdegno?

Una parte del mondo è che si giace
mai sempre in ghiaccio et in gelate nevi,
tutta lontana dal camin del sole;
là sotto i giorni nubilosi et brevi,
nemica naturalmente di pace
nasce una gente a cui il morir non dole.
    Questa se, più devota che non sole,
col tedesco furor la spada cigne,
Turchi Arabi et Caldei,
con tutti quei che speran nelli Dei
di qua dal mar che fa l'onde sanguigne,
quanto sian da prezzar conoscer dei:
popolo ignudo paventoso et lento,
che ferro mai no strigne
ma tutt'i colpi suoi commette al vento.

Dunque ora è 'l tempo da ritrare il collo
dal giogo antico, et da squarciare il velo
ch'è stato avolto intorno a gli occhi nostri,
et che 'l nobile ingegno che dal cielo
per grazia tien de l'immortale Apollo,
et l'eloquentia sua vertù qui mostri
   or con la lingua, or co' laudati 'ncostri.
Perchè d'Orfeo leggendo et d'Anfione
se non ti meravigli,
assai men fia ch'Italia co' suoi figli
si desti al suon del tuo chiaro sermone,
tanto che per Jhesù la lancia pigli;
che s'al ver mira questa antica madre,
in nulla sua tenzione
fur mai cagion sì belle o sì leggiadre.
Tu ch' ài per arricchir d'un bel thesauro
volte l'antiche et le moderne carte,
volando al ciel colla terrena soma,
sai da l'imperio del figliuol de Marte
al grande Augusto che di verde lauro
tre volte triunfando ornò la chioma
   ne l'altrui ingiurie del suo sangue Roma
spesse fiate quanto fu cortese;
et or perchè non fia
cortese no, ma conoscente et pia
a vendicar le dispietate offese
col figliuol glorioso di Maria?
Che dunque la nemica parte spera
ne l'umane difese,
se Cristo sta da la contraria schiera?

Pon' mente al temerario ardir di Xerse,
che fece per calcar i nostri liti
di novi ponti oltraggio a la marina,
et vedrai ne la morte de' mariti
tutte vestite a brun le donne perse
et tinto in rosso il mar di Salamina.
   Et non pur questa misera ruina
del popolo infelice d'oriente
vittoria t'empromette,
ma Marathona et le mortali strette
che difese il Leon con poca gente,
et altre mille ch' ài ascoltate et lette.
Per che inchinare a Dio molto convene
le ginocchia et la mente
che gli anni tuoi riserva a tanto bene.

Tu vedrai Italia et l'onorata riva,
canzon, ch'a gli occhi miei cela et contende
non mar, non poggio o fiume
ma solo Amor, che del suo altero lume
più m'invaghisce dove più m'incende,
nè natura può star contra 'l costume.
Or movi, non smarrir l'altre compagne,
che non pur sotto bende
alberga Amor, per cui si ride et piagne.

7. John Block Friedman, *Orpheus in the Middle Ages* (Cambridge: Harvard University Press, 1970).

8. Friedman, *Orpheus,* pp. 110–13.

9. Arnulf d'Orléans, "Arnolfo d'Orleans, un cultore di Ovidio nel secolo XII," ed. Fausto Ghisalberti, *Memorie del reale Istituto Lombardo di Scienze e Lettere de Milano* 24 (1932): 157–232 (my translation).

10. Isidore of Seville writes: "Unde et Lucanus ideo in numero poetarum non ponitur, quia videtur historias conposuisse, non poema" (even Lucan, then, is not counted in the number of poets, because he seems to have composed histories and not a poem) (*Etymologiarum sive originum libri XX,* ed. W. M. Lindsay [Oxford: Clarendon, 1966], 8.7, par. 10; my translation). For Dante's treatment of Lucan, see Giuseppe Mazzotta, *Dante, Poet of the Desert: History and Allegory in the Divine Comedy* (Princeton: Princeton University Press, 1979), pp. 47ff.

11. See the fascinating reading of Lucan's *Pharsalia* in W. R. Johnson, *Momentary Monsters: Lucan and His Heroes* (Ithaca, N.Y.: Cornell University Press, 1987).

12. I quote from *Rime, trionfi e poesie latine,* ed. Ferdinando Neri et al. (Milan-Naples: Ricciardi, 1951), p. 630. The translation is mine.

13. The translation is taken from *Literary Criticism of Dante Alighieri,* ed. and trans. Robert S. Haller (Lincoln: University of Nebraska Press, 1973), p. 49.

14. See the remarks on painting in chapter 1.

15. The *Rerum familiarum libri* records with utmost precision Petrarch's own steady involvement with music and the work of Vitry and Socrates. See, for instance, 1.1 and 9.13.

16. *The Didascalicon of Hugh of St. Victor: A Medieval Guide to the Arts,* ed. and trans. Jerome Taylor (New York: Columbia University Press, 1968), pp. 69–70.

17. For a detailed survey of the sound patterns in the *Canzoniere,* see the richly documented study by Maria Picchio Simonelli, "Strutture foniche nel 'Rerum vulgarium Fragmenta,'" in *Francis Petrarch, Six Centuries Later: A Symposium,* ed. Aldo Scaglione, Studies in the Romance Languages and

Literatures, no. 3 (Chapel Hill: Department of Romance Languages, University of North Carolina, 1975), pp. 66–104.

18. "Fabulae vero sunt quae nec factae sunt nec fieri possunt, quia contra naturam sunt" (Isidore of Seville, *Etymologiarum* 1.44.5).

VII.   Humanism and Monastic Spirituality

1. The contours of Petrarch's spiritual dilemma are drawn in his *Secretum*, a text that has of course attracted much critical attention. Some of the chief studies probing the cultural components of this confessional work are A. Bobbio, "Seneca e la formazione spirituale e culturale del Petrarca," *Bibliofilia* 43 (1941): 224–91; Carlo Calcaterra, "Sant'Agostino nelle opere di Dante e Petrarca," in *La selva del Petrarca* (Bologna: Cappelli, 1942), pp. 247–360; Pierre Courcelle, "Pétrarque entre saint Augustin et les Augustiniens du XIVᵉ siècle," *Studi petrarcheschi* 7 (1961): 58–71; Eugenio Garin, *L'umanesimo italiano* (Bari: Laterza, 1952), esp. pp. 31–37; Francisco Rico, *Vida u obra de Petrarca* (Chapel Hill: University of North Carolina Press, 1974); and Hans Baron, *Petrarch's "Secretum": Its Making and Its Meaning* (Cambridge: Medieval Academy of America, 1985).

2. The form of the dialogue in Petrarch has been studied in Aldo S. Bernardo, "Dramatic Dialogue and Monologue in Petrarch's Works," *Symposium* 7 (1973): 92–120. See also the most interesting remarks in Francesco Tateo, *Dialogo interiore e polemica ideologica nel "Secretum" del Petrarca* (Florence: Le Monnier, 1965), as well as the more recent Bortolo Martinelli, *Il "Secretum" conteso* (Naples: Loffredo, 1982), esp. pp. 79–86. More generally, see the theoretical debate on dialogue in *Bakhtin: Essays and Dialogue on His Works*, ed. G. S. Morson (Chicago: University of Chicago Press, 1986). See also the carefully documented and speculative Jon R. Snyder, *Writing the Scene of Speaking: Theories of Dialogue in the Late Italian Renaissance* (Stanford: Stanford University Press, 1989).

3. I am quoting from the translation by Aldo Bernardo in *Letters on Familiar Matters: Books IX–XVI* (Baltimore: Johns Hopkins University Press, 1982), pp. 57–68.

4. *Fam.* 10.3, trans. Bernardo, p. 59.

5. In Italian (as in French and Spanish), the semantic link between *modernità* and *moda* is self-evident. For a classical definition of contemplation, with which Petrarch was certainly familiar as his own texts on contemplative spirituality make clear, one should recall the following by Richard of St. Victor: "Contemplation is the free, more penetrating gaze of a mind, suspended with wonder concerning manifestations of wisdom" (*The Mystical Ark* 1.4). The quotation is taken from *The Twelve Patriarchs: The Mystical Ark*,

Book Three of the Trinity, trans. Grover A. Zinn, Classics of Western Spirituality (New York: Paulist Press, 1979), p. 157. On the question of contemplation, see Giuseppe Mazzotta, *Dante's Vision and the Circle of Knowledge* (Princeton: Princeton University Press, 1993), pp. 154–73. A recent book, Marjorie O'Rourke Boyle, *Petrarch's Genius: Pentimento and Prophecy* (Berkeley: University of California Press, 1991), stresses with considerable force the religious substance of Petrarch's work.

6. *Fam.* 10.3, trans. Bernardo, p. 58.

7. The text is available in English in Jean Leclerc, *The Love of Learning and the Desire of God*, trans. Catharine Misrahi (New York: New American Library, 1961). See also Pierre Courcelle, *Les Lettres grecques en Occident de Macrobe à Cassiodore* (Paris: De Boccard, 1948); H. I. Marrou, *S. Augustine et la fin de la culture antique* (Paris: De Boccard, 1949); and James J. O'Donnell, *Cassiodorus* (Berkeley: University of California Press, 1979). More generally, see Franco Simone, "La *reductio artium ad Sacram Scripturam* quale espressione dell'umanesimo medievale fino al secolo XII," *Convivium*, n.s., 2 (1949): 887–927.

8. The statement in which grammar is opposed to the Benedictine rule appears in *De perfectione monachorum*, in *Patrologia Latina* [*PL*] 145.306C. More generally, see Marie-Dominique Chenu, "Grammaire et théologie aux XIIᵉ et XIII siècles," *Archives d'histoire doctrinale et littéraire du Moyen Age* 10 (1953): 5–28, and Philippe Delhaye, "Grammatica et *Ethica* au XIIᵉ siècle," *Recherches de théologie ancienne et médiévale* 25 (1958): 59–110.

9. The quotations from Petrarch's *Fam.* 10.4 are taken from trans. Bernardo, pp. 69–75. For the eclogue, I am following the excellent translation in *Petrarch's "Bucolicum carmen,"* trans. Thomas G. Bergin (New Haven: Yale University Press, 1974), pp. 2–15.

10. The links between Saturn and contemplation are dramatically deployed in Dante's *Paradiso*. In the heaven of Saturn (*Paradiso*, cantos 21 and 22), Dante encounters contemplatives such as St. Benedict and Peter Damian. See Raymond Klibansky, Erwin Panofsky, and Fritz Saxl, *Saturn and Melancholy* (Cambridge: Nelson, 1964), and Siegfried Wenzel, *The Sin of Sloth: Acedia in Medieval Thought and Literature* (Chapel Hill: University of North Carolina Press, 1967).

11. Varro, *De lingua latina*, book 6.

12. The point is made in the excellent article by Thomas M. Greene, "Petrarch's 'Viator,'" which is included in *The Vulnerable Text: Essays on Renaissance Culture* (New York: Columbia University Press, 1986), pp. 18–45.

13. The etymological interpretation was first given by Fulgentius in *Mitologiae* in *Opera*, ed. Rudolf Helm (Leipzig: Teubner, 1898), 3.10.77. See also Isidore of Seville, *Etymologiarum sive originum libri XX*, ed. W. M. Lindsay

(Oxford: Clarendon, 1966), 3.17–23, for an extended review of music and its power and practice in biblical and pagan traditions. For the specific theme of Orpheus, see Boethius, *De consolatione philosophiae* 3.12, where Philosophy sings of Orpheus. The passage is important because later commentaries of Boethius, such as that of William of Conches, will describe the myth as follows: "What does Orpheus represent? He stands for wisdom and eloquence and because of that he is called *Oreaphone*—that is best voice." See John Block Friedman, *Orpheus in the Middle Ages* (Cambridge: Harvard University Press, 1970), esp. pp. 86–145.

14. The imaginative links between Orpheus, David, and Christ are documented in Friedman, *Orpheus*, 38ff. See also D. P. Walker, "Orpheus the Theologian," in *The Ancient Theology* (Ithaca, N.Y.: Cornell University Press, 1972), pp. 22–41.

15. Still valid studies of humanism in relation to Petrarch are Pierre De Nolhac, *Pétrarque et l'humanisme* (Paris: Librairie H. Champion, 1907); Umberto Bosco, "Il Petrarca e l'umanesimo filologico," *Giornale storico delle letteratura italiana* 120 (1943): 65–119; Guido Martellotti, "Linee di sviluppo dell'umanesimo petrarchesco," *Studi petrarcheschi* 2 (1949): 51–80; and Giuseppe Billanovich, "Petrarch and the Textual Tradition of Livy," *Journal of the Warburg and Courtauld Institutes* 14 (1951): 137–208. A good profile of Venetian classicism and Albertino Mussato has been sketched in Francesco Tateo, "L'incremento degli studi classici," in *Petrarca,* ed. Raffaele Amaturo (Bari: Laterza, 1974), pp. 39–57. For Mussato's sense of the relationship between poets and theologians, see his *Epistle* 7.11.15–44. Cf. Luigi Borghi, "La concezione umanistica di Coluccio Salutati," *Annali della Regia Scuola Normale di Pisa,* 2d ser., 3 (1934): 469–92, and J. R. O'Donnell, "Coluccio Salutati on the Poet-Teacher," *Medieval Studies* 22 (1960): 240–56. Finally, see Ernest R. Curtius, "Poetry and Theology," in *European Literature and the Latin Middle Ages,* trans. W. R. Trask (New York: Harper and Row, 1963), pp. 214–27.

16. St. Augustine's views in *The City of God* (18.14) are mentioned in *Invective contra medicum,* book 3, where Petrarch writes: "Primos numpe theologos apud gentes fuisse poetas et philosophorum maximi testantur, et sanctorum confirmat autoritas, et ipsum, si nescis, poete nomen indicat. In quibus maxime nobilitatus Orpheus, cuius decimoctavo civitatis eterne libro Augustinus meminit" (in *Opere latine di Francesco Petrarca,* ed. Antonietta Bufano, 2 vols. [Turin: Unione Tipografica-Editrice Torinese, 1975], 2:920).

17. *Fam.* 10.4, trans. Bernardo, pp. 69–70.

18. For a rhetorical-historical delineation of the tradition, see William J. Kennedy, "The Virgilian Legacies of Petrarch's *Bucolicum Carmen* and Spenser's *Shepheardes Calendar,*" *Early Renaissance, Acta* 9 (1982): 79–106.

19. The motif of the cloister as paradise on earth has been studied in Jean

Leclerc, *La Vie parfaite* (Turnhout, Belg.: Brepols, 1948), pp. 164–69. Other references can be found in Leclerc's other study, *Love of Learning,* trans. Misrahi, pp. 64–72.

20. The imaginative reversal of desert and garden has been probed in Giuseppe Mazzotta, *Dante, Poet of the Desert: History and Allegory in the Divine Comedy* (Princeton: Princeton University Press, 1979), pp. 113–33.

21. The line is from Vergil's *Eclogae* 1.6. Of great importance to my ideas about leisure is the philosophical meditation, Joseph Pieper, *Leisure: The Basis of Culture,* trans. Alexander Dru (New York: Pantheon, 1954). See also Michael O'Loughlin, *The Garlands of Repose: The Literary Celebration of Civic and Retired Leisure* (Chicago: University of Chicago Press, 1978), and Mihai Spariosu, *Literature, Mimesis, and Play: Essays in Literary Theory* (Tübingen: G. Narr Verlag, 1982). For some historical background, see Jean-Marie André, *L'Otium dans la vie morale et intellectuelle romaine* (Paris: Presses Universitaires de France, 1966), and Alberto Grilli, *Il problema della vita contemplativa nel mondo greco-romano* (Milan: Bocca, 1953). For further bibliography, see Giuseppe Mazzotta, *The World at Play in Boccaccio's Decameron* (Princeton: Princeton University Press, 1986), pp. 6–8.

22. *Letters,* trans. Bernardo, p. 201.

23. Jacob Zeitlin, *The Life of Solitude by Francis Petrarch* (Urbana: University of Illinois Press, 1924), emphasizes the Epicurean elements in Petrarch's ideal of solitude (see Introduction, esp. p. 71). O'Loughlin, *Garlands of Repose,* pp. 228–34, argues for a balance of classical and Christian ideas in the text.

24. *De vita solitaria,* book 1, in *Opere latine di Francesco Petrarca,* ed. Bufano, p. 306. The translation is mine.

25. On the question of the morality of monastic leisure, see Claude J. Peifer, *Monastic Spirituality* (New York: Sheed and Ward, 1966).

26. "Unum tamen non obmiserim, ne illis auros, aut animum accomodes, qui obtentu studii Theologici te nituntur a notitia literarum scholarium dehortari, qua ut sileam reliquos, si Lactantius atque Augustinus caruissent, neque illae superstitiones paganorum tam facile subruissent, neque iste Ciuitatem Dei tanta arte, tantisque molibus erexisset. Expedit Theologo praeter Theologiam etiam multa nosse, imo si fieri possit, pene omnia, quibus contra insultus carnalium sit instructus, certe sicut unus est Deus cui omnia subsunt, sic una est scientia, de Deo, cui bonae omnes aliae obsequunt. De his tamen libro secundo de doctrina Christiana, ipse idem disputat Augustinus. Lege ergo de illius consilio, quae potes sine propositi principalis praeiuditio, et disce quantum dum ne ingenium aut memoriam afficias, semperque memineris esse te Theologum non Poetam, aut Philosophum: nisi, inquam, tum uerus Philosophus uerae sapientiae est amator. Vera autem Dei patris

sapientia CHRISTUS est" (*Seniles* 15.6, in *Francisci Petrarchae florentini opera quae extant omnia* [Basel: Sebastian Henricpetri, 1581], pp. 733–34). See E. H. Wilkins, *Petrarch's Later Years* (Cambridge: Mediaeval Academy of America, 1959), pp. 256–57. On the question of true Christian wisdom, see Conrad H. Rawski, *Petrarch's Remedies for Fortune Fair and Foul* (Bloomington: Indiana University Press, 1991), book 1, p. 147, and book 2, pp. 224–25, n. 6. This splendid passage from the *Seniles* was brought to my attention by Professor Conrad H. Rawski, who also sent me its excellent translation, which I have transcribed verbatim. I have never met Professor Rawski, but I am deeply touched by his intellectual generosity, which appropriately expresses itself in the name of Petrarch, whose ideal was to promote intellectual conversation, and which I am delighted to acknowledge. The fact that Professor Rawski, as he writes to me, is, as am I, an old Cornellian and a friend of Cornell scholars and Petrarchists such as James Hutton, Morris Bishop, Thomas Bergin, Harry Caplan, Luitpold Wallach, and others explains to me, at least in part, the magnanimity of his spirit.

27. See on Boccaccio, Mazzotta, *World at Play.*

28. This is the way Joseph Pieper, *Leisure,* translates in the epigraph to his book.

29. See Giuseppe Billanovich, "Petrarca e il Ventoso," *Italia medievale e umanistica* 9 (1966): 389–401; Bortolo Martinelli, "Petrarca e il Ventoso," in *Petrarca e il Ventoso* (Bergamo: Minerva Italiana, 1977), pp. 149–215; Robert Durling, "'The Ascent of Mount Ventoux' and the Crisis of Allegory," *Italian Quarterly* 18, no. 69 (Summer 1974): 7–28; Thomas M. Greene, *The Light in Troy: Imitation and Discovery in Renaissance Poetry* (New Haven: Yale University Press, 1982), pp. 104–11; Jill Robbins, "Petrarch Reading Augustine: 'The Ascent of Mount Ventoux,'" *Philological Quarterly* 64 (1985): 533–53; Albert Russell Ascoli, "Petrarch's Middle Age: Memory, Imagination, History, and 'The Ascent of Mount Ventoux,'" *Stanford Italian Review* 10, no. 1 (1991): 5–43. More generally, see Kenelm Foster, *Petrarch: Poet and Humanist* (Edinburgh: Edinburgh University Press, 1984).

30. See the elaborate footnotes to song 366 in *Le rime,* ed. Giosuè Carducci and Severino Ferrari (Florence: Sansoni, 1960), pp. 512ff.

APPENDIX I: Petrarch's Song 126

1. The translation is from *Petrarch's Lyric Poems: The "Rime sparse" and Other Lyrics,* ed. and trans. Robert M. Durling (Cambridge: Harvard University Press, 1976), pp. 244–47.

2. The definition occurs in the *Didascalicon* 2.8. I quote from *The Di-*

dascalicon of Hugh of St. Victor: A Medieval Guide to the Arts, ed. and trans. Jerome Taylor (New York: Columbia University Press, 1968), p. 67.

3. *De regressu animae* is a text by Porphiry; see its fragments in *Vie de Porphyre,* ed. Joseph Bidez (Gant, Belg.: Van Goethen, 1913), pp. 25–44. For the motif of the port, see St. Augustine, *Contra academicos* 3.2.3. I quote from *Corpus Christianorum, series latina* 37 (Turnhout, Belg.: Brepols, 1981).

4. See chapter 3.

Index

Abelard, 16
Acteon, 62, 67–69, 175
Aeneid, 101
aesthetics: musical, 141–42
Africa, 36, 137–38
Agon, 154, 177
Alan of Lille, 56
Albertino Mussato, 86
Alexander, 124
allegory, 73, 76, 99–101, 153
alterity: of the Middle Ages, 15
Amaturo, R., 203 n.4, 204 n.16
amor. *See* love: etymology of, 63
amor de lonh, 49, 139
Amphion, 131–32, 141
anagram, 78, 206 n.38
analogy, 29, 66, 68
anaphora, 19, 177
André, J.-M., 220, n.21
Andreas Capellanus, 62, 204 n.14
antiquarianism, 24, 195 n.13; antiquities, 17, 111
apex mentis, 74
aphorism, 144
Apollo, 77
appearance, 62
Aquinas, Saint Thomas, 23, 33
archeology, 21
aretalogy, 118, 211 n.16
Aristotle, 16, 37–40, 80–83, 103, 106–107, 123, 151, 198 n.32
Arnold, V., 207 n.5
Arnulf d'Orleans, 29, 133, 199 n.38
ars dictaminis, 86
Ars nova, 143
arts, 5; debate of, 201 n.12; figurative, 23; liberal, 5, 23, 41; mechanical, 5, 41; "new," 8
Ascent of Mt. Ventoux, 174

Ascoli, A. R., 193 n.3, 201 n.17, 221 n.29
auctoritas, 37, 81, 104
Augustine, Saint, 21, 23–25, 51, 56–57, 74–75, 98, 118, 121, 123, 139–40, 142, 145, 155, 161, 163, 174, 196 n.18, 205 n.32, 208 n.1, 219 n.16, 222 n.3; fall of Rome, 196 n.18; and Rome, 122, 198 n.28
Augustus Caesar, 124, 127, 186, 187; and Petrarch, 123, 124
authority, 37
autobiography, 108, 111, 209 n.7
Averroes, 16
Avignon, 24, 26–27, 32, 113, 119, 122, 187–91, 211 n.18; etymology of, 25; as labyrinth, 24; and Rome, 32

Babylon, 130–31, 134
Bahti, T., 201 n.17
Baranski, Z., 208 n.11
Barbou, N. I., 209 n.4
Baron, H., 5, 193 n.1, 202 n.21, 217 n.1
Bartholomaeus Anglicus, 107
beauty, 30–31, 199 n.39
Bédier, J., 15
Benedict, Saint, 152
Berges, W., 212 n.23
Bernard, Saint, 165
Bernard of Chartres, 194 n.6
Bernard of Clairvaux, 16, 46
Bernard of Gordon, 52, 202 n.19
Bernardo, A. S., 207 n.10, 217 n.2
Bersuire, P., 26, 107, 143
Billanovich, G., 5, 211 n.15, 219 n.15, 221 n.29
biography, 6, 8, 108–109; on history, 108–11, 118
Bird, O., 202 n.19

Daedalus, 12
Damian, Peter, 152, 158, 165
Dante, 16, 17, 25, 30, 51, 53, 62–63, 73, 76, 97–98, 136, 140–41, 146, 164–65, 173, 177, 195 n.11, 197 n.27, 198 n.34, 205 n.28, 209 n.7, 212 n.19, 213 n.4
Daphne, 77–78
Daristot, T., 27
Davis, C. T., 196 n.17
death, 23, 99–100; and culture, 23. See also *Trionfi*
De Lacy, P., 207 n.6
Delhaye, P., 218 n.8
Democritus, 37–38
De otio religioso, 147, 161–63
De remediis utriusque fortunae, 142
De rerum memorandarum libri, 126
De Robertis, G., 203 n.3, 206 n.40
De Sanctis, I., 14, 60, 203 n.10
desire, 75; and language, 75
De viris illustribus, 102, 111, 115–19, 123–25
De vita solitaria, 43, 147, 159–62
dialogue, 7, 9, 62–63, 67–69, 147–48, 217 n.2
Diana, 204 n.19
dietetics, 90–91
Dino del Garbo, 52
Dionigi da Borgo San Sepolcro, 8
divinity, 99–100. See also *Trionfi*
docta ignorantia, 39
Dotti, U., 5, 212 n.18
Dragonetti, R., 204 n.22
dream, 100–101
dream-vision, 98–99
Dudley, D. R., 212 n.21
dulcedo (sweetness), 173. *See also* music
Durling, R., 3, 201 n.14, 203 n.5 and n.8, 221 n.29

Echo, 67, 79, 179–80, 184
ecphrasis, 26, 131
eloquence, 131, 133, 135; political, 129–33

Emerton, E., 213 n.24
encyclopedia, 7, 16, 106–108; failure of, 123
Ennius, 137
onvoi, 50, 133, 179
epic, 137–38; and lyric, 137
Epicurus, 37, 86, 159
Epistle to Posterity, 36–37, 126, 137, 181–92
epistolary genre, 86–87
Erasmus, H. J., 210 n.8
ethics, 80, 82–83, 89, 127; and the self, 87; of writing, 92
ethopoeia, 123
etiquette, 91
etymology, 51–52, 75, 78
Eurydice, 79, 132–33; etymology of, 133
exempla, 117
exile, 66, 72, 74, 187–92; and language, 66–67; and power, 187–92

fabula, 109, 217 n.18; and *historia*, 109
faith, 8, 38–39, 150, 199 n.39
Falco, G., 193 n.1
falsigraphia, 30
fama, 59, 124, 182; Clio, 135
fame, 99–100. See also *Trionfi*
Familiares, 88–89, 91–93; *Fam.* 10.3, 148–49; *Fam.* 13.7, 158–59; structure of, 84–86
familiarity, 181–82
fashion, 91, 149–51
favola, 144
fear, 9, 120–21
Ferguson, W. K., 194 n.8
Fiorentino, F., 5, 33, 199 n.1
Fontaine, J., 209 n.4
forgetfulness, 178
Forte, L., 211 n.16
Fortuna, 118, 122; and virtue, 118
Foster, K., 205 n.31, 221, n.29
Foucault, M., 12, 207 n.5
fragmentation, 2, 4, 19, 78–79; political, 46; poetics of, 204 n.19; and totality, 100–101; and unity, 4, 78–79

Mazzocco, A., 195 n.13
Mazzotta, G., 194 n.7, 196 n.17, 198
     n.28, 210 n.12 and n.13, 212 n.19,
     213 n.2, 216 n.10, 218 n.5, 220 n.20,
     221 n.21 and n.27
mediatrix: Mary as, 164
medicine, 7; and rhetoric, 201 n.13
medium aevum (Middle Ages), 17, 32,
     195 n.9
medulla, 76
Medusa, 74, 205 n.31
Meiss, M., 198 n.34
memory, 8, 9, 54, 61–63, 114, 123, 147,
     149, 174, 177, 201 n.18; as space, 54;
     as time, 53–54
metacosmesis, 136
metamorphosis, 66
metaphor, 67–68, 76
Michel, F., 15
mirror, 64–65, 204 n.21
Misch, G., 209 n.4
modernity, 15, 17, 127, 195 n.11, 217 n.5;
     and the word *modernus,* 183–84
Momigliano, A., 209 n.4
Mommsen, T. E., 194 n.8, 195 n.13,
     196 n.20
monasticism, 147–66
monolinguism, 3
Montaigne, M. de, 110
Montale, E., 204 n.13
Morson, G. S., 217 n.2
Musaeus, 155
Muscetta, C., 212 n.18
music, 8, 141–43, 145, 173, 219 n.13;
     etymology of, 173; and poetry, 141;
     and rhetoric, 10
musica humana, 143
musica instrumentalis, 143
musica mundana, 143
Mussato, A., 17, 157

name, 138; fragments of, 77–78; of
     Laura, 9, 76–78; power of, 10;
     proper, 77; of Rome, 119
Narcissus, 31, 64–65, 67, 79, 180, 205
     n.23

Neckam, Alexander, 107, 194 n.6
negotium, 159
Nero, 127
new, 17
Nicholas of Cusa, 15
Nietzsche, F., 12
nimbus, 178
Nimrod, 25
Noferi, A., 60, 202 n.21, 203 n.3 and
     n.9, 204 n.11
Nolhac, P. de, 211 n.15, 219 n.15
notitia vetustatum, 137

Ockham, 26
O'Donnell, J. J., 218 n.7, 219 n.15
O'Loughlin, M., 220 n.21 and n.23
On His Own Ignorance, 19, 39–42, 45,
     53–55, 80–83, 102–109
Oration, 113–14
oratory, 130; and culture, 130; and the
     sciences, 130
originality, 93
Orosius, 118
Orpheus, 79, 129–46, 219 n.13; ety-
     mology of, 132, 154–55
otium, 158–59, 161
Otto of Freising, 123; and humanism,
     158
Ovid, 29, 53, 62–63, 98, 127, 137, 152,
     180, 204 n.18

paideia, 108
painting, 8, 26, 30; and death, 30–31;
     and poetry, 26
palinode, 58, 144
Panofsky, E., 14, 193 n.2, 198 n.32, 218
     n.10
paradisus claustri, 158
Paris, G., 15
paronomasia, 10
Pascal, R., 209 n.4
Pasiphae, 25
Pasquini, E., 208 n.11, 211 n.18
passions, 9, 52, 153
pastoral, 153

Paul, Saint, 76, 98
peace, 35
Peifer, C. J., 220 n.25
peregrinatio amoris, 139
periodization of history, 193 n.1, n.2,
    and n.3
persona, 98, 151
perturbationes, 52
phantasm, 31
philosophy, 8, 24, 80–81, 83, 103–104,
    167–68; etymology of, 33–34; and
    hatred, 104; and history, 38, 104;
    as violence, 37–38
pictura: as *fictura,* 27
Pieper, J., 220 n.21, 221 n.28
Pietropaolo, D., 208 n.13
planctus, 72
Plato, 26, 37–38, 40, 42, 56, 146, 151,
    198 n.32
play, 161
Pliny, 107, 126
Plumpe, J. C., 202 n.20
poeta-theologus, 155–57
poetry, 42, 213 n.2; and the liberal
    arts, 42; and theology, 219 n.15
polemics, 7
Poliziano, A., 166
Polycletus, 28–29
pondus amoris, 74
Porphiry, 222 n.3
Post, G., 194 n.7
power, 37, 51, 184–92; and eloquence,
    111–12; and powerlessness, 139,
    185–92; of Rome, 122
praise, 213 n.4; rhetoric of, 163
Pratt, K., 211 n.17
prayer, 7, 12, 163, 165; and self, 165
Praz, M., 198 n.32
progress, 196 n.20
Prudentius, 35, 38–39, 99
Pseudo-Bede, 21–22
psychomachia, 11, 35, 56, 200 n.9
Pygmalion, 28–29, 31
Pythagoras, 37, 126, 151

Quintilian, 26, 38, 109, 140–41

Rabelais, F., 16
Raimondi, E., 98, 208 n.11
Rawski, C. H., 221 n.26
reason, 56
Rehm, W., 195 n.13
Renaissance: definition of, 193 n.2
    and n.3
renovatio imperii, 127
Renucci, P., 193 n.3
Rerum memorandarum libri, 102, 126
reticentia, 135
reverdie, 172–73
rhetoric, 8, 40, 53, 104–105, 139; and
    belief, 200 n.10; epideictic, 213
    n.4; and knowledge, 104–105; and
    logic, 106; and medicine, 41; and
    music, 8, 141, 146; and the Pessius,
    130; as power, 12; and theology, 157
rhythmica sonoritas, 141
Richard of St. Victor, 217 n.5
Rico, F., 5, 217 n.1, 202 n.21
Rigolot, F., 206 n.38
Robbins, J., 221 n.29
Robert, King, 126
Roche, T., 206 n.40
Roma aeterna, 119, 211 n.17
Rome, 19–21, 102–28; as Babylon, 21;
    and Cola di Rienzo, 112–13; eter-
    nity of, 21; fall of, 21–22, 196 n.18;
    future of, 114; historiography of,
    21; and history, 111–28; in the
    Middle Ages, 196 n.17; and Pe-
    trarch, 114; praise of, 122–23;
    Roma as amor, 139; *vetustas* of,
    120
Romilly, J. de, 201 n.13
Romuald, 152
Rudel, Jaufré, 139
ruins, 19–23, 102–28, 137–38; aes-
    thetics of, 22
rus et urbs, 87

Sabbadini, R., 211 n.16
Sallust, 110, 118
Salutati, C., 157
Sapegno, N., 203 n.8

INDEX

sapientia et fortitudo, 135

Saturn, 154, 218 n.10
Saxl, F., 218 n.10
Scaglione, A., 200 n.5
scholasticus, 36
sculpture, 29
Secretum, 11, 55–56, 202 n.21
self, 4, 5, 8, 58–79, 83–84, 149, 165,
    182–92; divisions of, 83–84; and
    echo, 94; fragmentation of, 85, 98;
    as subject, 68, 86, 101
Self-Portrait, 36
Semiramis, 25
Seneca, 24, 38, 55, 86–87, 89–93, 98,
    127, 151, 159, 207 n.5 and n.6
senhal, 63
Seniles, 220–21 n.26
sermo humilis, 81, 152. *See also* style
Sette, Guido, 88, 90
shame, 9, 145–46
signa amoris, 202 n.19
silence, 30
Simone, F., 194 n.8, 218 n.7
Simonelli, M. P., 216 n.17
sincerity, 92–93
skepticism, 40
Smalley, B., 198 n.31, 199 n.35
Smith, M., 211 n.16
Smurthwaite, J., 208 n.12
Snyder, J. R., 217 n.2
Socrates, 40, 83
solitude, 42–44, 97, 159–60
song, 141
sonitus, 141, 145
sonnet, 141
sound, 79, 140–41, 145
space, 19–20. *See also* time
Spariosu, M., 221 n.21
speculum naturae, 44
spirto gentil (song 53), 22
Starobinski, J., 206 n.38
statius, 132
Steiner, A., 212 n.23
stil nuovo. See "sweet new style"
stoics, 38, 55, 89–91

studia humanitatis, 33
style, 3, 7, 10, 17, 19, 35, 44, 72–73, 91–
    93, 97–98, 105, 145–46, 152–53,
    157–59, 173; and force, 105
Suetonius, 110, 118, 124, 212 n.21
Swain, J. W., 196 n.18
"sweet new style" (*stil nuovo*), 7, 17,
    51, 62–63, 176

Tacitus, 124, 212 n.21
Tateo, F., 217 n.2, 219 n.15
Taylor, Henry O., 15, 194 n.5
Tertullian, 196 n.19
Testament, 142, 199 n.34
theology: and literature, 155–57; and
    poetry, 156–57
thinking, 8, 9, 31; etymology of, 31;
    pensare, 31
Thorndike, L., 193 n.1
thought, 50–51, 201 n.14; as *cogo,
    cogito,* 51; and imagination, 50; of
    love, 50–51; and memory, 51
Thucydides, 110, 116, 209 n.5
time, 4, 19, 20–21, 97, 102, 138, 174;
    and being, 144–45; and con-
    templation, 155; fragmentation of,
    174
torpor lethargi, 178
totality, 79; and parts, 123
tradition, 94
translatio, 26, 126
Trimpi, W., 200 n.6
Trinkaus, C., 5, 200 n.5, 201 n.11, 203
    n.2
Trionfi, 98–101, 175
Trivet, Nicholas, 26, 132
truth, 36, 55–56; and time, 38
tyranny, 212 n.24

Ubertino da Casale, 25
unity, 5–6, 12, 34, 78–79; and frag-
    mentation, 2; of Middle Ages, 15

Valency, M., 204 n.22
Valerius Maximus, 118, 126

About the Author

Giuseppe Mazzotta is Professor and Chair,
Italian Language and Literature Department, Yale
University. He is the author of *Dante, Poet of the Desert,*
The World at Play in Boccaccio's "Decameron," and
Dante's Vision and the Circle of Knowledge.